DISCOVER
THE
MIDDLE EAST
AND ARABIA

PUBLISHED BY THE READER'S DIGEST ASSOCIATION LIMITED

LONDON   NEW YORK   SYDNEY   MONTREAL

DISCOVER THE MIDDLE EAST AND ARABIA

Translated and edited by Toucan Books Limited, London
for Reader's Digest, London

Translated and adapted from the French
by Michael Kerrigan

For Reader's Digest
Series Editor: Christine Noble
Editorial Assistant: Lucy Murray
Prepress Accounts Manager: Penny Grose

Reader's Digest General Books
Editorial Director: Cortina Butler
Art Director: Nick Clark

First English language edition Copyright © 2002
The Reader's Digest Association Limited
11 Westferry Circus, Canary Wharf, London E14 4HE
www.readersdigest.co.uk

Reprinted with amendments 2004

We are committed to both the quality of our products and
the service we provide to our customers. We value your
comments, so please feel free to contact us on 08705 113366,
or via our web site at www.readersdigest.co.uk
If you have any comments about the content of our books,
you can contact us at gbeditorial@readersdigest.co.uk

Copyright © 2002
Reader's Digest Association Far East Limited
Philippines copyright © 2002
Reader's Digest Association Far East Limited
All rights reserved

ISBN 0 276 42522 7

Discover the World: THE MIDDLE EAST AND ARABIA
was created and produced by
AMDS,and first published
in 2001 as *Regards sur le Monde: LE MOYEN-ORIENT*
Paris for Selection Reader's Digest S.A., Paris,

©2001 Selection Reader's Digest, S.A.
212 boulevard Saint-Germain, 75007, Paris

CONTENTS

TURKEY

CYPRUS

LEBANON   SYRIA

ISRAEL

JORDAN   IRAQ

IRAN

AFGHANISTAN

KUWAIT

SAUDI

ARABIA

BAHRAIN

QATAR

UNITED
ARAB
EMIRATES

OMAN

YEMEN

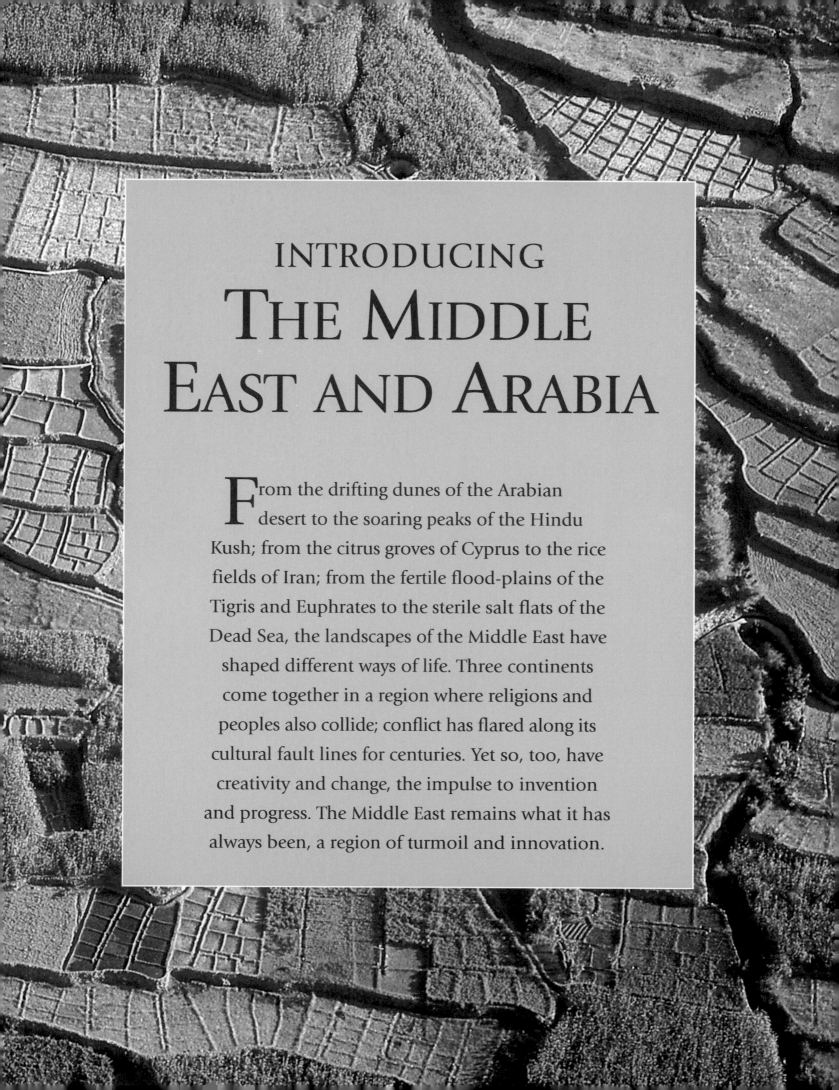

INTRODUCING
THE MIDDLE
EAST AND ARABIA

From the drifting dunes of the Arabian desert to the soaring peaks of the Hindu Kush; from the citrus groves of Cyprus to the rice fields of Iran; from the fertile flood-plains of the Tigris and Euphrates to the sterile salt flats of the Dead Sea, the landscapes of the Middle East have shaped different ways of life. Three continents come together in a region where religions and peoples also collide; conflict has flared along its cultural fault lines for centuries. Yet so, too, have creativity and change, the impulse to invention and progress. The Middle East remains what it has always been, a region of turmoil and innovation.

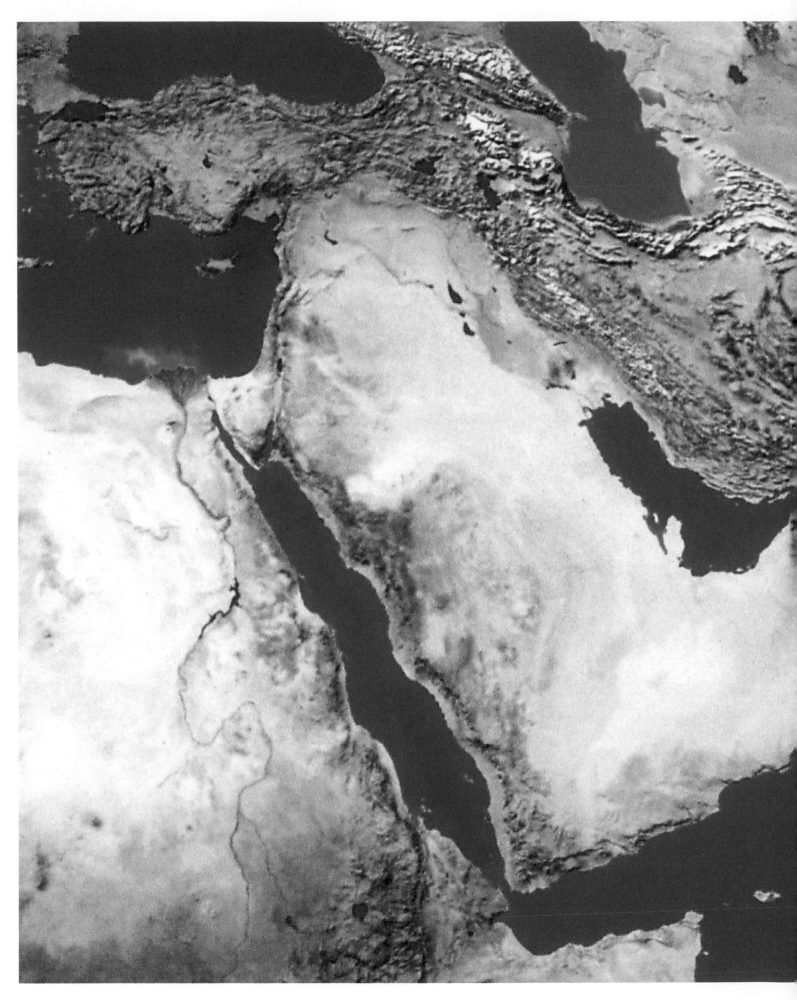

A land of empires

Civilisation began in the Middle East. History itself was invented here, more than 5000 years ago, when the ancient Mesopotamians first developed writing. Thanks to writing, people could record the size and condition of their flocks, the abundance or dearth of their harvests, the details of their commercial exchanges. In time, they also began to record the acts of their princes, their victories and defeats, their mythological stories and epics, and even the words of their gods. Without these written accounts we would have no insight into the lives of our ancestors other than speculation from the sparse record of archaeology.

Writing did not emerge here by accident. In fact, the Middle East had been at the very heart of the greatest revolution of the Neolithic Age for millennia before the first letters were shaped. It was in the Fertile Crescent, perhaps 10 000 years ago, that settled agriculture was first developed. Agriculture flourished here before it spread to the rest of the world. It created wealth, and encouraged the formation first of villages, then of towns and finally of cities and great empires. And agriculture also freed humans for the first time from the constant need to forage for food. It gave them the leisure to develop cultures and to find new ways – like writing – of passing on accumulated wisdom to their descendants.

The Middle East had another advantage, too – though at times it must have seemed like a curse to the people who lived there. The whole, vast region forms a kind of hinge between the Far East, Europe and Africa. Despite the inhospitable deserts of the Arabian Peninsula, this key position

has meant that the Middle East has always attracted people from outside, both near and far. Some came as peaceful traders, others as conquerors. As a result, the region has perhaps the most turbulent history of any on the planet.

The great ancient empires of Ur and Sumer, Akkad, Babylon, Assyria and Persia rose within the Middle East. Others, like the empire of Alexander and those of the Romans and the Byzantines, came from outside and incorporated all or part of the region. Then, in the 7th century, Islam spread from Mecca and Medina. Within a few decades, Arab horsemen had conquered Egypt, the Maghreb, Spain. First from Damascus and then from Baghdad the caliphs (and then the Ottoman sultans) ruled over three continents for centuries. But they had no more success than their Christian Crusader enemies in creating the peaceful, united realm their religion promised. Even when its political power began to decline, though, Islam remained the religion of the overwhelming majority of Middle Eastern people.

European colonialism in the 19th and early 20th centuries overlaid new borders on the successor states to these empires, creating the Middle East as we know it. The formation of the state of Israel in 1948 and the growth of the oil industry in the Gulf added new tensions. The spread of fundamentalist Islam and terrorist movements from the 1970s onwards raised the geopolitical stakes still higher. The Gulf War, the 2001 war in Afghanistan and the 2003 Iraq War have brought the region close to political explosion today.

The Middle East has known both glory and decline, but it has always returned to a kind of dynamic balance. Whether it can do so again depends above all on its young people, who form the majority in most states. Everywhere, they hunger for freedom and modernity. The road to greater peace and tolerance is hard, but the peoples of the region have a long history of innovation and adaptation.

Heart of the world *The core of the Middle East lies at the base of the Arabian Peninsula, the very centre of the ancient world. By both land and sea, it radiates outwards to north and south, east and west. The same expansive geography opens the region to influences from outside.*

Where the waters rise Though they are anything but lush themselves, the mountains of eastern Turkey are the source of the Middle East's fertility. It is here that the twin rivers of ancient Mesopotamia, the Tigris and Euphrates, rise. The waters that first brought life and plenty to the Fertile Crescent, far to the south, originate in unpromising landscapes such as this, in the valley of the upper Euphrates, near Kemah (left). Water never seems to linger on these slopes. The rain and the spring snowmelt pour away downriver without softening an arid mountain scene.

The high road Snow and ice and a spartan settlement in rough terrain torn by winds: a valley in Afghanistan's north-eastern Badakhshan province (right) presents an uninviting prospect to the Western visitor. But the native trader sees the perfect route for his mule or camel trains here. The winter-hardened earth and frozen rivers make a more reliable thoroughfare than he could hope to find in the claggy spring thaw or in the heat and dust of summer. What may appear a remote outpost is in fact a link in a longer chain of commerce, connecting communities in Afghanistan with others in Pakistan and even western China.

Mountain fortress The highest point in the ridge that walls the south-eastern corner of the Arabian Peninsula, Jabal Al-Akhdar (above) looks like a mighty fortification. Its rocky ramparts reach an altitude of 9777 ft (2980 m). They dominate the Gulf of Oman as though standing guard over the ships that ply back and forth between The Gulf and the Indian Ocean. These heights are a continuation of the range that buttresses the western edge of Iran before running on through the Kurdistan region to link up with the mountains of southern Turkey.

East or West? What might seem a vista from the American West (right) is actually a scene from Ma'lula, some 30 miles (50 km) north-east of Damascus. The vast Syrian plateau stretches out like a sea of stones. This is a typical Middle Eastern desert landscape; the only variety is provided by differing rock formations. Here the limestone and sandstone of the Anti-Lebanon mountains add a lighter tint to the plateau and rock outcrops alike; south-east of this region, the colours become greyer as volcanic rock begins to predominate.

A desert on the doorstep Within a day's travel of Tel Aviv, the Negev (below) looks as though it could be on another planet, with its weird plateaus, its wrinkled ridges and its dark dunes. The contrast with the region's rocky deserts could scarcely be more striking; the Negev landscape is softened by shifting sand. Yet the two distinct desert topographies are in fact complementary – shattered by frost and then wind-worn to powder, the debris of the rougher uplands finally drifts down here on the desert breezes to form the dunes that spread across the Dead Sea Valley.

Silken sandstone The structure of the famous 'Tomb of Silk' at Petra, Jordan (right), is so called because it looks like bales of silk stacked up in a draper's shop. The depth and colour of successive strata were dictated by the changing climatic conditions prevailing at the time of their first formation at the end of the Tertiary period, more than 1.6 million years ago. Despite the exposure of these ancient deposits, their colours remain vivid because of the dryness of the desert, which has prevented excessive oxidisation or growth of lichens. Between the 4th century BC and AD 106, when their kingdom was conquered by the Roman Empire, architects of the Nabataean trading city of Petra (the name is Greek for 'stone') learned how they could put these colourful sediments to work, carving astounding temples and tombs out of the cliffs and hillsides of the Jordan Valley. The most stunning effects could be created by exploiting the thickness of the different seams, and by varying the angles at which the craftsman cut across them.

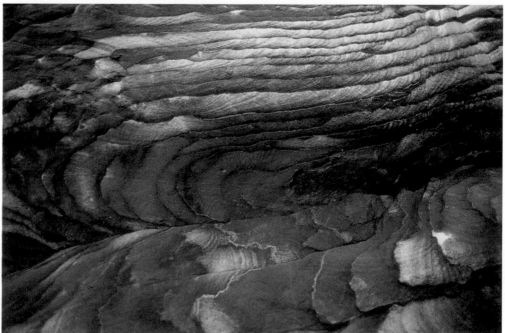

Coral threshold A line of islets (left) marks out the shallow shelf that spans the opening of the Strait of Hormuz, the continuation of a barrier reef that runs along the Oman coast to the north of Muscat. The islands appear unspoilt, but several were used as bases by Iran in the 'tanker wars' of the 1980s. Others have begun to attract developers, encouraged by the Iranian government's success in opening up the isle of Quechm to tourists.

Afghan steps A series of six lakes runs like a staircase down the valley of Band-i-Amir (below) in northern Afghanistan. The turquoise tint of the water contrasts with the rich ochre of the surrounding hills, and with the distinctive coffee-cream calcifications on the sills of rock that stand, like natural dams, between them. Such water as there is collects in the corrugations between the rocky ridges; the Hazarajat Mountains contain a surprising number of lakes.

Salt stains Seen here in an aerial view, the Dead Sea shallows (right) resemble a painter's palette, but the colour scheme is entirely natural – though irrigation is thought to have increased desertification in the Jordan Valley by diverting too much of the river's water. Modern ecological concerns thus recall the Biblical view that the river's disappearance was a punishment from God. In fact, there is no great mystery about what killed the Dead Sea, or what is drying up the lower Jordan. Stranded far below sea level in the deep declivity of the Ghor Rift Valley, the Dead Sea waits for the sun to evaporate it away. Until recently the flow of the Jordan was sufficient to replace the water that was lost, but now, because of irrigation, the supply from upstream has been greatly reduced. As the level drops, the wider waters subdivide into mudbound basins, each taking on its own tone and colour according to its depth and the concentration of salt it contains. Some conservationists suggest that the Dead Sea will have disappeared completely by 2050.

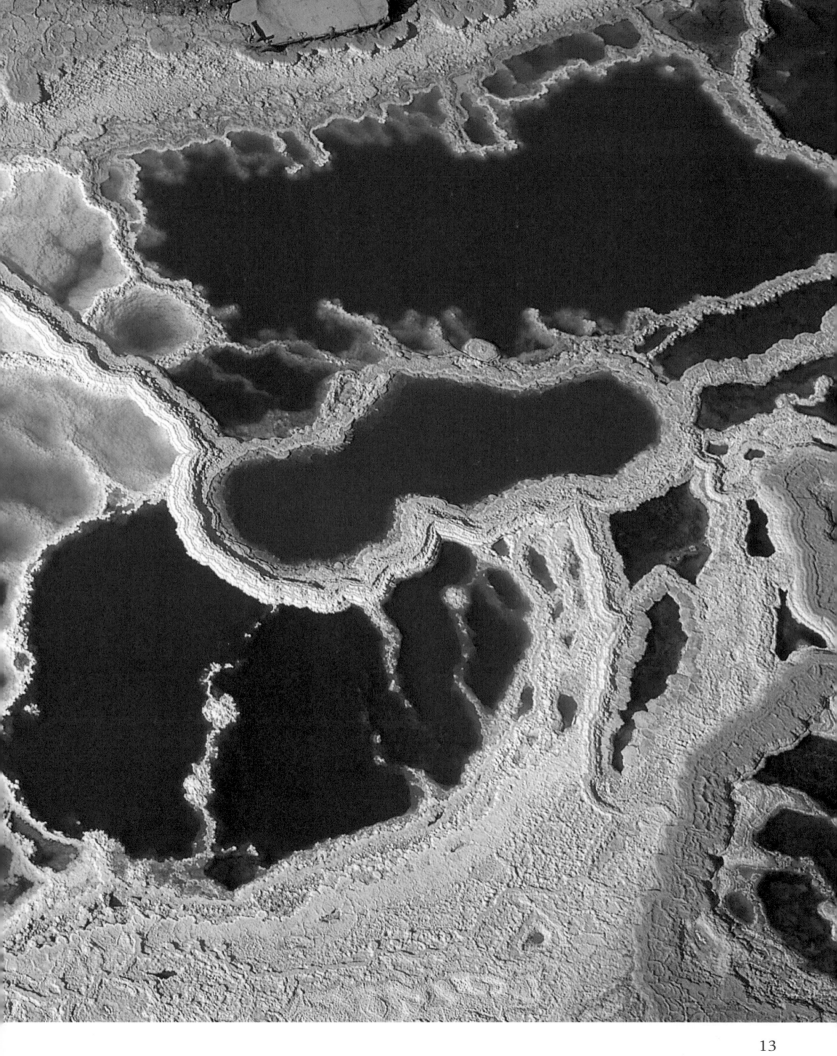

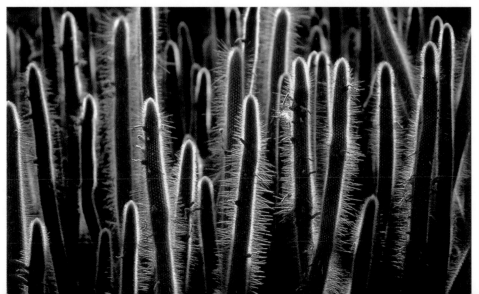

Desert blooms   In spite of its Biblical reputation as a 'land of milk and honey', the region comprising modern Israel and Palestine is actually very short of water. The human population has had to develop its own strategies for coping with this, but the native flora is perfectly adapted to dry conditions. Many plants are experts at trapping and storing every available drop of water. These Israeli cacti (left) have fleshy stems that serve as reservoirs and sharp protective spines that help to condense moisture from the morning dew. They even secrete poisons to exclude competing plants from their territory. Israeli botanists are studying such cacti, hoping to find clues to future biogenetic advances in both medicine and agriculture.

Fragile miracle The Gulf of Aqaba reaches right into the arid interior of southern Israel, a continuation of the same Ghor Rift Valley in which Lake Tiberias and the Dead Sea lie. Yet the sea here is anything but dead; the stunning richness of its coral reefs (left) is one of the region's most glorious natural treasures. There are proportionally more fish in the northern reaches of the Red Sea than in any other area of open water in the world; thanks to the plunging rift valley walls, deep-sea and reef fish live here side by side. Several hundred different species are to be found in the Gulf of Aqaba, including magnificent manta rays and fearsome sharks. Turtles, such as the loggerhead shown here, also abound in these warm subtropical waters.

Persian cat Lions, leopards, tigers and panthers all feature frequently in ancient artworks and pace menacingly through Middle Eastern legend. Gilgamesh lifted a lion above his head to show his strength, while the Hittite goddess Hebat was often depicted riding on the back of a leopard. For centuries hunted by princes for sport, and more recently killed by shepherds protecting their flocks, these majestic animals are now almost extinct. Found in the high forests of Iran's Zagros Mountains, this Persian leopard (right) is a rarity, the Iranian government's recent attempts at conservation seem almost certainly too late.

Living myth One of the largest and most elegant of antelope species, the white or Arabian oryx (right) was mentioned in the Bible, and was often taken for the legendary unicorn by European Crusaders of the Middle Ages. The confusion is easier to understand than it may seem: oryx bucks often lose a horn in the clashes of the rutting season. Today this beautiful creature survives only in small, isolated herds in the region's most inaccessible areas; these were photographed in the Hejaz uplands of western Saudi Arabia. Recently, however, the Israelis have been attempting to reintroduce the oryx to the Negev Desert in the south.

15

A brief history

The history of the Middle East begins on the flood-plain of the Tigris and Euphrates rivers. Here, on a flat expanse of sun-scorched clay, Mesopotamian culture came into being. The Greek name Mesopotamia means 'between two rivers', and the site was the key to the civilisation's success: the fertile silts laid down after the spring flood left the valley the perfect place for an agricultural revolution. Until around 10 000 years ago, the inhabitants of this area had, like other peoples of the time, lived as nomads, hunting game and gathering fruit and nuts in season – traversing vast territories in search of sustenance.

The first Noah
A mosaic of shells, the celebrated 'standard of Ur' (c.2600-2400 BC) shows Atra-hasis preparing for the great flood.

Ancient pottery
This vase, found at Al-Ubaq, Syria, is 4500 years old.

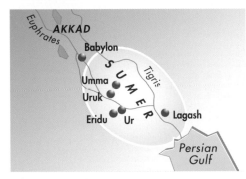

Once herding had begun to replace hunting, and the cultivation of crops to replace gathering them from the wild, human existence began to be transformed. With a more reliable supply of food, a larger and more complex community could be maintained. Surplus produce could be stored or traded with other communities. Where brushwood shelters had once been adequate, permanent settlements sprang up to accommodate a sedentary lifestyle. Mud bricks baked hard in the sun proved the ideal material for building an urban infrastructure; the new settlements expanded as irrigation schemes extended the cultivable area.

As well as working revolutions in food production and social organisation, these first farmers discovered the wheel, pottery and the plough. They equipped wooden vessels with woven sails to make their rivers into arteries of trade. Bartering food for copper from tribesmen in the hills, they also mastered metalworking skills.

Sumerian survivors *The Marsh Arabs of the Shatt al-Arab, southern Iraq, may be descended from the founders of Mesopotamian civilisation.*

The Fertile Crescent

Although Mesopotamia is generally acknowledged as the cradle of civilisation, it is conventional for archaeologists and historians to speak of the 'Fertile Crescent'. This area embraces the valleys of the Tigris and Euphrates, but also takes in the Anatolian foothills, sweeping south and westward to include much of modern-day Syria, Lebanon and northern Israel. Archaeological evidence confirms that cultural and economic commerce flowed in both directions along this crucial corridor. Researchers working at the region's many archaeological sites have found evidence of the gradual spread of innovative agricultural practices and new technologies, the gradual improvement of plant and animal stocks, and increasing urbanisation.

The Fertile Crescent

The Sumerians

Historians used to attribute all these advances to the civilisation of Sumer, which held sway in lower Mesopotamia from around 3500 BC. Today archaeologists emphasise the contributions made by other peoples living farther upriver – but there can still be no doubting the special part played by the Sumerians.

Their origins are obscure – perhaps from Oman, or even from the Indus Valley – but the Sumerians settled between the Tigris and Euphrates more than 7000 years ago. Here they built reed huts on the river banks and began to improve the primitive agriculture and animal husbandry of the region. They invented the wheel, built the first defensive walls of sun-dried mud bricks around their settlements and learned how to fire clay to make durable, multi-purpose pottery.

The Akkadian eclipse

By the middle of the 3rd millennium BC, the Sumerian settlement at Ur had grown into a fully fledged city-state. Uruk, a

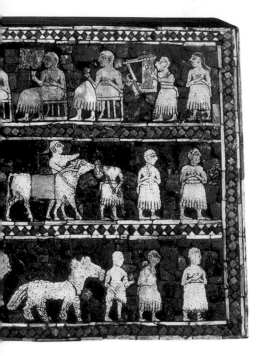

The written word

Before true writing was devised, the Sumerians are thought to have used a system of pictograms for keeping records of their exchanges of goods – an image of a cow's head to represent a cow, an image of a fish to represent a fish, and so on. These images were traced on clay, the universal material of the Sumerians. Then, about 3200 years ago, their scribes developed a system that was much faster to write, using ideograms, or stylised symbols that no longer imitated the objects they denoted. Writing in these conventional symbols is now known as cuneiform, because the symbols were impressed into soft clay using a wedge-shaped (Latin *cuneus*) stylus made from cut reed. Cuneiform quickly became a complete script, for use not only in bookkeeping but in the codification of law,

philosophical and mathematical enquiry and in literature. The example illustrated here is a clay tablet dating from about 2400 BC.

veritable metropolis, covered some 1000 acres (400 hectares) at the height of its power: its defensive walls had a circumference of 6 miles (9.6 km). Other Sumerian city-states had appeared – at Kish, for example, and at Nippur – but the centre of power was soon shifting northwards. Sumeria was not a single, unified realm but an aggregation of independent city-states, jostling for pre-eminence and power; it was dangerously vulnerable to annexation by a determined strongman.

The epic of Gilgamesh

Gilgamesh ruled Uruk around 2600 BC. A mighty warrior, he has the distinction of being the world's first literary hero: the epic poem in which he figures, first written down in Akkadian around 1600 BC, predates both the Bible and Homer. Many fragments have been found inscribed on clay tablets or carved in stone, and though there are gaps in the story, its themes of self-sacrifice, longing and loss still have great resonance. The epic tells of Gilgamesh's rivalry with his friend Enkidu, their battles together against the monster Humbaba and the goddess Ishtar, and Gilgamesh's vain search for the secret of eternal life. Gilgamesh's complex relationship with Enkidu, and his own mounting doubts and fears of death as the poem goes on, are profound and strikingly modern features of the poem.

In 2334 BC such a figure appeared in the person of Sargon, an Akkadian from the north. An official serving the Sumerian authorities in Kish, Sargon seized power in a coup; he then led his newly established kingdom in a campaign of conquest in which all of Sumer was brought to heel. Under Sargon and his sons, Akkadian influence was firmly in the ascendant, extending not only south through Mesopotamia but also westward towards the Mediterranean.

The Akkadians were the ancestors of such Semitic peoples as the Arabs and the Jews, but their history is obscured by later legend. Within the space of 200 years their empire had come and gone, torn apart by neighbouring peoples after the reign of Sargon's grandson, Naram-Sin (reigned 2254-2218 BC). But they had set a pattern of empire-building that was to dominate Middle Eastern history.

Sumerian leader   A statuette of Gudea, who rose to power in the southern city of Lagash in 2115 BC.

Abraham, father of the Jews

Perhaps the most famous inhabitant of Ur was not a Sumerian at all: tradition has it that Abraham, the Hebrew patriarch, was born in the city. Moving up the Euphrates with his family, he arrived in the northerly city of Haran. There, according to the Bible, God spoke to him in a dream: 'Leave your country, your family and your father's house for the land that I will show you.' That land was Canaan (modern Palestine), where a nation of nomadic

Monument in mud   The Ziggurat of Ur bears witness to Mesopotamian architectural skills.

shepherds and herdsmen, the Israelites, settled under the leadership first of Abraham, then of Isaac and Jacob and their descendants. Adopting the Semitic language of their Canaanite hosts, they were soon all but indistinguishable from the people they had settled among. Some scholars suspect that the story of Abraham and his Mesopotamian origins was a myth, but the tradition of outsidership, true or not, became vital to a Jewish nation that insisted on its special status as God's 'chosen people'.

Abraham and Isaac This illumination from a medieval manuscript shows how God tested Abraham's faith by demanding the sacrifice of his son, Isaac.

The Israelites did have one indisputable claim to uniqueness: their belief in a single god. Previous societies had given human forms to natural forces – earthquakes, thunder, storms, the sea – but the Israelites were the first to believe in a single, personal god with an interest in human affairs. Judaism was new in setting human standards of law and fairness; where other communities feared the arbitrary whims of irascible deities, the Jews believed they had only to keep the law of righteous conduct to maintain their god's approval. That law was codified on stone tablets by another great patriarch, Moses, on Mount Sinai, after he had led the Israelites to freedom from their enslavement in Egypt. Moses was not destined to live to see the 'Promised Land', but Joshua, the conqueror of Jericho, would claim Canaan in Moses' name, subjecting the country to Israelite law.

The people of the Book

So, at any rate, goes the biblical tradition. The truth appears to have been less clear-cut; monotheism, for instance, evolved only gradually over time. There is evidence that the early Israelites were eclectic in their observances to local deities wherever they happened to find themselves, while even Joshua may not have been quite as fanatical in his attitudes as the Bible – written piecemeal from about the 6th century BC – would have us believe. Even when the Israelite god Yahweh was established as the one god, his cult clearly owed much in its words and rituals to those of other deities in the region. Only in retrospect was the uniqueness of the Jewish people so clearly delimited.

Nonetheless, whatever its exaggerations and aggrandisements, the Bible is quite a reasonable guide to the broad sweep of Jewish history, in which the rule of the patriarchs gave way to that of the judges. Around 1030 BC, as the Bible states, Samuel anointed Saul the first king of Israel, and he steadily increased Israelite territory. His successor, David, took the city of Jerusalem in around 1000 BC and transferred to it the Ark of the Covenant, which held the stone tablets on which the laws of Moses had been engraved. He thus established what was already an ancient settlement as the sacred capital of the Jews. David's son Solomon built a temple in the

Legendary sage An illumination shows Solomon reading the Torah.

city to house the Ark. Solomon was celebrated as a wise ruler. Under his government, from 970 BC, Israel enjoyed a golden age – prosperous, politically united and militarily strong. But after his death in around 930 BC his realm split into two rival kingdoms, Israel and Judah, both overshadowed by the rising might of the Assyrians to the north and the Egyptians to the south.

The age of empires

Though Akkadian rule had faded in Mesopotamia, the Semitic language of Akkad had hung on to its dominance. When Hammurabi, ruler of Babylon between about 1792 and 1750 BC, set about emulating Sargon's imperialist mission, the language he established throughout his dominions was Akkadian. Hammurabi imposed a rigid code of law and a centralised system of taxation. Babylon became the centre of a rich and powerful empire, until its sacking by Mursilis I in 1595 BC. Mursilis was ruler of the Hittites, a people who had begun to spread from the hills of Hatti, in southern Anatolia, a century before. Their origins are mysterious: Indo-European immigrants, perhaps from far beyond the Black Sea, they seem to have been an exceptionally warlike race.

Empire-builder Sargon II extended Assyrian rule to the Mediterranean coast.

The Law Code of Hammurabi

A slab of black diorite over 6 ft (2 m) tall, closely inscribed with 282 clauses, the Law Code of Hammurabi, is the most famous monument of the Old Babylonian Empire. At the top, the king is shown receiving his laws direct from Shamash, the sun-god and patron of Babylonian justice. The code deals with matters such as property rights, divorce and the status of women. Some modern scholars suggest that, whatever its apparent concern for the orderly running of society, the code's real purpose was to justify the expropriations of Hammurabi himself.

The Hittites extended their realm through much of modern Turkey into Syria, Lebanon and Palestine. But from the 9th century BC Assyrian power was growing rapidly, and by the reigns of Sargon II (721-705 BC) and Sennacherib (704-680 BC) they had built an empire to rival ancient Akkad. Sennacherib's new capital at Nineveh boasted a marvellous palace complex, but this already seemed inadequate by the time Ashurbanipal (669-627 BC) came to survey his vast dominions. Esarhaddon's conquest of Egypt in 671 and Ashurbanipal's own vanquishing of the empire's eastern rivals, the Elamites, in 647 left the Assyrians in charge of an empire stretching from the shores of the Caspian to the valley of the upper Nile. The new palace of Ashurbanipal included a library of 25 000 clay tablets, containing not only diplomatic and legal missives, but also works of philosophy, science and literature. From inscriptions, it is clear that the king's agents were sent throughout the empire to seek works of learning and literature: Assyrian Nineveh was a centre of scholarship and culture, not just of government.

As his reign continued, Ashurbanipal's rule became increasingly tyrannical, and discontent spread throughout the Assyrian Empire. Egypt had regained its independence by 651 BC, and in 626 the Babylonians rebelled under their king Nabopolassar (ruled 626-605), with help from the Medes

The Temple

'Now, in the 124th year after the Exodus from Egypt, in the fourth year of his reign over Israel... Solomon ordered the building of the Temple of Yahweh.' There is no archaeological evidence for Solomon's Temple, but the Bible gives a good description. It was built of stone and Lebanese cedar, and decorated with gold, silver and ivory. The rectangular building consisted of a porch, the main hall (the 'Holy Place') and finally the raised, windowless chamber known as the 'Holy of Holies', where the Ark of the Covenant was kept. The Holy Place was lit by a great seven-branched candelabrum (the Menorah), shown here being carried off after the Roman sack of Jerusalem in AD 70.

of modern Iran; by 609 BC the Assyrian Empire had vanished, and a new Babylonian Empire had replaced it.

Nabopolassar's son Nebuchadnezzar II (ruled 605-562 BC) was a visionary and a builder in his own right. Under his rule, Babylon became the unrivalled metropolis of the Middle East, its awesome architecture a suitable setting for the outpouring of artistic, intellectual and scientific accomplishment that characterised the new empire. Though the magnificence of many Mesopotamian civilisations has not survived, enough of the blue-glazed brickwork of Babylon has endured – the Gate of Ishtar, for example – to give us a real sense of the grandeur of Nebuchadnezzar's city.

The Hanging Gardens of Babylon

One of the Seven Wonders of the World, the Hanging Gardens of Babylon are thought to have been built by King Nebuchadnezzar II, though Philo of Byzantium, the 3rd century BC writer on the Seven Wonders, attributes them to the legendary Queen Sammu-ram (Semiramis) two centuries earlier. There is no archaeological proof that the gardens ever existed, although several classical writers testify to their vast scale and spectacular appearance. Rather than 'hanging', they seem to have been raised up in tiers on the roof of the royal palace. An elaborate system of irrigation brought water from the nearby Euphrates.

Citadel of power Its elevated site a natural stronghold, the Hittite capital of Hattusas (left) was ideally suited as a hub of empire.

Imperial idyll Few tangible traces remain of the mud-brick cities of Mesopotamia. This is a 19th-century painter's vision of Nimrud.

The power of the Persians

Even as Babylon dazzled the ancient world, new nations were emerging in Iran, where first the Medes and then the Persians were in the ascendant. Under Cyrus II 'the Great' (556-530 BC), the Persians finally prevailed; by 530 their empire extended through Lydia and Babylon. The successors to Cyrus in the Achaemenid dynasty – named after its legendary founder, the hero Achaemenes – were as energetic as he had been, his son Cambyses annexing Egypt in 525. Under Darius (522-486 BC), the Persian Empire reached its greatest extent, stretching from the Indus Valley to the Balkans. Dividing the empire into 23 satrapies or provinces, Darius devolved power over everyday affairs to local rulers, while arrogating to himself authority over more eternal matters. Establishing a powerful cult of emperor-worship, he had his ancestors installed in impressive tombs in cities such as Persepolis and Susa.

Royal tomb Achaemenid resting place.

In 490 BC, angered by the disobedience of certain Greek cities in western Asia Minor, Darius decided to invade Greece – only to be defeated at Marathon. This setback was followed by a naval defeat for his son Xerxes at Salamis ten years later, and a further defeat on land at Plataea in 479.

Alexander and after

The lessons of the Greek triumph over Persia were not lost on Philip II of Macedon (ruled 359-336 BC). He united the Greek cities under Macedonian rule, preparing a formidable military expedition for the conquest of Persia. In 334 BC, his son and successor Alexander crossed into Asia Minor and defeated a Persian army on the banks of the River Granicus. Victory at Issus in 333 BC opened the way southward through Syria and Lebanon to Egypt; then Alexander turned eastward again to march against the very heart of the Persian Empire. Spurning Darius III's offer to cede all Persian territories

Full gallop The Parthians were superb riders and keen archers.

Alexander in action The young hero in the thick of things at the historic Battle of Issus, as recorded in a mosaic from Roman times.

west of the Euphrates, Alexander pushed on, routing a Persian army under Darius himself at Gaugamela in 331.

Even then, Alexander refused to rest: in 326 BC he crossed the Hindu Kush and pressed on into India. But by now his men were tired and restless, so Alexander turned reluctantly back. Alexander never saw Macedon again: he died of a mysterious illness in Persepolis. His body was barely cold before his generals began squabbling for succession. Without Alexander's commanding presence, the empire grew ungovernable, its subject peoples taking advantage of the confusion to cast off the conquerors' yoke. In the end, no single ruler was able to take over Alexander's realm. In Egypt Ptolemy seized power; he and his sons founding a lasting dynasty, while in Greece and the Aegean Antigonus and his heirs came to power. The Middle

The Parthians and Sassanids

Nomadic horsemen of the Central Asian steppes, the Parthians swept down to seize northern Iran in the 3rd century BC, raiding far and wide through what was left of the Persian Empire under Seleucid rule. A century later, under Mithridates I (shown in the medallion) they consolidated their grip on the region, but in AD 224 suffered defeat at the hands of a Persian client-ruler. Ardashir I quickly stamped his authority on the region, invading India and conquering Armenia, while making himself the unchallenged ruler in Persia, where he established Zoroastrianism as the state religion. Despite setbacks, Ardashir's Sassanid successors held back repeated Roman advances through the 3rd and 4th centuries, but were overwhelmed by the Ephthalites, or 'White Huns', at the end of the 5th century. Ephthalite dominance was finally brought to an end by Khosrau I, who embarked on a campaign of conquest, pressing westward to the Caucasus and the Black Sea coast, carving inroads into the Byzantine Empire.

Babylonian Empire, around 600 BC

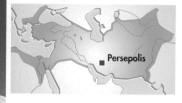

Persian Empire, around 500 BC

Seleucid Empire, around 300 BC

Greek influence
Statuary at Memrut Dagi, Turkey, testifies to Hellenistic rule.

East, including Persia, Syria, Mesopotamia and parts of Asia Minor, was fought over for 40 years before falling to the lot of Seleucus and his successors, who created a capital at Antioch. Though the Seleucids' Middle Eastern subjects were ready enough to let themselves be 'Hellenised', adopting Greek language and culture, the collapse of the Persian Empire and the wars of succession had left a legacy of political restlessness throughout the region.

Messages from the past Almost 2000 years after they were hidden by Essenes, the Dead Sea Scrolls were found by desert nomads.

Byzantine art This stunning mosaic shows Christ and his disciples at the Last Supper.

The coming of Christ

Judaea, the Seleucid province that included the ancient lands of the Israelites, was a typical centre of unrest. Here religious conflict between Hellenised and conservative Jews led to open Jewish revolt against the Seleucids in 161 BC. Under their leader Judas Maccabeus and his successors, the rebels eventually won an autonomy that lasted until the Roman conquest in 63 BC. The Romans also allowed the Jews a degree of independence within the empire.

The Judaism into which Jesus was born was riven by fierce faction-fighting between the adherents of different sects or systems of observance, including the punctilious

The Eastern Church

Many Christians in the East saw no reason to accept the authority of Rome, or its particular interpretation of the Gospels. With rival theological centres at Jerusalem and Antioch offering different rules, Christians were bitterly divided by the Emperor Constantine's time. The ecumenical council the emperor held at Nicaea in 325 tried unsuccessfully to reconcile the different groups.

In time, Eastern orthodoxy formally separated from Roman Catholicism. There was, however, no sudden schism. For several centuries the two Churches maintained an uneasy coexistence, and it was only in the 11th century that they finally ended all dialogue.

Orthodoxy has Greek, Bulgarian and Serbian branches – the Churches were given independence from the Byzantine patriarchite in the 19th century when those nations won their freedom from Ottoman Turkish rule. The Russian Church seceded in the 15th century; it was a state religion both under the tsars and under Soviet rule. There are also other Middle Eastern Christians – Chaldeans, Copts, Melchites, Maronites and many more.

Pharisees and the more Hellenistic Sadducees; Christ ultimately came into conflict with both groups. The nationalist Zealots, while representing a long-standing current of Jewish opinion, were relatively quiet in Christ's lifetime. The mystic Essenes withdrew from society; much of what we know about them dates from the discovery of the Dead Sea Scrolls near Qumran in the 1950s.

That Christ was inspired by the Essenes, as some have claimed, seems entirely possible, though his message was more one of engagement in society. Nonetheless, his teachings reach us only through the interpretative filter of the evangelists Matthew, Mark, Luke and John – and through the epistles of Paul, the man who made Christianity a religion acceptable throughout the Greek and Roman world. Though born a Jew, Paul was proud of his Roman citizenship, and spread his own version of the teachings of Christ throughout Asia Minor and Greece before finally reaching Rome. It was here that the new faith grew, despite intellectual opposition from Roman and Greek thinkers and occasionally brutal persecution by several emperors, until it became the official religion of the empire in the 4th century.

The Byzantine Empire

By this time the Roman world was beset by invaders all along its northern frontier. At the end of the 3rd century, the emperor Diocletian attempted to rationalise imperial government by dividing the Roman world into western and eastern halves. The first Christian emperor, Constantine, reunited the empire in 324, but six years later effectively turned his back on the western part, transplanting his capital to the old Greek colony of Byzantium – or Constantinople, as he renamed it. Standing on the shores of the Bosporus in the heart of what is now Istanbul, he effectively refounded the Roman Empire. Earlier Romans would have been staggered to see the Christian, Greek-speaking, Asiatic 'Rome' that Constantine had created, yet it would long outlast its predecessor, enduring for another thousand years.

The lawgiver Justinian I collected and codified the system of Roman law.

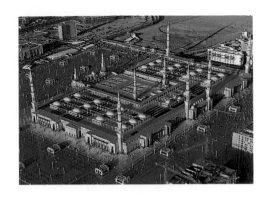

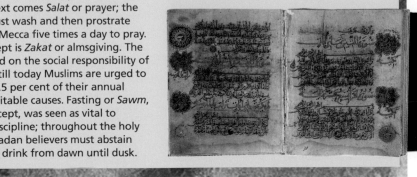

Burial place *Muhammad lies beneath the floor of the Mosque at Medina, one of the great holy places of Islam.*

Stone of pilgrimage *The black meteorite at the Ka'bah in Mecca was venerated in pre-Islamic times.*

A people apart

Arabia, with its nomadic herdsmen and traders, was more or less untouched by the rise and fall of the great empires. Its people were mentioned in the Assyrian chronicles and in the Bible, and at least one Roman emperor, Philip the Arab (ruled 244-9) came from their ranks. The Greek historian Herodotus, in the 5th century BC, had described their land as 'Arabia felix' ('Happy Arabia') – but by the 6th century advancing desertification had begun to deplete its small stock of cultivable land.

Most Arabs were polytheistic, though there were also important Byzantine Christian and Zoroastrian minorities. Their holiest shrine, a mysterious stone said to have been turned black by the sins of humanity, was at Mecca. In AD 610, according to tradition, a young trader named Muhammad began to experience divine revelations just outside the city that would make Mecca the spiritual and political centre of a new Islamic world. Muhammad, the Prophet, was inspired by the archangel Gabriel with a series of suras, the chapters of a new spoken scripture, the Koran. He began to preach rejection of polytheism in favour of worship of a single, all-powerful deity, Allah (*al-Ilah*, 'the god' in Arabic).

The Koran, from the Arabic *Qur'an* (recitation), is still transmitted orally and learned by heart. It was very much an oral inspiration for an illiterate people. Muhammad identified strongly with those earlier revelations recorded in the scriptures of the Jews and Christians; he was eager for Arabs to absorb the spirit of community he saw set down in Jewish law. None of these virtues, Muhammad felt, was much in evidence among the *Quraysh*, the elite of his tribe who controlled Mecca and its lucrative shrine.

Not surprisingly, far from embracing Muhammad's teachings, the *Quraysh* regarded him with contempt. In 622 he and his few followers were forced to make a migration (*hijrah*) to the northern oasis settlement of Yathrib, known to subsequent history as Al-Medinah or Medina, 'the city'. This migration is regarded by Muslims as the true beginning of their faith. It seems to have been in Medina, around 624, that, finding himself in theological conflict with the Jewish community, Muhammad came to realise how distinct from the Judaeo-Christian tradition his new Arabic faith was, for all its shared heritage. Muhammad himself became the political and military – as well as spiritual – leader of an Islamic community based in Medina; the new religion made no distinction between spiritual and secular power. However, Islam was soon having to fight for its own survival by force of arms. Muhammad's capture of Mecca in 630 represented a coming of age for the new religion, and it ushered in what was to be an astonishing period of conquest.

Written witness *The sacred book of Islam, the Koran, comprises 114 chapters or suras.*

The five precepts of Islam

'There is one god, Allah, and Muhammad is his Prophet'; this was the fundamental tenet of Islam and remains so to this day. *Shahadah,* or witness to the truth of this basic belief, is the first of the five spiritual duties of the Muslim. Next comes *Salat* or prayer; the worshipper must wash and then prostrate himself facing Mecca five times a day to pray. The third precept is *Zakat* or almsgiving. The Prophet insisted on the social responsibility of his faith, and still today Muslims are urged to offer at least 2.5 per cent of their annual income to charitable causes. Fasting or *Sawm,* the fourth precept, was seen as vital to spiritual self-discipline; throughout the holy month of Ramadan believers must abstain from food and drink from dawn until dusk.

Finally, at least once in a lifetime, the true Muslim should make the hadj, the pilgrimage to Mecca to offer the same ritual observances that Muhammad himself did so many centuries ago.

The Muslim triumph

Muhammad died in 632, and with no son to assume his place, his father-in-law Abu-Bekr was elected as his representative or *khalifah* – a word traditionally anglicised as 'caliph'. Completing the unification of Arabia, Abu-Bekr then turned to the north and east, sending expeditions to Iraq and Syria. Under his successor, Umar ibn al-Khattab (634-44), the Arab search for new lands became an extraordinarily swift and successful campaign of conquest.

The Christian view that Islam was a militaristic creed finds no support in the teachings of the Prophet himself. Nonetheless, Umar was only the first of many Muslim

For Allah Built between 706 and 715, the Umayyad Mosque, Damascus, is a masterpiece of Islamic art.

leaders to find in wars of conquest a way of uniting a quarrelsome tribal people with a tradition of raiding one another's settlements and camps. Umar's Arab armies swept into Egypt, Syria and Mesopotamia – all Byzantine provinces, ill prepared for the Islamic advance. Victory at Qadisiyyah in 637 opened the way into Sassanid Persia; the following year came the highly symbolic capture of Jerusalem.

Umar's successors in the Umayyad dynasty named after him continued his work, advancing along the coast of North Africa and across the Strait of Gibraltar to Spain, while Central Asia and north-west India were added to the empire in the east. Within a hundred years of Muhammad's death, the Prophet's teachings were treasured over a vast swathe of territories stretching all the way from the Pyrenees to the Himalayas.

The empire the Umayyads built was not just a military creation; a distinctly Islamic culture, rich and elaborate, had already evolved. Muslim teaching tended to frown on representative images that might encourage idolatry, so emphasis was placed on abstract ornamentation and on beautiful calligraphic expressions of the divine word. In ceramics, carpets, metalwork and jewellery, as well as in grand palaces, gardens and mosques, Muslim artists and craftsmen fostered a dazzling material culture, while poets and scholars wrote marvellous poems and made scientific and philosophical discoveries.

The caliphs of Baghdad

With such rapid expansion over a huge area, it is perhaps not surprising that there were soon stresses and strains within the Islamic Empire. These included serious spiritual differences – a growing band of believers known as Shiites argued that Islam had gone fundamentally wrong ever since Ali, Muhammad's cousin and son-in-law, was passed over as successor. In 747 the Persian province of Khorasan rebelled against Umayyad rule, beginning a process

Byzantine Empire in 565

Arab Empire in 750

Warriors of God In this colourful Persian miniature, Muslim horsemen prepare to charge, with banners unfurled and trumpets blaring.

Sunnis and Shiites

Just as different doctrinal and ritual traditions developed within Judaism and Christianity, so in Islam separate strands of belief evolved. Sunnis claimed a direct succession through the Umayyad caliphs from Abu-Bekr and from the Prophet himself. Followers of the *sunnah* or 'custom' recorded by Muhammad's family and friends from what they saw of the Prophet's life, they obeyed *Shariah* – Islamic sacred law – and its everyday social application in the laws of *Fiqh*. A breakaway sect of Shiites argued that this brand of Islam was corrupt from the start. They insisted that the succession should have passed through Muhammad's cousin and son-in-law Ali bin Abi Taleb. Though Ali had actually served a term as fourth caliph (656-61), his followers argued that he ought to have been the first, and that a different line of 11 imams should have come after him. An Umayyad supporter had in fact assassinated Ali and his son Hussein, thus preventing this potential succession. But Shiites believed that their imams still had Allah on their side: as infallible teachers, they should lay down the law for all believers.

Islamic astrolabe Muslim learning and inventions found their way to Europe through al-Andaluz, in modern Spain.

of political fragmentation. But even in 750, when the Abbassids of Khorasan organised a massacre of the Umayyads and seized control of the caliphate, the cultural and spiritual flowering of Islam continued. Indeed, governed from a new capital at Baghdad, on the banks of the Tigris in what had been Mesopotamia but was now Arab Iraq, Islam entered an Abbassid golden age. Under Harun ar-Rashid (786-809) and his successors, Baghdad became a centre of economic and cultural energy. Islamic scholars worked hard to preserve much of the learning of the ancient world and the orient and to translate it into Arabic, and did new work of their own in astronomy, philosophy, medicine and mathematics. Abbasid rule also brought new standards of racial and religious tolerance to Islam; followers of other religions were allowed far greater freedom in the Islamic world than their counterparts in the Roman Catholic or Byzantine Christian lands.

By the start of the 10th century the power of the Abbassids was on the wane and a new dynasty of Shiites had established itself in the Maghreb, Muslim North Africa. The Fatimids, they claimed descent from Muhammad's daughter Fatimah and his son-in-law Ali. Meanwhile the Buwayhids, a confederacy of peoples from the southern shores of the Caspian Sea, overran Persia (913) and Mesopotamia (945). The Abbassid caliphate's political power was at an end. But a new threat was arising in the east – the Turks.

Horse power The great strength of the Ottoman army lay in the quality of its cavalry.

The Turks take over

The Turks were nomad horsemen from the Steppes. They had adopted the Muslim religion, though the Arabic cultural values associated with Islam had proven rather less compelling. Led by the powerful Seljuk clan, the Turks were recruited as mercenaries by the Abbassid authorities in Baghdad, but by 1092 were *de facto* rulers of the eastern Islamic realms, their empire reaching well into Anatolia at its western limits. Their dominance tilted the balance of power within Islam back towards the Sunni tradition, while their conquest of Anatolia marked the beginning of the end for the Byzantine Empire. Seljuk power began to fragment after 1095, just as the first of the western Crusaders arrived in the Middle East.

Out of balance With their heavy armour and mighty chargers, the Crusaders (on the right in this miniature) were outmanoeuvred by their fast, lightly armed Turkish opponents.

Turkish stronghold This fortified base in Anatolia was built by the Ottoman Turks.

The Crusades

It was at the request of the Byzantine emperor Alexius Comnenus I in 1091 that Pope Urban II inaugurated the First Crusade. A disorganised crowd of pilgrims and adventurers answered his initial call, travelling overland through the Balkans to Constantinople. Though Alexius had hoped for assistance in expelling the Seljuk Turks from his empire, the leading Crusaders had different aims: the liberation of the Holy Places of Jerusalem from Muslim rule and – in many cases – their own enrichment. The Crusaders established a series of kingdoms down the coast of Syria and Lebanon. In 1099 a French-led army achieved its main objective, seizing Jerusalem from the Fatimids. However, the Second Crusade in 1145 ended in failure, with a French defeat outside Damascus by the Turks.

The fortunes of Crusaders and Muslims seesawed back and forth for the next two centuries. By 1187, the charismatic Kurdish leader Salah ad-Din or Saladin had restored Jerusalem to Islam. Despite the campaigns of England's King Richard I and other Christian kings involved in the Third Crusade of 1189-92, Saladin was able to hold on to his prize. The Fourth Crusade (1202-4) saw Crusaders sack the city of Constantinople, while the Fifth (1217-22) ended in failure. Two further Crusades in 1248 and 1270 were utter fiascos that ended the Crusading dream.

Fortress of faith Syria's Krak des Chevaliers was built by Crusaders in the 12th century.

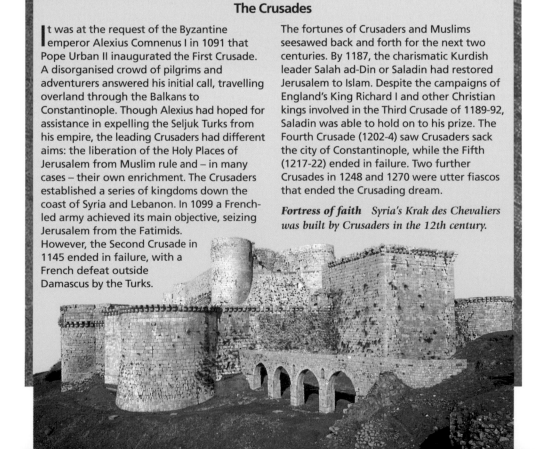

Mongols versus Mamelukes

From around 1220 the Mongols, another nation of nomads from the north Asian grasslands, burst in upon the lands of Islam under their leader Genghis Khan. They massacred the population of Nishapur in 1221 and, under Genghis's grandson Hulegu, took Baghdad in 1258. The Mongols stayed on in the eastern Islamic heartlands, adopting the Islamic heritage.

In the south, the Ayyubid dynasty founded by Saladin in 1177 ruled the former Fatimid lands until 1250. In that year, the Mamelukes – a caste of mainly Turkish slave soldiers – gained control of Egypt and Syria. They managed to turn back the Mongol advance at Ain Jalut, in northern Palestine, in 1260, and consolidated their power. Their empire lasted until 1517, and their caste identity until 1811.

Ottoman Empire in the 16th century

EUROPE

Constantinople

ASIA

AFRICA

Where continents meet
An exhilarating prospect
of the Topkapi Palace,
home of the Ottoman
emperors for 300 years,
highlights Istanbul's
dramatic situation on
the narrows of the
Bosporus.

Suleiman the Magnificent

Born in 1494, Suleiman the Lawgiver, as he is known to Muslims, ascended the Ottoman throne in 1520. In the 46 years of his reign, the empire reached its greatest extent, and its growth was accompanied by a cultural renaissance whose greatest monument is the stupendous Suleimaniye Mosque built in Istanbul in 1550-7. Painting, poetry, philosophy, scholarship and science also flourished in a time of astonishing creativity and learning, prompted in part by the sultan's openness to the ideas and innovations of the West. Yet it is possible to see even in Suleiman's leadership the seeds of the empire's decline. His retreat from active government to a more ceremonial role added to the mystique of the sultan, but over time was a recipe for lack of leadership and inefficiency.

Faithful to
the death
The Ottoman
armies owed
many crucial
triumphs to the
janissaries.

The Ottoman Empire

As Mongol power receded, the Turkish Ottoman dynasty came to the fore in eastern Anatolia, seizing extensive territories from the Byzantines in both Asia Minor and the Balkans. Their emperor Mehmed II finally captured Constantinople in 1453. The city he renamed Istanbul became the capital of a mighty Ottoman empire – its shock weapon the elite corps of janissaries, slave-soldiers raised from boyhood to fight for the Prophet like the Mamelukes before them.

In the course of the 16th century, the Ottoman Empire took over much of the western Muslim world. Though the Christian reconquest of Spain, the *reconquista*, had finally been completed in 1492, the Ottoman hold on the Holy Land was absolute. They also made themselves masters of the Mediterranean – the first major Muslim sea power since the 7th century.

For nearly 300 years, the Ottoman emperors waged almost constant war against the Christian powers of Europe – first the Spanish Habsburg Empire, then Austria and finally Russia. In 1529, and again in 1683, Ottoman forces came near to capturing Vienna. For much of the same period, they fought brutal wars against their Islamic neighbour to the east, the Shiite empire of Safavid Persia. By the mid 17th century, however, the empire was starting to fall behind its European rivals in wealth, technology and military power.

'The sick man of Europe'

Throughout the same period, Europe gradually developed maritime trading links with Asia. These increased European wealth while slowly reducing the Ottoman Empire to an economic backwater. Ever more formidable European armies drove the Ottomans from much of the Balkans, while the empire's North African provinces became increasingly independent. When

Napoleon invaded Egypt in 1798, his chief opponent was not the weak Ottoman Empire but Britain, France's colonial rival in the region.

In 1827 the European powers combined to smash the Ottoman fleet off Navarino, Greece. From this point the power of the Ottoman Empire was ebbing away. By the beginning of the 20th century a group of modernising army officers concluded that the only way to save the empire was to pull down its tottering power structures. The 'Young Turks', as they were known, were at first unsuccessful; in 1914 the 'sick man of Europe' drifted into the First World War on the Central Powers side, with its government almost paralysed by corruption.

Pomp and circumstance
Few foreign envoys came away
unimpressed by the splendour of
the Ottoman court.

When one of the Young Turks, Mustafa Kemal 'Atatürk', succeeded in resurrecting his country after the First World War, it was not as an Islamic empire but as a modern, secular republic.

A dream of Zion

By the end of the 19th century, Palestine, a province of the the Ottoman Empire, had some 350 000 inhabitants, of whom 85 per cent were Muslims, 11 per cent Christians and only 4 per cent Jews. The vast majority of the Jewish nation had lived in exile – mainly in Europe and other parts of the Middle East for nearly 2000 years. Meanwhile, in Eastern Europe, where the largest concentrations of Jews were to be found by the late 19th century, anti-Semitism was growing, and pogroms (organised attacks on Jewish communities) were frequent.

Many Jews chose emigration as an escape from these attacks. The 'Jewish homeland' of Palestine, a British protectorate after the

Old enemies The Yom Kippur War of 1973 was the fourth Arab-Israeli conflict.

Father of the Turks *Mustafa Kemal was the founder of modern Turkey.*

First World War, was the favoured destination for many. British rule made it a haven from pogroms, and the call of the ancient, Biblical homeland remained strong for many Jews. Theodor Herzl (1860-1904), founder of the 'Zionist' movement, proposed the creation of a modern Jewish state in Palestine, and the Balfour Declaration of 1917 committed Britain to the support, not quite of a Jewish state, but of a Jewish 'national home'.

After the Second World War and the horrors of the Holocaust, the steady flow of Jewish immigrants to Palestine became a flood. In 1947, despite fierce opposition from Arab states, the United Nations responded to the Zionist call by proposing the partition of Palestine between Jews and Arabs. The state of Israel was proclaimed in 1948.

The new nation was immediately at war with its Arab neighbours. Up to a million Palestinian Arabs were forced from their homes as Israel enlarged its boundaries in response to Arab invasions in 1948 and 1956. In the Six-Day War of 1967, Israel destroyed the armies and air forces of Egypt, Syria and Jordan. Egyptian and Syrian invasions in the Yom Kippur War of 1973 posed a greater threat, but Israeli forces again emerged triumphant.

Only in 1978, in peace talks overseen by US President Jimmy Carter, did the first signs of an end to Arab-Israeli hostility begin to emerge. At the Camp David summit in 1979, Egyptian premier Anwar Sadat and Israeli prime minister Menachem Begin signed a peace treaty between their countries, and Israel agreed to withdraw from occupied Sinai. Little by little, the Arab states began formally to acknowledge Israel's right to exist.

French and British mandates, 1920-23
◼ French mandate   ◼ British mandate

Home at last Jews celebrate the proclamation of the state of Israel on 14 May, 1948. Within hours their country would be at war.

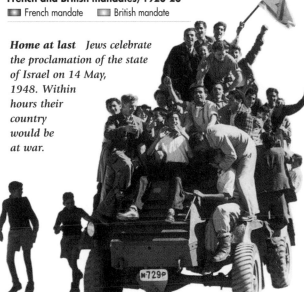

Afghan agony

The liberation of Afghanistan from a ten-year Soviet occupation in 1989, after a long and brutal war against the invaders, brought no end to the country's suffering. The disparate political factions that had maintained an uneasy alliance against the USSR soon turned against each other, and the country was further ravaged by civil war. The capital, Kabul, was a particular target.

The capture of the city in 1996 by the fundamentalist Islamic Taliban group was guardedly welcomed at first (pro-Taliban Kabulis demonstrate their support, above) – at least they brought peace. But the Taliban ruthlessly enforced a harshly repressive version of Islamic law, and openly supported international terrorism against the West. Finally, in late 2001, a sustained US-led air offensive again devastated Kabul and other Afghan cities, and Taliban military forces were routed by their Northern Alliance enemies.

The Palestinians

Driven into exile or refugee camps by Israeli armed forces, the Palestinians increasingly began to demand their own state, based on historical claims at least as strong as those of the Jews. The Palestinian Liberation Organisation (PLO), founded in 1964, began its armed struggle in the wake of the 1967 war and the Israeli occupation of the West Bank, previously a Palestinian territory within the kingdom of Jordan. PLO members were responsible for a series of 'skyjackings', bombings and other attacks worldwide. Yasser Arafat, their leader, was reviled in the 1970s as a terrorist,

Desert storm

Iraq protested when Kuwait was granted independence in 1961, making no secret of its claim that the kingdom was Mesopotamia's '19th province'. The Iraqi dictator Saddam Hussein maintained this claim throughout the 1980s, but in US eyes his Ba'ath regime seemed preferable to Ayatollah Khomeini's Islamic revolution, so the USA supported Iraq in the Iran-Iraq War of 1980-8.

Emerging from war victorious but bankrupt, Saddam sought loans from his wealthy Kuwaiti neighbours; in August 1990, when none was forthcoming, he sent his powerful army to annex their country.

Within weeks, an enormous allied land, air and sea force was assembled to liberate Kuwait. Saddam's actions had thrown the entire Middle East into confusion, and a number of Arab states joined Western powers like Britain in the US-led alliance.

Fire! *An oil well burns during the conflict.*

On January 17, 1991, alliance forces mounted a devastating attack – Operation Desert Storm – on Iraq's army of occupation. The Iraqi army collapsed, and it was all over in a matter of days. However, Saddam was left in power: the fragile alliance would not have survived an effort to oust him. Economic sanctions were imposed on Iraq, but critics have since objected that they punish the Iraqi people while Saddam's repressive regime continues to sponsor terrorism worldwide.

Israel and the Palestinian territories

Territory:
- ▨ under Palestinian control
- ☐ under joint control
- ■ Jewish settlements

Historic handshake *Brought together by Bill Clinton in 1993, Yitzhak Rabin (left) and PLO leader Yasser Arafat found common ground on the White House lawn.*

but subsequently won respect as one of the leaders – alongside the late Yitzhak Rabin of Israel – of a peace process sponsored by successive US presidents. After a historic agreement between Rabin and Arafat in 1993, Israel granted limited self-rule to the occupied Palestinian territories and agreed to withdraw its military forces.

Since then, the lack of progress toward full autonomy and Israel's policy of continuing to allow Jewish settlement in the Palestinian territories has led to new Palestinian unrest. Among the stone-throwing youths and suicide bombers behind this unrest, or *intifada* (popular uprising), are those that have little time for Arafat's PLO or a peace process they see as leading nowhere. Despite the Palestinian tradition of pragmatism and tolerance, they increasingly draw their inspiration from the fundamentalist Islamic rhetoric of the late Ayatollah Khomeini of Iran and his successors, or international terrorist leaders like the Saudi Osama bin Laden.

It is a matter of deep embarrassment to many Palestinians that the September 11, 2001, Arab terrorist attack on New York's World Trade Center was greeted with open celebration by young Palestinians in some areas of Gaza.

Football mania *Cheering on their team, these young Iranians burn as ardently for modernity as their parents did for independence and Islam.*

The Middle East today

In many ways, the young Palestinians protesting on the streets against Israel stand for the Middle East as a whole. Everywhere in the region, young people are the largest section of the population, and they represent the future. The rhetoric of Islamic fundamentalism attracts many because of its affirmation of their distinct identity and its rejection of an exploitative, commercial West. Yet at the same time their hunger for modernity and new experience leads them to reject the repressive attitudes of many of their elders. It is this dynamic balance of tradition and modernity that has always made the Middle East what it remains today: one of the crucibles of history.

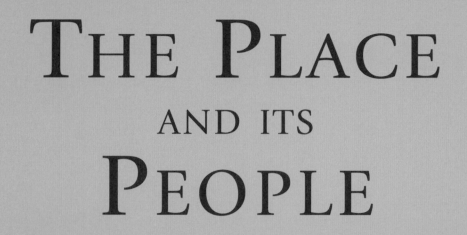

THE PLACE
AND ITS
PEOPLE

The Middle East is rooted in tradition, but it is also a place of startling modernity. Alongside souks straight out of the *Arabian Nights* are new cities built on oil wealth, with some of the most futuristic architecture in the world. From Cyprus to Afghanistan, from Turkey to Yemen, the region is home to some 270 million people, where the vast natural wealth of some is matched by the severe shortages of resources suffered by others. No single statistic adequately sums up the region as a whole, where the past jostles with the future, and contrast is the source of life itself.

CHAPTER 1

THE WONDERS OF NATURE

The landscapes of the Middle East are charged with memories. Every name seems to evoke a myth, a story, a sacred place. The Tigris, the Euphrates and the Jordan, mounts Ararat and Sinai, Lake Tiberias and Lake Van, the Dead Sea, the Bosporus, Cyprus, Socotra and the Arabian desert – all recall the ancient pagan gods and the origins of the great monotheist religions. Shaped by deep Earth forces that are still active, by extreme aridity and also by the miracle of water that makes the desert bloom, the landscape governed human life in the Middle East for thousands of years. Modern dams and lakes, pollution and exploitation have severely threatened this balance – but almost everywhere now programmes are in hand to safeguard the region's unique natural heritage.

Deserts, as here in Oman, make up the greatest part of the Arabian Peninsula.

Rivers of antiquity

In a region fragmented both naturally and culturally, the rivers have played a key role: they not only irrigated the sparse areas of fertile land, but they also acted as lines of communication between different peoples.

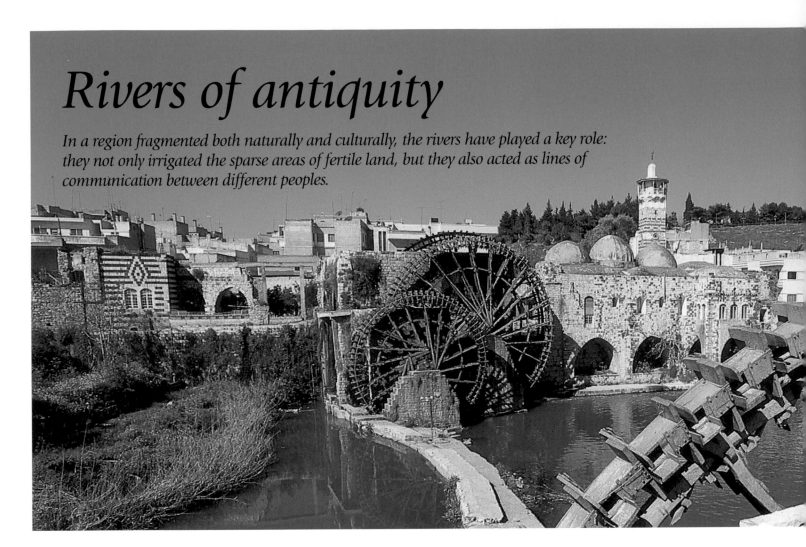

The Islamic vision of paradise is a garden with fountains and brooks. The very idea of running water holds an understandable appeal for those whose history and identity have been formed by the challenge of aridity.

The flow of progress

The peoples of the Middle East have risen to that challenge. It was here, on the plains of Mesopotamia, that agriculture was first developed. The Sumerians who worked out how to transfer some of the water from the Tigris and Euphrates on to the parched plains were the same innovators who built the first great civilisations. Monuments to their enterprising spirit can be found in the ancient norias on the River Orontes at Hama, in Syria. These giant wheels are driven by the force of the rushing current. They are rimmed with cup-like tanks, which raise water up from river level and pour it into a cistern high above, from where it flows through a series of pipes and aqueducts to supply the city. Introduced in around 300 BC, norias were once found throughout the Muslim world, with hundreds of them along the course of the Orontes alone. Now only 44 remain, in the vicinity of Hama, but, carefully maintained and their parts restored, they still supply the city and surrounding cultivated areas after more than 2000 years.

A new challenge

The challenge facing modern societies in the Middle East is not so much one of extraction as of conservation, of making sure that there will still be enough water for future generations. Another consideration is neighbouring states, as several countries may have a stake in the same river. The Orontes flows through Syria and also through Lebanon and Turkey – all three countries feel entitled to rights of extraction as well as some control over conservation issues. The river provides water for drinking, for irrigation and for hydro-electricity, and is also a means of transport and effluent disposal. In addition it is an important habitat for endangered wildlife. Overextraction near a river's source may well bring drought downstream, just as pollution in one place may result in problems hundreds of miles away. The River Jordan, for example, is slowly drying up, as Israel extracts more and more water to feed its national irrigation system. The river's flow is sluggish, and water levels in the Dead Sea and Lake Tiberias have begun to decline sharply.

Running dry

Fossil evidence suggests that some 5000 years ago, woodlands extended over much of the area that is now

Sumerian style   This type of boat, still widely used in the Euphrates delta, has been in use for more than 5000 years.

River at work *These ancient norias (giant water wheels) on the River Orontes at Hama, Syria, are proof of the long history of human efforts to control the waters of the Middle East.*

Downstream *Already a major river by the time it enters Iraq, to the north of Mosul (right), the Tigris still has a long, slow journey across the level plains of what used to be Mesopotamia.*

Twin rivers: the Tigris and Euphrates

The two great rivers of the Middle East share a birthplace, valley and delta. Their headwaters originate close together in eastern Turkey, while in their lower reaches they have been joined into a single flow by human engineers. Impressive though each may still seem to us in size, today's Tigris and Euphrates in fact represent only the last feeble tricklings of a single giant river. In prehistoric times, a huge torrent poured down from the mountains, carving out the whole valley of Mesopotamia as it rushed headlong to the Gulf. After 10 000 years of desertification, only these twin streams are left in the valley floor.

The Euphrates, whose course takes it south and west through Syria, is the longer of the two but the smaller when measured by volume. Fed by year-round run-off and spring snowmelt from the Iranian Zagros Mountains, the more easterly Tigris has a stronger flow that is less susceptible to seasonal variation. The first known human settlements were established on the Euphrates, and the cities of Ur and Babylon were built on its banks. On the Tigris stands the seat of the Assyrian Empire at Assur and its great metropolis at Nineveh. Beside the Tigris, too, the city of Seleucis was founded in the 1st century BC – later becoming Baghdad, the capital of the Abbassid caliphate.

desert; it was grazed by gazelles and giraffes, while huge herds of hippos wallowed in rivers that have long since ceased to flow. Desertification has taken place naturally over centuries, but it has gathered speed dramatically in recent decades. The region's growing population has imposed new demands, but modern economic development and industrialisation above all have reduced the total flow of water to a truly alarming extent.

The difficulty of reconciling the demands of modern societies with those of the natural environment has become one of the central problems of our time. But nowhere is the dilemma clearer than in the management of water resources. All the experts agree that meeting this challenge is becoming critically urgent in the Middle East.

An ecological disaster?

The fate of a substantial section of what was once the Fertile Crescent is a typical example. Ecological disaster is a real prospect in the plains of lower Mesopotamia, after countless generations of successful agriculture. Iraq's attempts to 'rationalise' the Tigris and Euphrates rivers artificially by damming and canalisation were perhaps misguided to begin with. These measures enabled water flow to be regulated, preventing both extensive droughts and destructive floods, but they also prevented the transportation downstream of fresh silt – the secret of the lower valley's fertility through some 10 000 years of intensive cultivation. The region that gave birth to the ancient myth of the

Holy water *The Bible indicates that Christ was baptised here, in the waters of the River Jordan.*

Garden of Eden is now slowly dying. In the end, the huge artificial reservoirs created in the upper reaches of these great rivers have multiplied by millions of times the water retention capacity of the ancient dams, and thus greatly increased the agricultural production of the irrigated areas – but the problems they have caused downstream have all but cancelled out any benefits gained.

Even worse, by trying to impose mechanical regulation on complex ecological systems, such projects make rivers vulnerable to breakdown and sabotage. This has certainly been the fate of the lower Tigris, canalised as the Shatt al-Arab waterway and consequently a key target for attack in both the Iran-Iraq War of 1980-8 and the Gulf War of 1991. Its concrete embankments were smashed at various points by bombs and shellfire, and the contained river overflowed its man-made boundaries to spread out for miles. The immense swamps that resulted formed breeding grounds for disease, and their vast open shallows caused water loss by evaporation on a scale impossible in rivers and canals – paradoxically increasing still further the danger of desertification in the flooded areas.

Mystic summits

Zion, Ararat, Sinai, Elburz, Zagros, Hadramaut – the names of many of the mountains and ranges of the Middle East conjure up symbolic or spiritual associations that transcend mere topography. Many of the region's mountains have long historical associations too, as the sites of early settlements, refuges from oppression or fortresses in times of war.

Mountain bird
Bonelli's eagle haunts the Middle East's peaks.

Once, the ancient Persians believed, the earth was flat and featureless, an open expanse that stretched to infinity without the slightest wrinkle. Nothing could improve this primal perfection, and so nothing changed or moved: the sun, moon and stars stood still in their spheres and all was silence.

Then suddenly, one fateful day, evil burst in upon the world like a terrible thunderbolt, exploding the original order and replacing it with wild chaos. Shattering the even surface of the earth, creating huge ravines and rippling up vast mountain ranges, the impact tore the planets loose from their heavenly moorings and set them circling ever after. At the epicentre of the shock, where the bolt had struck the solid ground, the earth began to rise – and continued to do so for eight centuries. The result was Mount Elburz. Though it was formed in evil, it offered hope to humankind, for from its summit ran the bridge by which the souls of the just would one day make their crossing from earth to eternity.

Higher things

From the earliest times, the scriptural records of the Middle East seem to have attached a special importance to mountain peaks. Almost every culture in the region includes some variant of the mountain temple of the Sumerians, the mountain of the god Baal of the Canaanites and Assyrians or the Mountain of Light beloved of the Persian and Afghan followers of Mithras. In the Jewish Bible, Moses climbed Mount Sinai to receive God's commandments, while Christ addressed his followers from another 'mount' – actually little more than a hill above the Sea of Galilee. Muhammad gave his own Sermon on the Mount when, just three months before he died in 632, he spoke on the upper slopes of Mount Arafat, outside Mecca. He had seen his first revelatory visions on another nearby hill, and in one experience in particular – his famous 'Night Journey' – had been transported to Jerusalem, to the top of the Temple Mount. From there a band of angels had whisked him up to heaven, where he visited Allah.

But even an atheist can appreciate the special qualities of the Middle East's mountains. Viewed from a scorching plain below, a snowcapped summit looks as if it belongs to the heavens rather than the earth. The magical, life-giving role of the mountains in much Middle Eastern culture is also easily understood. The mountains of this region seem to condense water from the parched air; they store it as snow and ice even in the baking sun, and release it as the streams and rivers that make agriculture possible even in the desert. It is only in the mountains, too, that certain plants rare

Cedar of Lebanon *A rarity now in the land of which it is the emblem, the cedar is today the subject of a campaign of replanting.*

Listening post *Mount Olympus in Cyprus lacks its Greek namesake's pantheon of deities. Instead, it is now dominated by a British listening post that can monitor the signals traffic of the entire Middle East.*

and precious in the Middle East since antiquity – incense and myrrh, kat, coffee and cedar – can grow.

It is also the fact that the mountain ranges of this part of the world provide particularly dramatic testimony to the titanic geological forces that have shaped the earth. It is easy to understand how the people who lived in such landscapes in an earlier age might intuitively have come to see the mountains themselves as evidence of vast supernatural powers. The extraordinarily regular, rectangular cliffs of the mountains of Palestine and Lebanon, for example – which stretch for nearly 300 miles (500 km) and seem to be brutally hacked from the depths of the Mediterranean and Dead seas – are evidence for us of the movement of tectonic plates. For the people of the ancient Middle East, they must have seemed just as clearly to be evidence of the slash of a divine sword, or the track of a supernatural thunderbolt.

Chain link *This jagged Afghan peak is a link in a lengthy chain of mountains that stretches from the Aegean coast to the Himalayas.*

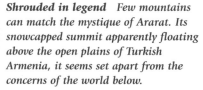

Shrouded in legend *Few mountains can match the mystique of Ararat. Its snowcapped summit apparently floating above the open plains of Turkish Armenia, it seems set apart from the concerns of the world below.*

Out of the earth *All along the geological fault that separates Arabia from Africa, dramatic volcanic cones break the horizon.*

Other, more modest summits in the Middle East owe their special place in legend and culture to more material qualities. In many cases, these hills provide hard rock for building, or crystals or rare minerals like gold that are absent from the monotonous lowlands of clay, sand or broken limestone. Thus, for example, the Yemenis hold sacred the rocky heights on which their ancient capital Sana'a is built. Similarly, the Jordanians attach special significance to Mount Nebo, which stands like a beacon above the depths of the Dead Sea on one side and the sterile expanse of the al-Asimah desert on the other.

Places of safety

Hilltop locations have of course also served as sanctuaries in times of danger and, equipped with man-made earthworks and walls, as defensive strongholds. How many sacred mountains in the Middle East owe their appeal to more mundane strategic factors we may never know. Archaeologists suspect that Mount Zion, for example, was a military citadel first and a spiritual one only second. The Christian monastery of St Catherine on Mount Sinai is another example of a mountain spiritual stronghold whose powerful defensive walls make its military function equally clear.

For the Armenians, Mount Ararat acquired a particular poignancy in the last century – not as a place of refuge, but as a symbol of their losses in the Turkish attempted genocide of 1915. The mountain also became an emblem of their lost homeland for the thousands who fled into exile to escape the massacres.

Many of the Middle East's great cities occupy hilltop sites: Jerusalem, for example, stands some 2560 ft (780 m) above sea level, covering a cluster of summits that include such famous

Mount Ararat and the Ark

When, according to the Bible, an angry Yahweh sent a deluge to engulf the earth, Noah, his family and a breeding pair of every animal species were saved in a floating Ark. The story recounts that the Ark came to rest on the summit of Mount Ararat, now in Turkish Armenia, when the waters abated. The entire population of the earth was renewed from the descendants of Noah.

The Armenians hold Mount Ararat sacred, and consider themselves the first race to have emerged after Noah's flood. An Armenian village was established high on the mountain, at the spot where Noah was believed to have built an altar of thanksgiving. Nearby, the Armenian Christian monastery of St Jacob was built in honour of a saint who was said to have tried unsuccessfully to reach the site of the Ark's remains.

Ararat was first climbed only in 1829, by the German Johann von Parrot, and both the village and the monastery of St Jacob were destroyed by an earthquake in 1840. Successful ascents have been made more recently, and some climbers have claimed to have seen the remains of the Ark.

In fact, the story of Noah was almost certainly derived from more ancient Mesopotamian flood myths. The oldest of all is the Sumerian tale of Ziusudra, who built a great boat and alone survived a flood sent by the god Enlil. The Akkadian story of Utnapishtim, which is mentioned in the Epic of Gilgamesh, offers even closer parallels to Noah: Utnapishtim not only survived the flood in a boat, but also sent out a swallow, a dove and a raven to find land as the flood receded. This story is known to have been current in Canaan before the Bible was written.

Mountain refuge Running along the whole length of western Iran, the Zagros Mountains have provided a sanctuary down the centuries for countless refugees, most recently the Kurds.

Devil's peak The ancient Persian hero Thraetaona imprisoned a fearful devil-dragon inside Mount Demavend, the highest peak in the Iranian Elburz range.

Biblical locations as the Mount of Olives. On the slopes of this hill is the Garden of Gethsemane, where Christ spent an agonising night of prayer before his arrest. Temple Mount, or Haram ash-Sharif, is not only the site of the Jews' main temple, but also the spot from which Muhammad is traditionally held to have ascended to heaven. (While his flight is attested to in the Koran, no actual starting point is specified.)

Whatever the truth, the event is commemorated by the majestic Dome of the Rock, built on the site – and one of the holiest shrines in the Islamic world. One of the world's great monuments, the Dome can be seen as an assertion in architecture of Islam's claim to be counted among the great religions of the world. As such, it has been resented by fanatical followers of the other creeds; a Christian tourist set fire to it in 1969, while a group of Jewish zealots conspired to blow it up in the early 1980s.

Other hilltop cities include Riyadh (1919 ft/585 m) and Medina (2096 ft/639 m) in Saudi Arabia, and the Syrian capital of Damascus (2267 ft/691 m). The Jordanian capital, Amman, and the Turkish capital, Ankara, both stand at 2788 ft (850 m), some way behind the Iranian metropolis of Tehran (3800 ft/1200 m). Two other Iranian cities are sited still higher – Isfahan (4600 ft/1400 m) and Shiraz (4875 ft/1485 m) – while the Afghan capital, Kabul, is higher than both with an altitude of 5905 ft (1800 m). But the most elevated city in the Middle East is the Yemeni capital, San'a, which stands 7500 ft (2286 m) above sea level.

Sanctuaries for the oppressed

If mountain-tops make readily defensible positions, larger areas of upland afford protection of a different kind. Fugitives can disappear in remote and marginal lands, while outcasts can escape persecution. The mountains of the Middle East have always had their brigands and warlords, but at one time or another they have been joined by larger groups of refugees whose only crime may have been one of religious belief or national identity.

Always mountain-dwellers, the Kurds have been pushed into the bleakest areas of their former territories, where they have had to abandon their seasonal migrations. Their sense of their own nationhood is felt as a threat by those states – Turkey, Iran and Iraq – across whose modern borders the Kurds are spread. National boundaries established on maps by 19th-century colonialists and 20th-century diplomats often failed to acknowledge the ethnic loyalties of those peoples actually living in the areas; there has arguably been no single more important cause of war.

Such difficulties are intensified where, as in much of the upland Middle East, the tradition of settled existence is a comparatively recent one. Those Kyrgyz traders who drive their camels across the high passes of the Hindu Kush today range freely across the frontiers of Afghanistan, Pakistan, Tadjikistan and even China. They went about their business equally unheeding, even at the height of the Cold War.

Where the nomadic and the nationalist spirits combine, the result can be very difficult for organised government to deal with – hence the readiness of the former Soviet-backed government of Afghanistan to brand as 'bandits' the *mujahideen* resistance. Propaganda aside, city-based bureaucrats always find it hard to understand a people in whom national pride goes hand in hand with an obstinate indifference to all the normal national institutions.

Vertigo Rising to 10 000 ft (3000 m), the Oman mountains have been deeply scored by rain. Here a path zigzags down a rocky spur.

Desert dreamscapes

From Arabia to Afghanistan, arid conditions are the norm in the Middle East. However, the desert landscape is anything but uniform. There is a world of difference between the sands of the Negev and the rocky plateaus of central Syria, or the salt pans of Iran's Dasht-e-Kavir. The one thing these landscapes share is an austere beauty that has haunted Western travellers down the centuries.

'Vast, echoing and godlike,' wrote T.E. Lawrence of Jordan's desert region, the Wadi Rum, 'a processional way greater than imagination.' His reverence has been shared by many travellers in the deserts of the Middle East. Geographically, the Middle Eastern desert is no more than an eastern annexe of Africa's Sahara, extending from the sands of southern Arabia's Rub al-Khali to the Negev in the north. It continues eastward – the valleys of Mesopotamia are only an interruption – across the central Iranian plateau into Afghanistan. But there is more to the desert than mere geography; a desert journey can be a transcendent personal experience.

The desert experience

Thomas Edward Lawrence (1888-1935) made a speciality of the Middle Eastern desert. His campaigning with the Bedouin rebels fighting to throw off Ottoman rule during the First World War won him world renown – and the romantic title 'Lawrence of Arabia'. Much of Lawrence's glamour came from the company he kept – for if the desert has mystique, so too do its nomadic inhabitants, known in Arabic as *Badu* (desert men) or Bedouin. Their flowing robes, which wrap them from head to foot, offer protection not only against the blazing sun and wind-whipped sand, but also against the curiosity and comprehension of outsiders. Lawrence's acceptance by such people marked him out as a unique hero of the war, but for all his work among the tribes of the desert, he came to Arabia alone.

Dangerous salt pans The kavirs of central Iran conceal quicksand traps for the unwary traveller.

Desert excursion Jordan's Wadi Rum (right) is now a tourist attraction.

An important player in the game of imperial intrigue, Lawrence sought to destabilise Germany's ally, the Ottoman Empire. He could thus hardly have been more actively involved in Great Britain's affairs of state. In the desert, though, he found a sense of solitude that, far from being lonely, was liberating. When he put on his Bedouin robes, he put aside his former self completely. 'It's clean,' he replied when asked what appealed to him personally about the desert – and it is hard to resist a suspicion that he sensed in its emptiness the possibility of escape from the clutter of customs and conventions that defined him as English.

Another Englishman, Alexander Kinglake, striking south from Gaza in 1835, had similarly lost himself in the monotony of his journey. 'The hills and the valleys are sand, sand, sand, still sand, and only sand, and sand, and sand again. The earth is so samely that your eyes turn towards heaven – towards heaven, I mean, in

Beyond the highway Black lava and golden sand give the desert of southern Yemen its characteristically mottled appearance.

Deserts and arid zones

Desert dilemma The dry Negev accounts for half the land area of Israel – a country in which lack of space is a chronic problem.

Desert impacts

The Bedouin guides who offered in 1932 to take Harry St John Philby to the site of the lost city of Ubar were as good as their word. They brought him to a scene of great devastation. But amid all the strange rock formations strewn about the desert site there was no trace whatever of human occupation. After long weeks of arduous travel deep into the heart of Rub al-Khali, Philby realised that he had found not the ancient city but the impact crater of a meteorite.

Philby was crestfallen, but modern geologists do not share his disappointment. The site (now known as Wabar) has made a unique contribution to our understanding of the mineral structure of meteorites and those

substances (here a sort of jet-black glass and a hard white stone) formed by their sudden impact with the Earth's surface. Though still difficult to get to, the site has now been closely studied by scientists. There is no doubt that a meteorite ricocheted off the desert sand at this precise spot.

Some scientists think that the five huge, isolated volcanic craters that mark the Negev Desert far to the north may also have been formed in eruptions triggered by ancient meteorite impacts near the giant Ghor fault.

Titanic forces The gigantic rock formations of Jordan's Wadi Rum testify to the seismic activity of past millennia.

Rare beast The oryx is a protected species in Arabia.

the sense of sky. You look to the sun, for he is your taskmaster, and by him you know the measure of the work that you have done, and the measure of the work that remains for you to do... No words are spoken, but your Arabs moan, your camels sigh, your skin glows, your shoulders ache and for sights you see the pattern and the web of the silk that veils your eyes, and the glare of the outer light.'

Did Western travellers in earlier centuries find the same sense of ecstatic intoxication in their desert trips that they found in that other great Middle Eastern experience, the smoking of hashish? There is certainly something hallucinogenic about mirages, those glittering lakes and green oases seen by desperate wayfarers in the desert. British director Sir David Lean, in his film *Lawrence of Arabia* (1962), was clearly fascinated by the strange cinematic properties of the desert light. The sight of Omar Sharif atop a camel apparently floating into focus through the shimmering haze may represent a milestone in film-making history, but in the desert such scenes are nothing out of the ordinary. The gaunt sparseness of the desert is deceptive; this is, in every way, a much richer landscape than meets the eye.

Flora and fauna

A remarkable number of creatures have succeeded in adapting to desert life. Cacti, such as Israel's national symbol the sabra, are the best known of a large number of such plants. Their fleshy leaves, ideal for storing water, are often protected by sharp spines, which both ward off unwelcome attention from grazing animals and help to condense dew from the cold night air.

The low profile of what are generally ground-hugging creepers or short shrubs enables them to avoid the worst effects of desiccating breezes; by contrast, their roots thrust far underground in search of water. Rather than following regular seasonal cycles, desert plants tend to flower and seed in a rush; after a sudden rainstorm, the desert landscape may be carpeted with brightly coloured flowers.

Many animal species follow these erratic rhythms with a form of hot weather hibernation known as estivation – lying dormant in the earth between brief bursts of frantic activity. Some small reptiles and rodents pass more than eight months in every 12 this way; others, such as the jerboa or kangaroo rat, so called because of its long, leaping hind legs, are active all year round, finding food in the slightly damper conditions of the desert wadis or dried-up river bottoms. These small creatures support carnivores such as lynxes and foxes; lions, cheetahs and panthers have long since been hunted from the region. Larger herbivores were once surprisingly prevalent in much of Arabia, given the limited amount of available grazing, but they too have been driven to the edge of extinction by hunting in recent years.

Slow progress *A donkey and rider make their way across Yemen's Wadi Mur in a sandstorm.*

The empty quarter

There is one desert region, however, that is close to sterility: the Rub al-Khali area of southern Arabia. The Arabic name for this extremely arid zone translates as 'the empty quarter'. As one of the world's most hostile environments, it remains one of the least explored, but scientists believe that there are areas within it too dry to support animal or plant life.

An enormous expanse of real desert sand dunes, the Rub al-Khali was feared and shunned even by the desert Bedouin, though rumours persisted that the ruins of the lost city of Ubar lay somewhere here. Famed in the folklore of the Middle East, and mentioned in both the Koran and the *Arabian Nights,* Ubar was said to have been a bustling trading centre erased from the earth by some mysterious catastrophe.

All attempts to find what T.E. Lawrence called the 'Atlantis of the Sands' failed – the conditions were too difficult and the evidence too sketchy. Not until the end of the 1980s was it possible to embark on a scientific search. With a film-maker's eye for a story, documentary director Nicholas Clapp scripted a true-life desert adventure in which old-fashioned derring-do and modern technology went hand in hand. Calling on the assistance of the explorer Ranulph Fiennes, Clapp also asked for NASA's help in tracing out long-abandoned desert trails. The US space agency's state-of-the-art remote sensing satellite equipment detected several forgotten caravan routes, hidden by hundreds of years' worth of wind-blown sand.

A number of these converged near a tiny oasis called Ash Shisr, near the eastern edge of the Rub al-Khali, and here Clapp's expedition duly found the remains of what appeared to be a 4000-year-old fortified settlement buried deep beneath the dunes.

The existence of such a city confirms the long-standing view that the Arabian Peninsula has undergone significant desertification even during recorded history – it is inconceivable that a significant urban centre would be sited there now. Yet Ubar – if Ubar it really is – does not appear to have been the victim of long-term climatic change; rather, it actually does seem to have been swallowed up, as the legends claim, in an Atlantis-like catastrophe. Evidence uncovered by Clapp suggests that a vast limestone cavern underneath the earth suddenly collapsed in the course of an earthquake, burying the city and its inhabitants in the sand.

Dry seas

Still more treacherous underfoot are the great salt pans of Iran's Dasht-e-Kavir. Though streams flow into these almost rainless regions from the mountains to the north and east, they peter out as they make their way across these searing plains, the evaporation leaving behind a residue of salts. Where such pans or *kavirs* have fully dried out, the ground is safe enough, but a firm surface is no indicator of real stability. Salt deposits beneath the surface may still be drawing moisture from marshy ground below, so that what seems like solid earth may be no more than a brittle crust that may give way at any moment, pitching the explorer into a quicksand of chemical sludge.

Southward from the Dasht-e-Kavir stretches an even more forbidding desert, the Dasht-e-Lut, perhaps the most desolate place on earth. All that remains of an enormous inland sea, it is an eerie place even by desert standards; the Bedouin regard it as a home of spirits or jinn. To stand here and see the display of light reflected off the salt in every direction is to wonder whether one might not after all be in some otherworldly dreamscape.

Desert of deserts *South-eastern Arabia's Rub al-Khali is a sea of sand whose wind-blown waves are massive dunes reaching heights of over 1000 ft (300 m). Much of the area is still unexplored.*

Islands and peninsulas

Shipping and coral reefs are as much a feature of the Middle East as are deserts. A collection of beautiful islands and peninsulas forms the focus of maritime life; though few in number, they loom large in the region's history.

Aphrodite's bay *By tradition, the Greek goddess of love emerged from the waves here at Paphos, Cyprus.*

One morning many centuries ago, according to the Greek poet Homer, the Trojan princes woke up to find that their besiegers had gone. The High King Agamemnon and his Greek army had camped outside Troy for ten years, and fierce fighting had claimed the lives of heroes on both sides. Overnight the Greeks had simply melted away. Outside the city walls they had left a large wooden horse – presumably some sort of peace offering. The exultant Trojans dragged the horse inside, and as they were celebrating their delivery, the Greek Odysseus and his men climbed out of their hiding place in the belly of the horse to open the city gates. The Greek fleet slipped from its anchorage behind the nearby island of Tenedos. By the time the Trojans woke up to their plight, their city was in flames and their citadel seized.

Offshore influences

Modern archaeologists disagree over precisely which collection of ancient stones on the southern shore of the Dardanelles represents the ruins of Troy, but all acknowledge that there was once such a city, and that it stood roughly where Homer claimed. Tenedos is now known by its Turkish name, Bozcaada.

Long after the sack of Troy described in Homer's *Iliad* and *Odyssey* (and Virgil's *Aeneid*), it was used as the base for a naval attack on Greece by the Persian emperor Xerxes. His fleet was smashed off another island, Salamis, in the

Saronic Gulf near Athens, in 480 BC, a defeat that set a limit to his empire and ushered in the Athenian golden age. If one thing unites the very different islands and peninsulas of the Middle East, it is the influence they have exerted on the history of the region – and, in many cases, the wider world.

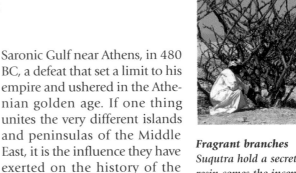

Fragrant branches *These trees in Suqutra hold a secret: from their resin comes the incense burned in religious ceremonies worldwide.*

Just across the Dardanelles strait from Bozcaada, for example, is the peninsula of Gelibolu, known to a generation of servicemen from Britain and the Commonwealth as Gallipoli. In 1915 an Anglo-French fleet landed an army here to relieve pressure on their Russian ally by knocking the Ottoman Empire out of the action in the First World War. More than 120 000 lives were lost in this inglorious and ill-conducted campaign – many from the Anzac forces of Australia and New Zealand. The repercussions of the Allied failure did not end there. The expedition's failure to open a southern supply route to Russia helped to speed up the disintegration of the tsarist state that reached its climax in the 1917 revolutions. Gallipoli also prolonged the Allied campaigns in Palestine and Mesopotamia until 1918, and meant that a subsequent attempt to establish a second front at Salonica was woefully half-hearted.

Desert shore *From Aden to Muscat, the southern coast of the Arabian Peninsula is largely undeveloped.*

Aegean paradise   The Turkish shore of the Aegean Sea consists of a multitude of islands, archipelagoes and peninsulas, as seen here. Its fascinating and historic shores attract tourists by the thousand.

The Strait of Hormuz and its islands

The narrow neck through which shipping passes between The Gulf and the Indian Ocean, the Strait of Hormuz has long held great strategic significance. It attracted the attention of the outside world in 1984, when a 'tanker war' that had simmered for some time boiled over in a spate of attacks by Iran and Iraq on one another's shipping. The Iraqis launched air raids on the main Iranian oil terminal at Kharg Island to the north and attacked Iranian shipping farther south, while the Iranians sent gunboats to harass tankers bearing Iraqi oil in the Strait of Hormuz. Vital as bases for these operations were the islands of Greater and Lesser Tunb and Abu Musa, which had been occupied by Iranian forces after British withdrawal from the Gulf in 1971. All three islands officially belong to the United Arab Emirates, but Iran has resisted demands for their return ever since.

Island orchid   The late spider orchid, Ophrys fuciflora, *grows in Cyprus and the Turkish islands.*

Aden emergencies

Another Middle Eastern peninsula whose name lives on in the British memory is that of Aden, a rugged volcanic promontory jutting from the southern coast of what is now Yemen. With a commanding position overlooking the approaches to the Red Sea, Aden was prized by its original Arab rulers, who built Seira Castle here in about 1173. Aden became a major centre for the trading empire carved out by the Arab merchant princes along the Indian Ocean seaboard. A number of imperialist rivals cast covetous eyes on the rock; in the 15th and early 16th centuries the Portuguese attacked it unsuccessfully several times, while the Ottoman Turks proved more effective in 1538, retaining control until 1730.

From 1839, Aden became a strategic base of the British Empire, a key port of call on the voyage to colonies east of Suez. Britain's tenure became increasingly bitter after the Second World War, and by 1965 the British government realised they had a full-scale 'Aden emergency' on their hands. In 1967, Aden and its rocky hinterland won a sort of freedom as the Arab world's only Marxist republic, the People's Republic of South Yemen. After many years of antipathy, the communist state managed to patch up its differences with the Arab Republic of Yemen – the former Ottoman colony to the north – the two coming together as the Republic of Yemen in 1990.

The island of Socotra lies 400 miles (643 km) offshore in the Indian Ocean. The remarkable flora that has flourished here in isolation has proved invaluable to modern medicine and science: 216 of Socotra's 680

plant species are unique to the island. Unfortunately, the introduction of modern farming methods and tourism have left a third of Socotra's endemic plant species endangered. Conservationists are attempting to call the world's attention to what they regard as a real ecological emergency.

Cyprus in love and war

The Middle East's largest island is Cyprus, celebrated in antiquity as the birthplace of the Greek goddess of love, Aphrodite. The Roman general Mark Antony made a present of Cyprus to his Egyptian lover, Cleopatra. Given away like a bit of jewellery, it was seized back for Rome by Antony's sworn enemy Octavian. Down the centuries, the island has been fought over repeatedly. Its strategic position in the eastern Mediterranean has meant that Cyprus has occupied a pivotal role in a series of international rivalries: first between the Christian powers and Islam, then between the British and Ottoman empires and finally between the two opposing power blocs in the Cold War.

Cyprus still seems no closer to finding real peace. The Cold War tended to obscure the island's own home-grown difficulties, notably an implacable enmity between its Turkish-descended northerners and southerners of Greek extraction. Turkey invaded the island in 1974, and in 1983 the north seceded as the Turkish Republic of Northern Cyprus. The state remains unrecognised by the world community and is bitterly resented by Cyprus' Greek majority to the south of the 'Green Line' that divides the two communities.

Stone sentinels   The Pigeon Rocks at Raouché, Beirut's seaside resort, are one of Lebanon's most celebrated landmarks.

Surrounded by seas

Encircled on all sides but the east by seas and oceans, the Middle East could almost be considered a continent. Parts of its interior also contain expanses of salt or fresh water large enough to count as inland seas.

The maritime horizon plays a large part in Middle Eastern myth and culture, geography and economics. The waves of the surrounding waters provide a conceptual counterweight to the endless undulation of the desert sand dunes, and the word for 'sea' in the ancient Mesopotamian myths is closely linked with the word for 'mother'. The term 'sea' is almost too general here: it has to encompass expanses of water that range from the vast openness of the Indian Ocean to the tight rectangularity of the Red Sea, and from the extreme salinity of the Dead Sea to the faint bitterness of the freshwater Lake Van.

East meets West *The Bosporus has been a cultural junction for 5000 years.*

Though the centre of the Indian Ocean lies well to the south of the Middle Eastern landmass, the sea seems to thrust its way right into its heart, the Persian Gulf and the Red Sea following the great faults that mark the two sides of the Arabian Peninsula. At the northernmost extremity of the Red Sea, the Gulf of Aqaba juts out like a pointing finger, indicating the line along which the Ghor Rift Valley cleaves the western edge of the Asian continent. In its depths are Lake Tiberias (the 'Sea' of Galilee in the Bible, an imprecision matched by the Kurdish definition of Lake Van as their 'sea') and the Dead Sea.

The Black Sea is almost landlocked, but does connect with the Mediterranean and ultimately with the Atlantic far to the west. To the south-east, however, high up in the mountains, Lake Van in south-eastern Turkey (the Kurdistan region) and Iran's Lake Urmia have no communication with the oceans of the outside world at all.

Black Sea, dark secrets

The ancients called it *Pontus Euxinus*, 'friendly, hospitable sea', but the Black Sea lives up to its more modern name. What looks as though it ought to be a safe and sheltered stretch of water has an unpredictable microclimate in which severe storms can be whipped up out of nowhere at a moment's notice. But its turbulence pales into insignificance beside the violence of its formation – if the theory of American geologists William Ryan and Walter Pitman is to be believed.

Their view is that the sea came into being abruptly some 10 000 years ago. The end of the last Ice Age set sea levels rising worldwide and sent water cascading into the basin of a lake almost 100 miles (160 km) inland. Rising up along the fault line still readily apparent in the form of the Sea of Marmara and the Bosporus, the waters would have spilled over the rocky shelf at the strait's northern end like a gigantic waterfall. Any settlements in the lakeside region would have been inundated, their inhabitants heading for the hills. The tradition of a fearful deluge – Noah's flood – would have entered folk memory.

True or fanciful theory? The facts certainly seem to add up: the ice ages are known to have locked up enormous quantities of water, which subsequently thawed to produce a rise in sea level. Robert Ballard, finder of the *Titanic*, set out to test the truth of the theory by underwater exploration, and has found signs of human habitation deep beneath the surface of the sea. The story of Noah's flood really does seem tantalisingly close to being confirmed.

Noah's flood revisited *Between 1978 and 1995, the level of the Caspian Sea rose by about 8 ft (2.4 m), drowning many industrial installations as well as settlements like this, in Iran.*

Seas and lakes

1 Black Sea
2 Caspian Sea
3 Sea of Marmara
4 Lake Tuz
5 Lake Van
6 Lake Urmia
7 Lake Assad
8 Lake Tiberias
9 Dead Sea
10 Dacht-e-Kavir

The little egret

Undiscovered *Turkey's Black Sea coasts have remained one of tourism's best-kept secrets.*

Kurdish sea *Lake Van in eastern Turkey is high up in the mountains, a typically large Middle Eastern lake.*

untreated into the River Volga. This toxicity combined with a rising sea level is affecting the 400 species unique to the sea and its wetlands. The impoverished states around the Caspian sea are understandably keen to see an oil and gas boom. The fear is, however, that this might destroy an environment already reeling. The Convention for the Protection of the Marine Environment of the Caspian Sea, agreed by all Caspian countries in 2003, may be the first step to halting the damage.

Lake or sea?

The Caspian Sea completes the ring of salt water around the Middle East at its north-eastern edge. About 1000 miles (1600 km) long from north to south, and over 200 miles (320 km) across at several points, it is the largest inland body of water on earth. So, should it properly be considered a lake or a sea? The question is of particular interest to the five countries that share its shores: Iran, Azerbaijan, Russia, Kazakhstan and Turkmenistan. By international law, where two countries abut a lake a line is drawn down the middle to divide its waters up equally between them; if it is a sea, however, the rules of territorial waters apply. Applying that principle to the Caspian, a small area at the centre counts as 'high seas', open for exploration by all – a point that Russia was anxious to press home in early negotiations at the start of the 1990s.

The Soviet Union had effectively occupied all but the Iranian southern shore; the disintegration of the USSR after 1991 made things more complicated, at a time when the ailing Russian economy needed all the benefit it could get from the Caspian's oil and gas reserves. Too impoverished and lacking in infrastructure to exploit their own reserves, the former Soviet republics made deals with American oil companies allowing them to organise extraction. Outnumbered and out-argued, Russia backed down in 1993, after it became clear that, were the Caspian to be designated a sea, the Volga-Don river system would have to be kept open to the shipping of all nations. The arguments raged on until 1998 when an agreement of sorts was reached which split the bed of the Caspian into national territories while leaving its surface unpartitioned.

The region's huge oil reserves are estimated to be up to 200 billion barrels – however, it will be expensive to reach this bonanza, and there is the potential for great environmental impact. The sea is already severely polluted in parts: half the population of Russia, and most of its heavy industry, has for years emptied its waste

Sea of records

The Sea of Judaea was renamed the Dead Sea by the Crusaders, to whom it must have been a strange sight. At 1296 ft (395 m) below sea level, it is the world's lowest-lying spot. Its waters are saltier, denser and warmer than those of any other body of water, and the most sterile. The sea lies at the bottom of the world's deepest geological fault, the Ghor. The River Jordan flows into it, but there is no exit: the water collects and is evaporated by the sun, leaving a saturated solution of mineral salts that discolour the water and build up into salt encrustations. The level of the sea has been falling naturally for thousands of years, but the process has been accelerated by channelling off water from the Jordan for irrigation schemes upriver. Some fear the Dead Sea will have disappeared by 2050.

Sterile sea *The Dead Sea is too salty to support life.*

Nature under threat

Eruptions and earthquakes, deluges and desertification – the Middle Eastern landscape has largely been fashioned by natural catastrophes. But most Middle Eastern governments have only recently woken up to the damage modern industry and agriculture have wrought in the region.

In the first flush of revolutionary triumph in 1978-9, everything suddenly seemed possible for the people of Iran. The years of political tyranny, of spiritual subservience, of economic exploitation were at long last over. The country's new leaders began to set out their glorious new vision for a country that was certain to grow in prosperity as it was to grow in piety and faith. A number of environmentalists ventured to sound a note of caution, to stress the need for care, but their concerns were brushed aside by a leading figure in the government's Environmental Protection Agency. Had not Allah himself created all of nature? And would he not protect all the creatures in it? 'Brothers,' he concluded, 'there is no reason to fear or to take any action.'

Such complacency was truly shocking, even to religious Iranians. Citing the minister's comments in an article in Tehran's English-language *Morning Daily* on February 14, 2001, journalist Mehri Haqani called on Iranians to wake up to the plight of their wildlife heritage. Iran should be a remarkable bank of biodiversity: between the peak of Demavend, at 18 376 ft (5601 m) above sea level, and the shores of the Persian Gulf, there is a marvellous range of habitats. The country does still have an enviably varied flora and fauna, with more than 8300 plants and 160 mammal species, but many are now fighting for survival. The panthers and wild asses that adorned the sculpture of the Persian emperors now seem likely to go the same way as the Iranian lion, with the zebra, black bear and yellow deer almost certain to follow. Measures aimed at preserving these larger species have been treated with contempt, while the conservation of habitats has lost out to the rush towards economic development. Large-scale irrigation

Wear and tear *Heavy maritime traffic pollutes the waters of the Mediterranean.*

Drying out *The coastal wetlands of Mesopotamia are in danger of drying out completely, placed in jeopardy by the construction of barrages upstream on the Tigris and Euphrates rivers.*

Ancient eco-disasters

The Bible recounts a number of cataclysmic natural events. Scientific explanations for some of these can be found in the Middle East today. For example, the fire from the sky that destroyed Sodom and Gomorrah may be connected with volcanic activity in the Negev, known to have occurred in the 14th century BC. Craters left by these now-dormant volcanoes can clearly be identified in the area.

schemes have worked agricultural miracles, but also wrought ecological tragedies in so doing; overgrazing has led to the desertification of delicate scrubland habitats.

A catalogue of disasters

Other states in the region have been every bit as complacent. Wealthy hunters long since decimated the large mammals of the Arabian desert. Around the coasts, meanwhile, mangrove swamps

Endangered species *The ibex survives under strict protection in certain Middle Eastern sanctuaries.*

Desert detritus

Lawrence of Arabia, asked what he most liked about the desert, said 'It's so clean'. He would hardly give the same answer were he to see it now. Huge amounts of scrap iron litter much of the desert landscape of the Middle East. Some of the giant oil installations and pipelines are still in use, but many have simply been abandoned as wells run dry or processes become obsolete. Machinery connected with irrigation schemes, too, is often in use only for a year or two, and then abandoned when the earth is exhausted. The Kuwaiti desert is also littered with thousands of mangled Iraqi tanks and personnel carriers.

Repopulating the wilderness

At Hai-Bar, in the Israeli Negev, a conservation programme is currently under way. Its aim is to preserve the existing ecology and to restore it to something like its splendour in Biblical times. The Negev's impoverishment since the days of the prophets is clear. Where are the ostriches in the wilderness of Lamentations; the wild asses we read of in Hosea or the Book of Job? Along with the oryx, both animals have been reintroduced to the Negev in recent years. Under the strictest supervision, they are settling in reasonably well, but staff stress that this is a long-term project and they are expecting difficulties. The wild ass is temperamental and tricky to breed, while the ostrich

Survivor *The wild ass or onager survives in northern Afghanistan.*

has to be kept corralled for fear of the effects of chemical run-off from the region's intensive farms. The 'wilderness' is not what it was in Biblical times, and this scheme to repopulate it with native fauna conflicts with the earlier Israeli drive to 'make the desert bloom'.

Israel has in fact come full circle in its attitude to its landscape. The early kibbutzniks set out to colonise what they saw as a wasteland. They pioneered intensive methods of cultivation that were copied throughout the region, taking pride in coaxing crops out of uncooperative soils. More recently, a new generation of environmentalists worldwide has questioned the desirability of such agricultural systems. Calling for farmers to attune themselves to the needs of nature they urge a policy of 'sustainability', even where this means slightly lower crop yields. Conservation has thus begun to take on an ideological significance, with many Israelis anxious to assume the role of custodians of their country's fragile natural inheritance.

have been uprooted to make way for oil installations and tourist resorts. One that remains, the Khor Kalba swamp, which spans the Oman-United Arab Emirates border, illustrates some of the problems of conservation in the region as a whole. Its peculiar ecosystem includes rare crabs and beautiful bird species found nowhere else on earth. There are no fewer than five types of turtle, as well as important populations of fish and crustaceans. Although the swamp itself is nominally protected, the

Modern plague *Plastic has even invaded the Arabian desert.*

salt flats on either side are not, though they are crucial both as a buffer zone and as a habitat in their own right. By building next door to the mangrove swamps, developers have kept the letter of the conservation law, but ignored its spirit. Commercial fishermen from the cities seem not to have understood the purpose of the wildlife sanctuary at all. Large areas once rich in flora have already been laid waste.

Similar ecological disasters can be found throughout the region. Water quality in the Gulf of Aqaba has been threatened by pollution from port facilities at Eilat in Israel and Aqaba in Jordan, while the offloading of ballast by ships in

Cyprus cedar *The cedar still grows in Cyprus, where a programme of protection has succeeded in saving it.*

the Red Sea poses a serious threat to coral reefs. The growth of the tourist industry is also having a devastating effect. Development on the Egyptian coast of the Gulf of Aqaba is already taking its toll, with recreational divers damaging those stretches of reef not already destroyed by the construction of modern beach resorts.

CHAPTER 2

A REGION'S RESOURCES

When one thinks of the Middle East today, one thinks of oil. Saudi Arabia, Iraq, Iran, the United Arab Emirates, Oman, Kuwait – all have seen their fortunes transformed by the discovery of 'black gold'. But long ago, this was the region that witnessed the birth of agriculture. The Fertile Crescent remains today as fertile as ever, and it still depends on sophisticated irrigation to get the best out of the soil. The Middle East's maritime resources remain comparatively unexploited, but progress has been made in opening up the region to tourists. Pilgrims have long poured in their millions to Mecca and to the Holy Land; now sun-worshippers also flock to the coastal resorts. Many more superb coasts and great archaeological sites remain to be opened up to the tourist trade.

These traditional boats at Bi'r 'Ali in the Yemen are typical of those still used by the region's fishermen.

Going for growth

The Fertile Crescent of antiquity arches through the modern states of Israel, the Palestinian Territories, Jordan, Syria, Lebanon and Iraq. While technological advances bring new possibilities – and new problems – the essential challenge remains the same: how to harness the rich potential of the region's parched soils.

Crop circles *Circular irrigation produces high yields, but quickly exhausts the desert soil.*

Not all Middle Eastern states have grown rich from oil: many must still find their livelihood, as the Bible warned, in the sweat of their brow. Now, as in the days of Genesis, agriculture is the focus for their labours, although modern techniques have made their work both more productive and less onerous. Israel, whose Zionist founders made intensive cultivation central to the national project, still leads the region as a producer of fruit and vegetables. Despite the slogan about 'making the desert bloom', Israel has made few agricultural inroads on its most arid zones: what it has done is pioneered techniques to maximise yields from more marginal, semidesert soils.

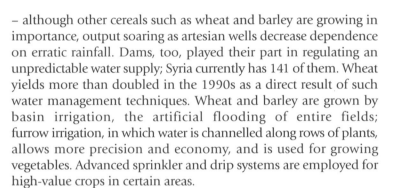

The last drop Drip irrigation targets moisture directly at plant roots.

Syrian statistics

Others have followed in Israel's footsteps. Syria, though an implacable enemy of the Jewish state, has been eager to emulate its example with regard to agriculture. Syria is an important producer of rice – it was from here that Arab traders first took rice to Europe – although other cereals such as wheat and barley are growing in importance, output soaring as artesian wells decrease dependence on erratic rainfall. Dams, too, played their part in regulating an unpredictable water supply; Syria currently has 141 of them. Wheat yields more than doubled in the 1990s as a direct result of such water management techniques. Wheat and barley are grown by basin irrigation, the artificial flooding of entire fields; furrow irrigation, in which water is channelled along rows of plants, allows more precision and economy, and is used for growing vegetables. Advanced sprinkler and drip systems are employed for high-value crops in certain areas.

Terraces of plenty
An elaborate system of terracing ensures that every inch of cultivable earth on this Omani hillside is exploited.

Starting young *In rural areas, children are soon initiated into the rhythms of agricultural work.*

Drug addiction

The raw ingredient for cannabis or marijuana, hemp has been grown for centuries in Turkey and in Iraqi and Iranian Kurdistan. In Lebanon it has been rising in importance in recent years as farmers seek to make a living from a rural economy otherwise in ruins. In Yemen the mildly narcotic *kat* is a national addiction; cultivation of the source plant *Catha edulis* puts extra pressure on scarce water resources.

Battery cows *Saudi Arabia has the world's largest dairy farm. This gigantic facility employs all the most sophisticated techniques of modern livestock rearing.*

Staple diet *Many of the great cuisines of the Middle East are based on rice. Iraq, Syria and (below) Iran all have extensive paddy fields.*

State of the art *Israel's intensively farmed flowers, fruit and vegetables are exported far and wide. Here labourers bring in a crop of tomatoes.*

Other countries find themselves facing similar challenges. Jordan, for example, has been unable to capitalise on agricultural advances because of a lack of processing facilities and a failure to find export markets. The country's isolation was increased when its government decided to support Saddam Hussein's invasion of Kuwait – a prudent enough move in regional terms, perhaps, given the unpredictability of the dictatorship next door, but a major diplomatic error in the eyes of the international community.

Ploughshares and swords

The Middle East has been one of the modern world's political flashpoints, and Jordan is not the only country whose agriculture has been affected by war. Iraq was an important agricultural producer before two Gulf wars left roads and bridges destroyed, river banks broken and productive land flooded. Subsequent economic sanctions have resulted in shortages of farm machinery, parts, pesticides, seeds and fertilisers.

Iraq was once the world's leading producer of dates, with an output of 400 000 tonnes a year. Its production has now slumped to less than half that total. In the past ten years the country is believed to have lost 29 million date palms, killed by pests because of shortages of insecticide. Dates were an important luxury export, but were also vital to the daily diet of many ordinary Iraqis. The UN's Food and Agriculture Organisation has become increasingly concerned about the near famine in several areas that has followed the imposition of Western sanctions.

Blessed by nature in every respect, Lebanon should have been a highly successful agricultural nation. That it is not is in part the fault of its ruling families. For too long they were happy to live in urban affluence without investing either thought or finance in those rural estates from which their riches flowed. At a time when other ruling elites were waking up to new economic realities, Lebanese landowners found themselves looking on helplessly as their country slid into a civil war that lasted from 1975 to 1991. The Israeli invasion of 1982 intensified the destruction; the whole traumatic experience left the country's infrastructure in ruins. Now, although schemes are in hand to reinstate distribution networks and to upgrade production, Lebanese farmers find themselves trying to catch up with competitors in the region, struggling to stay afloat, they say, in a market flooded with cheaper, lower-quality (and sometimes smuggled) imports.

With scant oil resources of its own, Syria relies on exports for hard currency. Its leading cash crop, cotton, has also benefited enormously from modern developments in irrigation. Syria ranks tenth in the world as a producer of cotton, but can claim a higher position in terms of quality. Its cotton is largely organically grown and picked by hand; production is labour-intensive, and employs around 20 per cent of the working population. Until recently, much of Syria's cotton was exported in its unmanufactured state – a missed opportunity for the wider national economy. Now a growing textile and clothing industry is adding value at home before shipment abroad, and Syria is beginning to reap the full benefits of its cotton harvest.

Many more such changes remain to be made. Syria has, for example, some 63.7 million olive trees, producing more than 750,000 million tonnes of olives every year. But with insufficient presses to extract the oil and inadequate facilities for refining it, the country has failed to make the most of this rich bounty. An ambitious investment programme targeted at the agricultural sector includes plans for olive oil refineries, as well as new plants for packaging delicate fruit. Along with enhanced cargo-handling facilities at seaports and airports, such measures will help Syria to cash in on a resource that, until now, has been underexploited.

Water wars

The Mesopotamian god Marduk, who first made humankind, did so because he needed someone to build irrigation ditches and make the earth productive. Water may be taken for granted in much of the world – in the Middle East, however, it has always been a scarce commodity, guarded and fought over.

Golan Heights
■ Syrian territory annexed by Israel in December 1981

In 1977, Saudi Arabia's Prince Mohammed al-Faisal established a company to tow a 100 million tonne iceberg from the Antarctic ice shelf to the port of Jeddah. Though the plan was never put into action, that it existed at all highlights the concerns of a Saudi state with large amounts of money but very little water.

Israel's plan to import water from Turkey in 20 000 tonne tankers seems almost humdrum by comparison. The government agreed in 2004 to purchase 1765 cu ft (50 million m³) of fresh water from the the Manavgat river in Anatolia each year for the next 20 years. This will be transported to a specially built facility at Ashkelon, from where it will be pumped directly into a national system that has been on the verge of crisis for some years. Although this is an enormous amount of water it still only accounts for three per cent of Israel's current needs. The daily supply of water in today's Middle East is an issue that can have profound political consequences; the next war in the region, say analysts, will be fought not over oil, but over water.

Heights of anxiety

Once the Israelis feared that their Arab enemies would drive them into the sea; now their main fear is being left high and dry. The country's coastal aquifer has been badly contaminated by nitrate run-off from fertilisers used in intensive farming, and 40 per cent of Israel's 'fresh' water is actually undrinkable. Hundreds of wells used primarily for drinking water have been shut due to the intrusion of seawater and boron contamination is turning into a large-scale problem. The annexation of the Golan Heights from Syria in 1981 was originally justified by the argument that their elevated position overlooking Israel's northern plain posed a strategic threat. But that apprehension has paled into insignificance beside the realisation that, without the Golan, Israel would lose control of a third of its water supply. Some 10 600 cu ft (300 m³) annually drain from the Golan Heights into Lake Kinneret (Tiberias) and the upper Jordan Valley.

Tzvi Ortenberg, Chairman of the Kinneret Authority, said in an April 2000 briefing: 'A potential Syrian success in diverting the sources of the Jordan and the Kinneret would mean only one thing: the destruction of Israel without resorting to military or political means. It is our deterrent capability, stemming from our presence on the Golan Heights, that makes Syria think twice before acting rashly.' An exaggeratedly apocalyptic view? Perhaps – but such pronouncements cannot be judged by the standards of Western Europe or North America. In the Middle East, increasing populations makes the need for fresh water a source of bitter conflict.

Stronghold *Lake Assad was constructed by the Soviet Union to assure its Syrian ally self-sufficiency in hydroelectric power.*

The water carrier *The task of bringing water from the well tends to fall upon women and children.*

The Ilusu Dam

The construction of the Ilusu Dam on the upper Tigris in Turkey has attracted adverse publicity despite its wealthy backers. A well-organised international campaign against the project has highlighted the fact that the resulting reservoir will not only damage the ecology of this part of eastern Turkey, but will also drown the ancient town of Hasankeyf, with 10 000 years' worth of archaeological remains. Still more important, they say, it will result in a human rights disaster, forcing 25 000 people – mostly ethnic Kurds – to abandon their homes in the area of the reservoir.

Some critics claim that the project is not about water, but part of a long-running strategic plan on the part of the Turkish government to suppress the Kurdish nationalist movement. Whether or not this is the case, the dam will certainly have an impact on

Holding tank *In western Yemen cisterns carved out of the rock store water from the monsoon rains.*

Troubled water *Israel would be lost without the water from Lake Kinneret (Tiberias).*

water supply – not just in Turkey, but also downstream in Syria and Iraq. Their populations need water as well, and their governments view the development with grave concern. Syria stands to lose 40 per cent of its water from the Euphrates, Iraq up to 90 per cent. Turkey actually stopped the flow of the river completely for a month in 1990 to fill one reservoir. Tensions have long been high between Syria and Turkey, in particular. Turkey accuses Syria of secretly supporting Kurdish subversion, while Syria complains that Turkey's dams reduce the flows of both the Tigris and Euphrates. The barrage complex of which the Ilusu Dam forms part will undoubtedly reduce the flow still further, so it is hard to see this dispute being readily resolved. That Turkey is sending supplies to Syria's enemy Israel has only added insult to injury for the Syrians.

Desalination plants

However dry its interior, the Middle East has no shortage of seas. But desalination plants are prohibitively expensive to all but the richest countries. After careful pre-treatment to remove any solid

Black tentacles *Like some giant, inky squid a Kuwaiti desalination plant sends out its trail of sodium chloride effluent, extracted from sea water in the process of purification.*

impurities that might damage the expensive equipment, water is forced at high pressure through thick walls of cellulose acetate. This substance acts as a semipermeable membrane that holds up salt molecules while allowing pure water through to the other side.

A pioneer of this process, Saudi Arabia leads the world in output volume; its desalination plants now produce well over 700 million gallons (3200 million litres) of fresh water every day. Water is piped into the Arabian Peninsula, with Riyadh receiving desalinated water from the Gulf almost 300 miles (500 km) away.

Irrigation honours

Ma'rib, the capital of Saba, or 'Sheba', must have been an imposing sight in its heyday in the 1st millennium BC. Yet the Yemeni kingdom's crowning glory was neither a palace nor a temple but a mighty dam. Standing at over 50 ft (15 m) high, it held back a lake that provided irrigation for farmlands supporting some 50 000 people. In more recent times, with Soviet assistance, Syria has constructed a dam almost four times as high. Yet neither ancient Yemenis nor the Soviet engineers found out how to prevent evaporation of irrigation water. That discovery was left to Israeli irrigation engineers working with American researchers. Drip irrigation allows moisture to be delivered direct to the growing root – having been brought from a source up to a mile (1.6 km) away.

Harvest of the seas

Fishing has been part of the Middle Eastern way of life since the beginnings of history – the practice is mentioned in the poems of ancient Mesopotamia. It remains largely unchanged in the Middle East of today, for the most part not yet industrialised even in the face of modern political and environmental pressures.

Sea food *Fish remains a vital foodstuff.*

Christ's ministry began in earnest the day he walked along the shores of the Sea of Galilee and saw two brothers, Peter and Andrew, casting a net into the sea. 'Follow me,' he told them, in the words of Matthew's Gospel, 'and I will make you fishers of men'. Soon afterwards, these first apostles were joined by a further two fishermen, James and John, whom Christ had found mending their nets aboard their father's ship.

Fishermen still cast their nets into the Sea of Galilee. Known since Roman times as Lake Tiberias, in honour of the emperor Tiberius, the Sea of Galilee is referred to by modern Israelis by its Old Testament title of Kinneret. This name comes from the Hebrew *kinor*, 'harp', which it resembles in shape. Today the lake is a thriving fishery, though this does not operate without controversy. How long will stocks hold up in the face of pollution from agricultural chemicals and a falling water

level caused by excessive extraction from the River Jordan? And what rights should Syrian fisherman have to these waters? The Golan Heights escarpment extends down to the lakeside, 2000 ft (600 m) below sea level; its annexation by Israel has deprived Syrian villagers of their own traditional navigation and fishing rights in the lake.

Tempestuous times

Fishing is also at the economic front line in the longstanding conflict between Israel and the Palestinians. In response to the Palestinian *intifada*, Israel has claimed the right to seal off access to the supposedly self-ruled Gaza Strip, in order to restrict the movements of suicide bombers and other terrorists. It has therefore imposed a virtual blockade of the Gaza coast. This blockade has had a serious impact on the Palestinian population as a whole. Israel's leaders brush all concerns aside, pointing to the activities of the militants of Hamas and Islamic Jihad; nevertheless, the suspicion remains that they are attempting to smother Palestinian sovereignty at birth.

For almost as long as Gaza has existed as an autonomous territory, its ancient fishing industry has thus been paralysed by restrictions imposed by the Israeli navy. The Israeli authorities warn that

---

Jewels from the deep

In the early 1930s, the Gulf States were reeling from the impact of Japan's newest industrial product, the cultured pearl. Consumers in the developed world were willing to ignore the vastly superior quality of the natural pearls that had been the Gulf's main export, and the real article began to lose lustre in a fashion market flooded with cheaper imitations.

For the divers of Bahrain, the Gulf's main pearling centre, this new development was calamitous. Their conditions of employment were tantamount to slavery, but the crisis in the industry meant little hope of improvement.

In 1932, however, Bahrain's first oil strike occurred. It rescued the country from an uncertain economic future at a stroke. In recent years natural pearls have

been making their way back as a prestige product, but even so the industry is now far smaller than it was in former times.

Prince of foods

No delicacy is more prized by connoisseurs than caviar, the distinctive black roe, or eggs, of the sturgeon. And none is better than caviar from the Caspian Sea. 'Ordinary' caviar – if there is such a thing – sells at around $650 a lb (450 g) on the international market; when it comes from the great Beluga sturgeon it fetches well over $1000. Caviar cannot simply be removed from the fish and exported in bulk; it has first to be carefully prepared, strained and washed and then 'matured' by salting. The craftsman kneads it gently together with salt crystals until exactly the right consistency is attained, judging not by taste but by touch when that moment comes. Worked even a fraction too roughly or too long, the roe is reduced to an unpleasant mush. It takes years for an apprentice to learn the secret of perfect caviar.

Rare luxury The Caspian fishery is threatened by over-exploitation.

Ageless Back in harbour after a day at sea, Yemeni fishermen prepare to unload their catches: this is a scene that has scarcely changed in a thousand years.

all boats venturing more than a mile (1.5 km) out to sea are liable to be shot at and seized – and they put this threat into action on a number of occasions. The justification for these measures is that they will protect innocent lives by preventing wanted terrorists from slipping out to sea – but they are certainly destroying many thousands of Palestinian livelihoods.

Gaza's fishermen are not alone in having to navigate stormy political waters: boats setting out from the harbours of northern Syria must also steer a particularly careful course. Immediately to the west lie waters claimed by the Turkish Republic of Northern Cyprus. Several vessels have been seized and their crews imprisoned by the authorities there.

Ships from the past

Today a few steel-hulled trawlers and factory ships operate in Middle Eastern waters, but for the most part the region's fishing boats have seen few changes in the past thousand years. Though the industry is large overall, fishing remains a small-scale, family concern built around the distinctive vessel of the Arabian world, the shallow-draughted dhow. With its graceful curves and its lateen-rigged sails, this ancient craft lends glamour to the most workaday tasks. The ships that once plied trade routes from Zanzibar to India and China are still in use off Middle Eastern coasts for trade and transportation. Thousands of smaller dhows also put to sea each day to fish the waters of the Red Sea, the Gulf and the inshore areas of the Indian Ocean. Apart from an outboard motor, most dhows are outwardly identical to their ancient predecessors. Looks can be deceptive, though. Before the 16th century, dhows were 'shell-built', their slender planking sewn together with palm fibres for flexibility as well as strength. Since the arrival of Europeans in the Indian Ocean, however, the hulls have been constructed around a rigid wooden frame using iron nails.

Fresh from the sea Turkish fishermen in the Bosporus sell their produce direct to passers-by.

Oil's ups and downs

For many people, the Middle East means oil. But many countries in the region have no significant reserves, and those that do have learnt that oil does not necessarily shield them from the vicissitudes of the world economy. The challenge has been to use oil income as a platform on which to build a more stable prosperity.

Marco Polo saw oil oozing from the rocks of the Caspian Basin as he crossed it seven centuries ago, but it did not occur to him then that he had found a Middle Eastern El Dorado. Not until the final decades of the 19th century were the possibilities of refining crude oil explored in the United States. The invention of the paraffin lamp opened up what seemed like a significant market for oil in the 1870s, but by 1882 the electric light bulb had replaced it. It was only when the first motor cars were invented, in the 1890s, that the demand for oil really took off.

Twentieth-century tale

The Middle East's involvement in the oil boom began in 1901, when the Englishman William Knox D'Arcy set out in search of oil in the Iranian desert. His uncanny instincts as a prospector had already made him a very rich man; he had discovered a major seam of gold in Australia. His Midas touch appeared to have deserted him as he searched fruitlessly for seven years, but in 1908 he finally found oil in south-west Persia.

Heavy traffic Enormous quantities of oil are shifted daily to keep the wheels of Western industry – and the regional economy – moving.

Oil boom The desert sand can scarcely be seen in places for the thicket of pipelines, derricks and other hardware.

The Anglo-Persian oil company, formed the following year, won the backing of the British government, which saw a partnership with Anglo-Persian as a way of guaranteeing oil supplies for the Royal Navy. By the time the First World War began in 1914, oil was already becoming the focus for a new wave of western colonialism.

Britain bought a controlling interest in Anglo-Persian just as it merged with the Turkish Petroleum Company (which, despite its

The OPEC club

The Organisation of Petroleum Exporting Countries (OPEC) is unquestionably the most powerful organisation ever created by the developing countries. Even if it has never quite managed to gain complete control over the world market for crude oil, it still has a major influence over oil's price per barrel.

OPEC was founded on September 14, 1960, at Baghdad, by five oil-producing countries (Saudi Arabia, Kuwait, Iraq, Iran and Venezuela). The cartel was soon joined by Qatar, the United Arab Emirates, Libya, Indonesia, Nigeria and Algeria.

Ecuador and Gabon both joined OPEC then left, and other major producers like Russia have refused to join. As a result, OPEC's fight to maintain oil prices continues to be a difficult one.

There for the taking In some parts of the Middle East, as here in the Gulf, oil reserves lie almost at the surface.

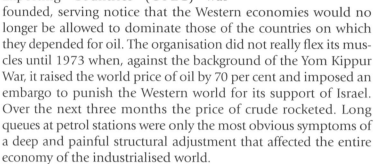

Manpower   The profits that well up in the Middle East may trickle down across a much wider area; some sparsely populated states now have more migrant workers than nationals.

exploration range, investigating the possibilities not only of smaller Gulf reserves but of such far-flung fields as those of Alaska and the North Sea.

In 1960 the Organisation of Petroleum Exporting Countries (OPEC) was founded, serving notice that the Western economies would no longer be allowed to dominate those of the countries on which they depended for oil. The organisation did not really flex its muscles until 1973 when, against the background of the Yom Kippur War, it raised the world price of oil by 70 per cent and imposed an embargo to punish the Western world for its support of Israel. Over the next three months the price of crude rocketed. Long queues at petrol stations were only the most obvious symptoms of a deep and painful structural adjustment that affected the entire economy of the industrialised world.

The effect of this first 'oil crisis', and of a second following the Iranian Revolution of 1979, was to make the West more prudent in its use of oil, working to increase fuel economy and to develop alternative energy sources. Concern about greenhouse gases and global warming added to the West's determination to make the industrialised economies less dependent on Middle Eastern fuel. The extent to which times had changed was underlined when Iraq's invasion of Kuwait in 1990 initiated a third 'oil crisis' – which, in the event, never really occurred. Braced for serious disruption in supplies and spiralling prices throughout the economy, analysts were taken aback by how little impact the episode actually had. Current political instability, the War in Iraq and the potential for the oil industry to be a target for terrorist attacks across the Middle East has intensified the need for alternative oil sources. Areas such as West Africa are being considered.

name, owned valuable concessions in Iraq). In 1938 huge reserves were discovered in neighbouring Kuwait – a British protectorate since 1899. The British were joined in Middle Eastern oil exploration by American oil companies during the 1930s. The American company Standard Oil had been drilling in Saudi Arabia for some years before the first big strike was made there in 1938, and it was well placed to exploit what was rapidly becoming an oil boom.

Over the next 30 years, the countries in which oil was found experienced economic development at an extraordinary pace. Some of the Middle Eastern states also underwent a political transformation from tribal-based feudalism to full modern statehood. In the worldwide climate of nationalism and anticolonialism that followed the Second World War, however, many in the Middle East began to resent the hold that Western oil companies had established on their countries.

In 1951, a new Iranian government nationalised its entire oil industry, spreading alarm throughout the financial world. The Iranian government finally reached an agreement with Anglo-Iranian (now British Petroleum or BP). The crisis brought a new degree of realism to a somewhat cavalier industry. Companies began to extend their

Self-help   One of OPEC's aims is to help states to take greater control of the more profitable refining processes. This refinery is in Dubai.

People versus petroleum

Despite the amount of oil that has been extracted in the middle east and the large amounts that remain to be exploited, the oil boom has done little to underwrite sustained regional development. Many undoubtedly benefited from oil-associated construction and service jobs, and from the impressive mosques and hospitals built on oil wealth. Most states did little, however, to create diversified industrial economies that might withstand a long-term decline in oil prices. And though there are exceptions to the rule, per capita incomes remains obstinately fixed in the Third World range, little changed from 1992 when the Arab world as a whole (including North Africa) plus the other countries of the Middle East had an average per capita income of US$2124, compared with US$20738 for the countries then comprising the European Union.

55

Kingdoms of commerce, cities of the future

Some states in the Middle East, even if they have not benefited from the oil boom, have developed other economic activities. Dubai, with its free trade port and Internet City, serves as a model for others to follow in an age of globalisation.

Cashpoint *Banks and bureaux de change are everywhere in Dubai – even in the street.*

The second largest of the seven city-states that make up the United Arab Emirates, Dubai struck it lucky, like so many of its neighbours, in the oil boom of the mid 20th century. But Sheik Rashid bin Saeed al-Maktoum, who ruled the emirate from 1958 until his death in 1990, was determined never to forget the austerities of the desert life from which his people had come – and to which they could so easily return.

Though great, the oil reserves of Dubai were not infinite; they offered only a few decades' prosperity. The sheik was unusual in being able to see the dangers of overdependence on oil revenues. 'My grandfather rode a camel, my father rode a camel, I drive a Mercedes,' he said. 'My son drives a Land-Rover, his son drives a Land-Rover, but his son will ride a camel.' This seems unlikely now, because the sheik defied the derision of his critics to establish Dubai as the 'Hong Kong of the Middle East'.

Free trade and tourism

Al-Maktoum was a visionary, but also a realist; his strategy for the future was built on the emirate's historical role in the region. Dubai had always been a trading centre, the dhows plying up and down the Gulf, farther afield to the East, or down the Swahili coast of Africa. Now, at a new Port Rashid, he developed the harbour to service modern ships, with a dry-dock facility adequate for even the largest tankers. Just outside the city at Jebel Ali, the sheik had the world's largest man-made harbour built, the centre of a free trade port that trades in everything from cars to textiles.

Part of Dubai's achievement has been to act as intermediary between unlikely trading partners; for example, much of its business involves the re-exporting of Western-produced goods to Iran.

Ashore, meanwhile, the sheik's World Trade Centre cut a dismally incongruous figure at first – the Middle East's tallest skyscraper towering above empty sand dunes. Not for long, though; the detractors were soon silenced as glass-and-steel office blocks started springing up.

International hotel chains sought the most prestigious sites in a city whose hinterland was also taking shape in the form of five-star beach resorts and world-class golf courses. The sheikdom has been promoted as the ideal base for regional companies, but its first-rate leisure facilities have also attracted the wealthiest tourists.

The sheik's son and successor, Maktoum bin Rashid al-Maktoum, has shared his father's vision, laying emphasis on the development of tourism. To the west of the city centre a vast new marina has been built, with mooring for up to 800 ocean-going craft. With its glitzy hotels and swish shopping malls, the Dubai Marina represents the last word in consumerism. None of this development would have been possible, of course, without a minor revolution in cultural tolerance. Dubai's free trade and tourism has necessitated greater freedom in social behaviour. Women are allowed to drive and, if foreign, to go unveiled – a licence extended even to visiting Muslim women. Alcohol is readily available, and the sexes mingle on the beach.

The old way... *The grand bazaar in Istanbul is one of the greatest markets in the world – a treasury of traditional crafts and antique objects.*

...and the new *People flock from all over the world to avail themselves of Dubai's duty-free shopping facilities. Japanese electronic hardware is especially sought after.*

Dubai.com

Because the present sheik is every bit as forward-looking as his father, Dubai has continued to have an eye to the future. October 2000 saw the opening, on a site next to the Dubai Marina, of a stunning new development, the Dubai Internet City. The world's first free trade zone for e-commerce, it was billed as offering not only superlative accommodation and high-tech infrastructure, but also a tax and regulatory environment designed to tempt the world's foremost IT companies. The ultimate city science park, it was envisioned as a centre for research and development, the physical home to the world's first Internet university.

The worldwide downturn in the dot-com industry means that Dubai will have to take things more slowly than expected, but the outlook for Internet City remains promising. Relatively late arrivals to the industry, Middle Eastern e-companies have not seen their shares blown up by the hype that inflated the American dot-com bubble. Whatever the short-term ups and downs of the industry, the trend to digitisation is irreversible, they say, and Dubai is well placed to take a lead in its steady development.

The newest jewel in Dubai's crown is the planned Burj Dubai which is set to open in 2008. It will be a spectacular site containing the world's tallest building, Burj Dubai Tower, in addition to the world's largest shopping mall complete with an indoor aquarium, the largest indoor gold souk and an artificial lake. The complex is expected to attract 35 million visitors in its first year of opening.

The emirate has nevertheless felt the chill: neither of the United Emirates' neighbours, Saudi Arabia and Iran, approves of Dubai's relaxed way of doing things – and the latter, in particular, is an unpredictable geopolitical presence. With an average per capita income well in excess of US$20 000, Dubai's native population has reason to be content, but they are outnumbered more than ten-

Merchant city *Dubai's success at modernising has been an inspiration for other ancient seaports of the Gulf. Sharjah (above) is just a few miles along the coast.*

Only the best *Dubai's wealth is such that even the public telephones are gold-plated.*

fold by an expatriate population that is for the most part nothing like so generously paid. The state shows no signs of intending to naturalise any of these immigrants, however long their residence – or to offer them rights to political representation or (in most cases) property ownership. Indian and Pakistani workers predominate in this community, with a substantial minority of Iranians. European and North American expatriates are smaller in number, though higher in status. Though the communities rub along together well enough for now, the fear must be that in the event of a serious economic downturn, Dubai would very abruptly come to seem a much less comfortable and harmonious society.

Striking a balance *Globalisation has not completely done away with old traditions.*

Israel online

Fibre optics, telecoms, the Internet, bio-engineering – Israeli expertise in all these cutting-edge fields is acknowledged everywhere. Geared up as it has been for military conflict, Israel has always set a high premium on high-tech development. The result is an unusually energetic and innovative IT sector. But old enmities hold the 'new economy' back; the Tel Aviv stock exchange is small, and investors among Israel's wealthy Arab neighbours impossible to find. The country's entrepreneurs therefore have no alternative but to look to the West, to the venture capitalists of Frankfurt, London, Paris and, of course, New York.

The tourist trail

Where the Crusaders once came in hopes of conquest, their Western successors come with cameras. The Middle East has history, culture and natural beauty in abundance – a sustainable tourist industry would safeguard this unique inheritance.

In 1971 the Shah of Iran marked the 2500th anniversary of the first Persian Empire with a huge celebration out in the desert near the site of old Persepolis. Building a small city of 50 luxurious tents for the purpose, he brought together leading figures from all over the world, Prince Philip and Princess Anne rubbing shoulders with presidents Tito of Yugoslavia and Ceausescu of Romania. Emperor Haile Selassie of Ethiopia was there, as was Vice President Spiro Agnew representing the United States.

Built at an expense of around US$300 million, their tents boasted marble bathrooms and beautiful French furnishings. Priceless Persian carpets lent an air of orientalism to their sumptuous interiors, but this was a celebration, not of Iran but of the Peacock Throne – the Iranian monarchy itself. Even the catering staff were flown in specially: 165 chefs from Maxim's of Paris prepared a

Amazing landscapes   The bizarre and amazing rock formations that are found in Cappadocia were caused by volcanic eruptions over millions of years. Early civilisations became established here more than 10,000 years ago.

Sackers of the cities

Some 750 years have passed since the Mongols swept down from their Central Asian homelands; 800 since knights of the Fourth Crusade destroyed Constantinople. Today's visitors to the Middle East are more welcome, and for the most part far better behaved, but a minority still seems to come in search of pillage. Stolen from mosques, museums and churches or archaeological sites, thousands of objects every year find their way out of Middle Eastern countries to end up in the collections of connoisseurs in London, Paris, New York or Tokyo.

banquet at which a tonne of Caspian caviar was washed down by gallons of champagne. The undoubted social event of the year, the only thing the party lacked was Iranian guests; the majority of the shah's subjects were by then living in fearful poverty.

Though it looks a little tatty and faded by now, this extravagant tent city still stands, preserved by the revolutionary regime as a monument to monarchist decadence. Provincial officials are planning to rebuild it as an attraction to entice moneyed tourists to Iran from all over the world. The new development will be more culturally sensitive – 'We want to turn them into Iranian tents,' a spokesman told the *New York Times* – but its main selling point will be its air of imperial splendour. The authorities acknowledge that

Holy Land   Christians visit Jerusalem today as they have done for centuries, to walk in Christ's footsteps and visit the holy sites.

Ancient visitors   The Middle East's heritage includes much more than its own indigenous civilisations. Roman ruins, for example, abound at Ephesus (right) in Turkey.

this is not exactly a revolutionary aim. But a country cannot afford to be too censorious if it wants a buoyant tourist industry.

In recent years, Iran has taken a lead in attempting to establish an all-Islamic tourist industry for travellers from within the Muslim world. Hotels in which sexual segregation is strictly imposed, women must go veiled and alcohol is outlawed may find an appreciative clientele in certain Muslim countries. 'Why should we look upon tourism from a Western point of view?' asked Mohammed Muezzeddin, the deputy culture minister. Like many other countries in the Middle East, Iran has enormous potential as a tourist destination, but its government has some difficult cultural dilemmas to resolve if it is to attract Western tourists.

Pilgrims' progress

Nonetheless, a growing number of non-Muslim Western travellers are braving the Islamic restrictions of Iran or Saudi Arabia. Some have even been prepared to put up with the inconveniences of travelling in sanctions-hit Iraq, finding their way through the ruins of a modern state to those of the world's first civilisations.

A new breed of secular pilgrims, ready to journey in cultural curiosity and more open-minded respect, has joined the crowds of believers still flocking in their hundreds of thousands to Jerusalem and Mecca. Syria's imposing Krak des Chevaliers, the astonishing reefs of the Red Sea, Jordan's Petra ruins or the empty expanse of the Wadi Rum – none of these may be religious sites, conventionally speaking, but in their different ways they all inspire a certain reverence, and those who come here seek an experience that is not far from spiritual. Damascus's Ummayad Mosque or Saint Sofia's Basilica in Istanbul may be religious monuments, but they are also triumphs of human aspiration and artistic endeavour.

The economic implications of more traditional forms of pilgrimage cannot be overlooked, either. However unworldly the motives that draw them, modern pilgrims make an important contribution to the local economy, spending money in hotels, shops, cafes, restaurants and all sorts of other places. Bethlehem, the birthplace of Christ, has some 600 000 visitors annually.

Turkish delights

Even by the standards of the Middle East, Turkey has an unusually rich historical and cultural inheritance, with relics from the prehistoric, Persian, Greek, Roman, Byzantine and Ottoman periods. Turkey has also set itself the target of making its Aegean coast the region's first centre for mass-market tourism. After enormous investment through the 1990s, the number of visitors to Turkey reached a new record in 2003, at just under 14 million, with receipts of $12 billion. Impressive though this may sound, the Turkish government is thinking still bigger, expecting 25 million visitors to spend $20 billion by 2010.

Jericho, Nablus, Hebron and Qumran have all taken on something of the quality of religious resorts, drawing great numbers of Christians eager to see for themselves and find inspiration in the land of the Bible. Jerusalem's associations are threefold – Jews and Muslims also making the pilgrimage here. The Dome of the Rock and the Al-Aqsa Mosque are among Islam's holiest shrines, while the city of David is the centre of the Jewish world.

The pilgrims of medieval times would be astonished to see such huge numbers of their descendants arriving today, by jumbo jet. But the purpose of their journeys remains essentially the same, and so do the implications for a region of the world whose religious significance has for centuries been a matter of crucial economic importance.

Something for everyone   From far-flung shores ripe for exploration (right) to bustling beach resorts and holiday villages, the Mediterranean coasts can cater to just about every touristic taste.

High spot   Cappadocia in central Turkey attracts visitors from all over the world.

Grand tourists

The Middle East has always attracted tourists. Enterprising spirits in the 18th century added the Ottoman Empire to the established Grand Tour, by which the cultivated young gentlefolk were supposed to complete their education with visits to Europe's most important capitals. Goethe and Lord Byron both came here, as did 19th-century novelists such as Gustave Flaubert and William Thackeray, finding colour and exoticism – and in some cases comedy – on the tourist trail.

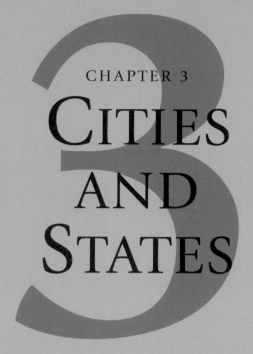

CHAPTER 3

CITIES AND STATES

Wind and rain long ago erased the cities of ancient Mesopotamia, but the idea of the city has endured. Islam was an urban religion from its start. Baghdad flourished at the end of the 1st millennium AD, only to be left in ruins by the Mongols a few centuries later; it was blasted again by the Western allies at the end of the 20th century. At least three great civilisations have contributed to the metropolis we now call Istanbul, while Jerusalem has been fought over by the followers of three world religions. Such changes in fortune are common in many Middle Eastern cities. In others, the memory of a nomadic life seems to persist – modern Riyadh still has something of the flavour of the ancient caravanserai. The bustling streets and souks, the roar of traffic, the cry of the muezzin calling Muslims to prayer – there is something unique and exhilarating in the Middle Eastern city.

Tradition and high-tech find equal expression in the design of Riyadh Airport.

Everything stops for kat

The streets of San'a are littered with discarded leaves; this unexpected sight in a city not exactly well endowed with trees is a sign of Yemen's national addiction to the chewing of kat. No more than a mild intoxicant, kat has been tested by America's National Institute of Drug Abuse and found to produce no indications of negative side effects. The consequences for the Yemeni economy have been more damaging, however, for the 'chew' brings every working day to a near halt each afternoon, while kat cultivation extends across acres of valuable agricultural land and soaks up vast amounts of much-needed water.

San'a, the mountain citadel

High up in the mountains of southern Arabia, in a natural amphitheatre among awesome peaks, nestles the ancient Yemeni capital, the stronghold city of San'a. The unique atmosphere of the setting, enhanced by the beauty of the city itself, has given San'a its reputation as a place of mystery and magic.

A nation addicted Life in San'a shifts down a gear or two for the afternoon 'chew'.

In *The Thousand and One Nights*, Sheherezade tells the tale of a Persian prince who, having upset a sorceror, was swept heavenwards on an enchanted ebony horse. When he finally gained control of his mount, the first landing place he saw was a palace roof in a strange and far-off city, where a fair princess slept in her chamber. Love at first sight, trials, tribulations and triumphant union ensued. Perhaps inevitably, the place where the prince landed was San'a, a city closer to heaven than any of the other mountain citadels of the Middle East.

A vertical city

San'a stands 7500 ft (2286 m) above sea level on a narrow plain, itself surrounded by peaks several thousand feet higher still; everything reinforces the visitor's sense of altitude. As if the city were not high enough already, its population long ago chose to live in towers. The ancient Ghumdan Palace is said to have had 20 floors: it could, according to legend, be seen from Medina, 700 miles (1126 km) away. One must allow for the exaggeration of myth – but of the 14000 old buildings still standing in San'a, many have up to eight storeys. Crenellations, arches and elaborate

Family business The souk has been a place of trade for many generations of San'a craftsmen.

patterns picked out in the brickwork add to the effect of verticality. The soaring minarets of the city's mosques and the many beautiful terraced gardens reached by staircases from the narrow streets below enhance the impression of a mysterious city in the skies. The fact that new buildings have always been constructed on the remains of old has only increased their elevation.

A jewel worth preserving

Mud-brick buildings, when carefully maintained, may stand for centuries, but they can literally be washed away by running water. A coating of limewash affords protection against the monsoon rains, and the resulting white glaze lends the finishing touches to a city of unsurpassed beauty. In 1984, the old city of San'a was selected by UNESCO as a world heritage site, and efforts have continued since then to protect its unique architecture for future generations.

Reputedly founded by Shem, the son of Noah, the city dates back at least as far as the 1st millennium BC. An important staging post on the caravan route between Aden and Mecca, San'a (the name means 'fortified place') was a strategic stronghold in the lawless mountains of southern Arabia. Since then the city has been forced to defend itself many times and been subjected to innumerable sackings. Today the greatest threat is to its historic heritage, under siege from modern developers.

Muscat, pearl of Oman

Since the accession of Sultan Qaboos bin Said in 1970, the emirate of Oman has opened out on to the wider world, taking full advantage of its situation at the mouth of the Gulf. Yet Oman's enthusiasm for the new has been matched by its reverence for tradition; its capital Muscat is, if anything, more beautiful than ever.

Preservation *Lovingly tended gardens typify the sultanate's protectiveness towards its natural and human heritage.*

The words of the Prophet echo in the minds of visitors to Muscat's Sultan Qaboos Grand Mosque: 'Whoever builds a mosque, desiring thereby God's pleasure, God builds the like for him in paradise.' However pious its intentions, this astonishing building serves a worldlier function as well, signalling a transformation in what was once one of the region's most stagnant backwaters. Completed in 2001, the mosque represents a remarkable collaboration between Oman and the outside world; an astonishing contract between modernity and tradition.

Engineers from Britain and elsewhere raised the building's arches and central dome; local craftsmen saw to every exquisite detail of its interior. Koranic verses in cut-tile calligraphy; stained-glass patterns and stunning mosaics: every surface assaults the senses and takes the breath away. Some 600 women worked by hand to make the 5098 sq yd (4263 m²) carpet that covers the entire floor of the main prayer hall in a single stretch. Outside, five minarets rise skywards above a marbled esplanade; at night the latticed dome becomes a lantern for the city. The whole extravagant pile can indeed be seen as Oman's beacon to the world – the sultan's vision for his state caught in glass and stone.

The sustainable sultanate

Crucial to that vision is respect for the past. Like Sheik Rashid bin Saeed al-Maktoum in Dubai, Qaboos has built a new port for supertankers and ocean-going freighters, but he has been careful to preserve the ancient harbour. The rulers of the Gulf sometimes seem intent on a glitzy modernity at any price, but Qaboos has endowed a major international prize for environmental preservation. His caution has stemmed in part from the fact that, by Gulf standards, Oman's oil reserves are modest. He has accordingly ensured that Oman's agricultural sector should not be neglected: Oman still produces the succulent muscat grape, for instance, along with other such exotic commodities as frankincense. The country's coastal fishing industry remains important, and diversification into other areas – notably tourism – has been encouraged. Where the other wealthy emirates have flooded their service sectors with low-paid and politically disenfranchised foreign immigrants, Oman has followed a policy of 'localisation'. Though there are workers from East Africa, India, Pakistan and elsewhere, the native presence in Oman's services is far stronger, a recipe both for economic sustainability and political stability in the longer term.

Safe haven *The harbour of Mutrah, Muscat, has hardly changed in a thousand years. Sinbad the Sailor was, some claim, Omani-born.*

Land of castles

On guard *The fort at Jabrin.*

Oman is famous for its forts, some built by the Portuguese to protect their shipping, others constructed much earlier by local rulers. Many were little more than decorative castles, though the fort at Nizwa saw fierce action against the Persians. Built in the 17th century, Jabrin looks more dramatic than Nizwa, but its history is tamer. It is actually a fortified palace, with stunning interiors and ornamented façades that are well worth a visit.

Situated 240 miles (386 km) from the Gulf in the Najd – the arid interior of Arabia – Riyadh has few of the geographical advantages one would expect to find in a capital city. It owes its rise to prominence to the ascendancy of the chieftains of the al-Saud dynasty and to the expanding influence of the Wahhabi religious movement in the peninsula as a whole. When Saudi Arabia won its independence in 1932, the seat of the al-Sauds became the country's official capital, but not until the modernising reign of King Khaled, from 1975 to 1982, were the offices of government and diplomacy transferred here.

Megalopolis   A small oasis a century ago, Riyadh is now a huge city.

Riyadh, the desert metropolis

The old city   The explosive expansion of Riyadh since the 1970s has changed the face of Saudi Arabia's capital city almost beyond recognition. But traces of the old settlement can still be found among the superhighways and high-rise office blocks.

In the space of a century, a small oasis settlement has become a modern metropolis with 3 million inhabitants: its explosive growth underlines the awesome rise of Saudi Arabia – and its continuing contradictions.

Riyadh ('the garden'), the capital of Saudi Arabia, is situated in the very heart of Arabia's huge Najd Desert. It extends over an area of nearly 200 sq miles (500 km²) and continues to grow rapidly. The city is home to an extraordinary mix of peoples: Arabs from the desert drawn by the bright lights of the city and the promise of oil wealth and luxury; mountain people from neighbouring Yemen; homesick Palestinians; Egyptians, Philippinos and Sri Lankans working as domestic servants; and a floating population of Westerners working in technical and service industries. This population forms a mosaic of communities within the city, separated by urban geography, social status and culture. Riyadh itself is divided into distinct districts – administrative, diplomatic, university, commercial – that further fragment its society. The city's physical appearance reflects an odd, contradictory mix of influences, with severe Wahhabite austerity awkwardly juxtaposed with American-style urbanism.

A place apart

In 1902, when King Abdul Aziz bin Abdul Rahman al-Saud brought together the tribes of central Arabia, Riyadh was a desert settlement with 10 000 inhabitants. In recent decades oil wealth has seen it transformed into one of the world's most modernistic cities. From the start this was a paradoxical place: how could there be a city of Bedouin nomads? Western visitors puzzle over the contrast between Riyadh's ultramodern architecture and the archaic sex segregation and liquor laws. In appearance an outward-looking, cosmopolitan city, Riyadh retains at heart the strongly Islamic identity stamped on it by the Saudi monarchy.

The Western democracies have chosen to ignore the ideological contradictions of a country that, whatever its faults, possesses 26 per cent of the world's known oil reserves. Within Saudi Arabia itself, meanwhile, if the higher echelons of officialdom have had divided loyalties, popular opinion has implacably opposed the country's close engagement with the West. The absence of any legitimate forum for debate has meant the suppression of such views, but to outsiders the signs have been clear for some time. As early as November 1979 a radical group seized the holy shrine of Mecca and had to be removed by government forces. Terrorist attacks on US personnel and interests in the 1990s increased the pressure on a Saudi state walking a tightrope between its economic allies and its neighbours in the Islamic world. The fact that the destroyers of New York's World Trade Center on September 11, 2001, were led by Saudi citizens emphasises the self-deception in which both Saudi Arabia and its Western friends have connived. The popular opposition to the West that has lain beneath the surface of the Saudi state now stands exposed: difficult times lie ahead for the Prophet's homeland.

Islamic style   Modern internationalism and Islamic traditionalism come together in Riyadh's architecture.

Ankara, Kemal's Turkish capital

Ankara is dominated by the mausoleum of Mustafa Kemal, also known as Atatürk, 'Father of the Turks'. The visionary Atatürk founded the modern Turkish Republic, and in 1923 made this small provincial town its capital.

Monumental architecture *Kemal's mausoleum combines the traditions of Asia Minor and the modernity of the new Turkey.*

The Ottoman Empire finally collapsed in the aftermath of the First World War, after several centuries of slow decline. Mustafa Kemal was determined to construct a new and modern nation state free from the pretensions and problems of its predecessor and true to its ethnic origins in Asia. His Turkish Republic would not suffer the ignominy of being an 'empire' without effective dominion, because it would content itself with building a strong and coherent domestic state structure.

Kemal could have chosen Istanbul for his capital, but along with its many splendours the city on the Bosporus also brought centuries of accumulated historical baggage. Not only had it been the administrative and commercial centre for a discredited Ottoman Empire, but before that it was the centre of the Greek Byzantine Empire. On the other hand, the city of Ankara, high in the Anatolian Mountains in the heart of Asia Minor, had been settled since the Bronze Age, when it was a centre of the Hittite Empire. It had been occupied by later waves of migrants from the steppes, all of whom had Turkish credentials that could hardly be questioned.

A blank page

Determined as Kemal was to avoid his nation being overshadowed by its Byzantine past, he was equally adamant that the country's Islamic heritage should not loom too large. While representing all the different strands in Turkish tradition, Ankara had the virtue of not giving too much prominence to any of them – and, equally

The heart of Turkey

Kemal's choice of Ankara as his capital was made largely for historical and cultural reasons, but its position at the geographical heart of Turkey also came into the reckoning. The centre of a centrist state, the mountain citadel of what was clearly destined to be a militarised nation – both these images figured in his calculations. Another was the city's inaccessibility to foreign aircraft: Turkey had a large, well-equipped army, but its air force was tiny and technologically backward at a time when aerial warfare was coming into its own.

important, of being a sleepy backwater. This was a place upon which Kemal would be able to imprint whatever identity he chose. As such, it can now be seen to represent both the best and worst of his achievement.

From a population of 30 000 in 1930, Ankara has grown into a metropolis of more than 3 million. Its orderliness and austerity may smack of authoritarianism for the modern visitor – as do the bold street plan with its sweeping boulevards, the gigantic civic sculptures and the neon-lit portraits of the great leader above many streets. But at the time it was built, Ankara represented the sense of coherence that Atatürk's new republic had conferred on a disintegrating nation.

The city does have its lighter side, with impressive shops and a busy nightlife. Its Children's Festival is famous throughout the world. There remains the sense, however, that this is institutionalised enjoyment, that this is a metropolis that has to work hard at its fun. Ankara's worst offence as a city, perhaps, is to be a little severe, a little too worthy; it has fine avenues and superb museums, imposing public buildings and mosques – but where is the buzzing, disordered life, the living history and excitement of Istanbul?

Military bearing *The streets and buildings of Turkey's modern capital are regimented, verging on uniform, in their design.*

Istanbul, a city between two continents

Unique in its history, its architecture and its setting, Istanbul is a metropolis of extraordinary diversity and vitality. Here, where Europe and Asia meet, the cultures of a colourful past come together with those of the modern world.

In the 17th century BC, merchants ventured out from Megara on the Greek mainland to establish an outpost of their home city on the Bosporus. They called their colony Byzantium, and traded with a native population that had lived there for 4000 years. Civilisations have come and gone since then, but Byzantium – since called Constantinople or Istanbul – has transcended cultural differences with ease: Greek, Roman, Turkish, Christian, Muslim and secularist strands can all be found in its history. Today around 9 million people live in this cosmopolitan metropolis which, while not the official capital of its country, nevertheless represents the face of Turkey to the outside world.

Sensual feast *Shoppers savour the exotic colours and aromas of the Spice Bazaar.*

The city on the sea

Hagia Sophia, the Topkapi Palace, the Suleimaniye Mosque, the Grand Bazaar: Istanbul has many attractions, but its greatest asset is its setting, as anyone who has looked out over the Bosporus on a soft summer's evening will testify. Leander's Tower, just off the Asiatic shore, calls to mind the famous legend of Hero and Leander. Falling in love with Hero, a priestess of Aphrodite, Leander swam across the strait to see her each night, guided by a lamp she placed for him on the European shore. One night it blew out in a storm and Leander, disorientated, was drowned. Despairing at her loss, Hero cast herself into the waves and she too died.

The sea is not merely a feature of Istanbul, but the essence of its

Shopping mall *In the thronged arcades of Istanbul's famous Grand Bazaar, you can find everything from carpets to jewellery, leather goods to tobacco pipes.*

identity. 'Nowhere else does the sea come so home to a city,' wrote Alexander Kinglake in 1844. 'There are no pebbly shores, no sand bars, no slimy riverbeds, no black canals, no locks nor docks to divide the very heart of the place from the deep waters.' His account of his travels in the Middle East, *Eothen*, first published in 1844, was an inspiration to successive generations of travellers from W.M. Thackeray to Paul Theroux.

For British diplomat Lord Hardinge, too, Istanbul was defined by its relationship with water. He wrote: 'It would be impossible to describe the wonderful beauty of the moonlit nights, the outlines of the hills on the Asiatic shore, the cries of fishermen signalling passage of fish, the song of the nightingales and the sparkling movements of the dancing fireflies.'

The Topkapi Palace

According to the 19th-century novelist William Makepeace Thackeray, the Topkapi Palace was 'no palace at all' but 'a great town of pavilions, built without order, here and there'. His disappointment at the sight of the Ottoman emperors' great palace may well have been justified. When the emperor moved to the more modest Dolmabahçe Palace by the Bosporus in 1853, the Topkapi Palace was allowed to fall into ruin. Thackeray was particularly put out by the shabby state of the harem or seraglio, a place of enduring fascination to the Western visitor, for whom it symbolised the exotic sexuality of the Orient. Today, the Topkapi Palace is anything but disappointing: its stunning interiors and artworks bear testimony to the extravagance and exuberance of the Ottoman Empire.

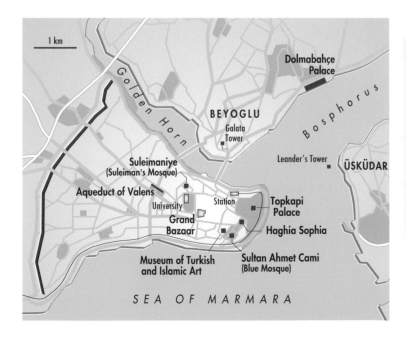

Standing guard

A pair of Ottoman castles once stood sentinel on either side of the Bosporus – the Anadolu Hisari, 'The Fortress of Asia', and the Rumeli Hisari, the 'Fortress of Europe'. With the decline of Ottoman rule, both forts became redundant: the Anadolu Hisari fell into ruin, while its European companion became a prison. Since 1953 it has served a much happier function as a museum.

Famous landmark *The dome and minarets of Hagia Sophia rise over the Bosporus.*

Whatever its appeal to visitors, the Bosporus is not so much a strait as the main street of a watery city. It has always been very much a working waterway. The Megaran colony came into being as a bustling commercial port, and so it has continued to this day. Where wooden galleys and caiques once skipped across the waves, giant container vessels now make their way, while commuters ply back and forth each day by river bus.

The strait divides a city that belongs to both Europe and Asia – and to neither. Turkey's greatest living writer, Orhan Pamuk, is in no doubt where his loyalties lie. 'I realised it was still better and still more lovely to see the two shores at once,' he writes. 'Speaking to each shore without completely belonging to either, this unveiled the finest scenery of all.' For him, the Bosporus is not a barrier but a bridge, a tie to bind European and Asian opposites, modern Turkey's symbol of plurality and cultural richness.

A grim reality

The old centre of Istanbul is still a buzzing bazaar of art and history, guaranteed to thrill the visitor. The vast aqueduct of Valens was built in 378 BC to help to assure the water supply of a Roman capital threatened by external invaders. A link between the Byzantine and Ottoman worlds, the great basilica of Hagia Sophia has seen service both as church and mosque in its 1500-year history, having been converted in 1453 after the Ottoman Turks took over the city. The building was turned into a museum in 1932, a secular shrine to Turkey's historic heritage. But the city's

Harvest of the sea *Istanbul has a small-scale but significant fishing fleet. Much of the catch is bought by the public direct from the boats.*

Muslims have no problem finding other places of worship, for mosques abound in Istanbul. The Sultan Ahmet Cami, or 'Blue Mosque' (1609-17), just a short walk across the square from Hagia Sophia, is one of the acknowledged architectural wonders of the Islamic world. A little farther to the west stands the Suleimaniye, erected on the orders of Suleiman the Magnificent between 1550 and 1557. Across the Golden Horn, on the hillside of Beyoğlu, stands the great bastion of the Galata tower; from the top, visitors can see the entire city laid out in all its glory.

But all this splendour is under threat from the pressures of the modern world. In the 1970s and 80s, highways were built through the heart of some of the city's most picturesque and historic

Communications centre *If Istanbul is the junction of East and West, Eminönü is its hub. From here you can get a boat to Beyoğlu or the Asian shore, a coach to the country, or a train to just about anywhere.*

A boat ride away At the northern end of the Bosporus, just before it opens out into the Black Sea, can be found waterside suburbs like Anadolu Kavagi on the Asian shore, where the houses have their own jetties.

Cafe society In Istanbul, coffee and conversation have gone together since as long ago as the 9th century. Hours are whiled away each day discussing everything from politics to poetry, from fine arts to football.

quarters. Town planners flattened other ancient neighbourhoods to clear the way for public housing projects, while private developers bribed officials for permission to throw up office and apartment blocks on key sites around the edge of the old city. Old Istanbul is now no more than the touristic core of an immense industrial and commercial city. The noise and fumes of traffic are as bad here as in any other metropolis, while effluent compromises the limpid blue of the Bosporus and Golden Horn.

The many faces of Istanbul

If there are Greek, Roman and Ottoman Istanbuls, there is also Istanbul the modern Third World city, where men, women and children work long hours in sweatshops and live in housing as poor as that in any Third World city. Despite its role as Turkey's financial and commercial centre, cultural heart and tourist magnet, Istanbul exhibits all the problems and hardships of cities that have grown too fast in the 20th century.

Though the worst of these social evils remain unseen by tourists, the effects of overcrowding and pollution are so evident that they are unavoidable. Istanbul has always had charm – Western visitors in earlier centuries were excited by the glimpse of Oriental exoticism and decadence – but the experience of visiting Istanbul today can be a difficult one. Journalist James Pettifer cites a survey of British holidaymakers which found that, of all major tourist destinations, the city had the highest percentage of visitors who did not wish to return. 'If the view of the 19th-century poet Lamartine was that you see the skyline of Constantinople and die,' he observes, 'some visitors now find that you encounter the city and then leave as soon as possible.' But there have been signs in recent years that the city is at last beginning to pay attention to its image.

Architectural wonder Built on the orders of Sultan Ahmet I in the early 19th century, the Blue Mosque is even more spectacular inside than outside. The huge dome casts an almost surreal light over the interior.

Relatively new Standing on the banks of the Golden Horn, the Yeni Cami or 'New Mosque' (right) was in fact built between 1597 and 1600.

Towards a better future

The Turkish government, having invested a great deal of money and energy in the tourist trade, has been attempting to arrest Istanbul's decline, working hard to improve public transport and amenities for citizens and tourists alike. But, even were the state so minded, it would be harder to reverse the damage done to the city's age-old cosmopolitan glamour by the hounding-out of so many of the Greek population in the wake of the disputes over Cyprus since the 1950s. Istanbul's great allure – and its great problem – is that it is so profoundly un-Turkish in the modern, Atatürkian sense. Turkey finds it hard to know how best to take advantage of a tourist resource whose appeal it recognises but cannot readily understand.

Tel Aviv, the secular city

The first capital of the state of Israel, Tel Aviv is a wholly modern city, surprisingly secular in its outlook. In 1967 Jerusalem took over as the official capital, but many Israelis prefer to live less hemmed in by historical and religious tensions.

Rendezvous *Cafés are always busy.*

In the last decade of the 19th century, building was already under way on the sand dunes outside Jaffa. The project was inspired by a mix of entrepreneurship, religious piety and pioneering nationalism. A brochure described the builders' intentions to create the world's first Hebrew town '100 per cent Jewish populated, where Hebrew will be spoken, and purity and cleanliness maintained'. It also outlined more material recommendations: the town would be nothing less than 'the New York of Eretz Israel. In this town, we will set out streets having roads and sidewalks, with electric lighting'. Tel Aviv has been the urban embodiment of a distinctive approach to Israeli life: steadfastly Jewish, yet worldly and unspiritual.

One of the reasons why Tel Aviv feels so relaxed is that it is some distance away from the modern zones of conflict. While patriotic zealots camp out in front-line settlements on the West Bank and puritans make pious observance at Jerusalem's sacred places, Tel Aviv's citizens are more preoccupied with dating, going to see the month's big movie or eating at the latest fashionable restaurant. But the air of frivolity masks a serious commitment to tolerance, that attitude of live-and-let-live that is for many a founding principle of the Israeli nation. Tel Aviv's dethronement as capital in 1967 in favour of a largely Arab-controlled Jerusalem did not merely represent a civic slight, but a rejection of this ideal of easy-going urbanity.

Architect's paradise *The Azorieli Center comprises two office towers, eight cinemas and a shopping mall.*

Lazy days *The citizens of Tel Aviv make time for relaxation and fun.*

An architecture in exile

Built on sand in an astonishingly short space of time, Tel Aviv is unsurpassed in the richness of its modern architecture. The Bauhaus style came, like so many of Tel Aviv's citizens, from Germany. Developed between 1910 and 1930 by Peter Behrens, Walter Gropius and Ludwig Mies van der Rohe, it was exported to the USA as the 'International Style'. The simplicity of Bauhaus was well suited to the new development beside the Mediterranean, its aesthetic of 'beauty through function' ideal for a young country that wanted comfort and convenience without old-fashioned fuss and ostentation. No one could have guessed that, in the 1930s, the architecture, like the Jews, would fall foul of the Nazi regime. Bauhaus found its home in exile here, and 17 architects ended up working in Tel Aviv. More than 1500 of their buildings are preserved as architectural monuments.

A mini Silicon Valley

Today, with 2 million inhabitants, Tel Aviv is a multicultural melting pot of Jews from all the different diaspora nations. There is also a sizable Arab population, and immigrants drawn from countries as far afield as Romania and Russia, Thailand and the Philippines. For them the magnet has been the economic opportunities afforded by one of the world's fastest-growing cities. In the absence of oil-wealth and willing trading partners in the region, Israeli entrepreneurs have been compelled to exercise originality and ingenuity in their thinking. 'Some say that Silicon Valley's most serious global competitor is the mini-sprawl around Tel Aviv,' reports America's *Newsweek* magazine. 'High-tech start-ups are the new Zionism,' one entrepreneur is quoted as saying.

Hemmed in *Old Damascus is now absorbed into a chaotic metropolis.*

Damascus, a paradise lost?

The old city has been surrounded by a 20th-century sprawl; its image tarnished by three decades of dictatorship. But whatever shocks modernity may have brought, a surprising amount of Damascus's heritage of history and culture still endures.

The narghile *Enjoying a pipe.*

The Prophet Muhammad refused to enter the city of Damascus, having seen it spread out before him from a nearby hilltop. In a place so delightful, might he not be tempted to forgo altogether the joys of that paradise of which he preached, and settle instead for the earthly attractions of the world's sweetest city?

A visitor to Damascus today is confronted with noise and traffic fumes, drab grey concrete, government posters and advertising hoardings. But if you push a little deeper through the development of the past five decades or so, Muhammad's rapture seems more comprehensible. The Syrian capital abounds in ancient buildings and streets, with monuments dating back to the Romans and beyond. The Umayyad Mosque, the ancient citadel, Saladin's mausoleum, the 18th-century Ottoman governor's palace – the city has architecture from all but the earliest stages of its lengthy history. And when earlier generations saw Damascus as heavenly, they were thinking not only of the beauty of its buildings, but the savour of its cuisine, the smells of its spice stalls, the sheen of its elaborately patterned silks, the touch of its fine-tempered steels and leathers. To describe the city as paradise would be an exaggeration – yet few other cities lift the spirits in quite the same way that Damascus does.

Damascene diversity

The famous conversion of St Paul from persecutor to apostle of Christianity may not actually have occurred on the road to the city (it seems 'Damascus' also referred to a site near the Dead Sea). Nonetheless, the city of Damascus has more than 200 mosques, as well as scores of Christian churches of different denominations. Druzes, Shiites, Aramaeans, Armenians and Jews all have their neighbourhoods, a fascinating mosaic of ethnic groups and religious traditions. The secular socialism of the Ba'ath party, Syria's dictatorial rulers since coming to power in a coup of 1963, has obscured this diversity in Western eyes without seriously threatening it at home. The anti-Western pan-Arabism of the government of Hafez al-Assad from 1970 to 2000 was only part of the Syrian story. The dictatorial Assad has been succeeded by his more circumspect son Bashar. The capital he has inherited may not be a paradise, but Damascus already shows signs of casting off the somewhat purgatorial air it had under his father. It may actually be reverting to its ancient rich diversity.

Rich heritage *Damascus still holds many treasures for the visitor. The Umayyad Mosque is the most famous of its splendours.*

Beirut, risen from the ashes

Beirut was for years a millionaires' playground, but in 1970 the city was plunged into almost two decades of war. Now, after ten years of peace, the old spirit has succeeded in reasserting itself. There is still a long way to go, but this is a city in renaissance.

A past revealed *Among the rubble, 5000 years of history is uncovered.*

With its elegant boulevards and spacious parks, its exclusive shops and cafés and its sumptuous hotels, Beirut was the most stylish and sophisticated of the Middle Eastern cities. After the break-up of the Ottoman Empire, Lebanon fell into the French sphere of influence, but the easy-going cosmopolitan quality of its capital city was also due to demographic pressures that originated much nearer home. A steady drift of Maronite Christians, Druze and other Shiite Muslims from the mountains all had to get along with a rising number of Sunni Muslim Palestinians displaced over the years by the bitter conflict across the Israeli border.

Into the inferno

The moment at which a lively and fruitful cultural diversity became a cockpit of religious and cultural intolerance is hard to pin down, but by 1970 the city was sliding into civil war between rival militias. For the next ten years, egged on by Lebanon's powerful neighbours Syria and Israel, Beirut became an inferno. Artillery batteries on the heights above the city pounded away at the great hotels, while on their balconies sharpshooters picked off targets in the streets below. Other fighters strafed pavements and shopfronts from the backs of cars, hurled grenades into shops and restaurants, or lobbed mortar bombs at the international airport.

By 1976, some 45 000 people had died in Lebanon's civil war, a further 100 000 were injured and an estimated half a million driven into exile. While the 'peace agreement' of that year may have brought the main organisations and their international sponsors together, the fighters themselves continued a factional war that increasingly defied political analysis. A 'green line' through the centre divided Beirut into Christian (east) and Muslim (west)

sectors, but the division meant little for a city in anarchy. Then, in 1982, the Israelis invaded Lebanon to put down PLO terrorists they claimed were attacking their territory; of more than 20 000 killed in the operation, the vast majority were civilians.

Through the 1980s the bloodshed went on – and the interference from outside. Iranian-backed Islamic Jihad and Syrian-sponsored Hizbollah were soon adding their own violent nuances to a war that seemed set to run indefinitely. In the end, ironically, the conflict was defused by the invasion of Kuwait by Iraqi strongman Saddam Hussein, an event that went some way towards redrawing the political map of the Middle East.

Beirut reborn

When the dust and smoke began to clear in 1990, large sections of the city centre were heaps of rubble. The green line lived up to its name: grass, shrubs and even small trees had sprung up among the ruined buildings. But soon, the old city of Beirut began to renew itself. The shops were restocked with perfumes and designer clothes; the five-star hotels, refurbished, reopened their doors; the yachts began to reappear in the city's marinas. Now, though still a shadow of its former self, Beirut is becoming a bustling centre of sophistication and style, the Paris of the Middle East once more.

Port of call *Back on the itinerary of the international yachting set after years of civil war, Beirut has been busily rebuilding its vital tourist industry.*

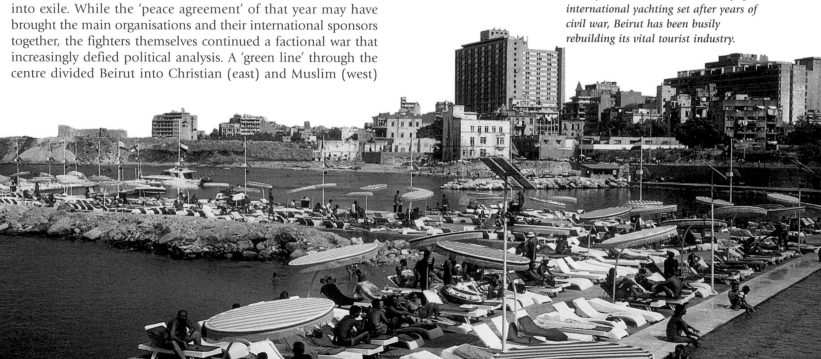

Tehran, the Muslim megalopolis

Spread across the lower slopes of the Elburz Mountains, Tehran has little to recommend it in the way of fine architecture. Its great resource – today as throughout its history – is the irrepressible life and energy of its people.

The revolution unbends After years of religious rule, there have been signs that the regime is prepared to allow some relaxation in the strict austerity.

Iran owes its identity as an Islamic nation-state to Shah Ismail (1502-24) and to his successors of the famous Safavid dynasty. The founder's son, Tahmasp I, passing through a one-horse town on the southern slopes of the Elburz Mountains in the course of a religious pilgrimage, decided to put Tehran on the Muslim map. He built an impressive set of city walls, measuring 6000 paces in circumference and protected by 114 fortified towers, one for each sura or chapter in the Koran. But the city has never quite been able to carry off its majestic role. The English traveller Isabella Bird put the problem accurately in the 1880s when she remarked that 'I never went through those mean outskirts of Tihran which are within the city walls without being reminded of a man in shabby clothes preposterously too big for him'.

Part of the trouble is the city's setting, dwarfed by the Elburz Mountains in the background. And it was doomed to spread out from the start, having been established on comparatively low-lying ground that was liable to flooding. The richer classes were soon rushing to build on drier – and cooler – sites on the slopes above.

Trials and tribulations

Tehran has been the Persian capital since 1786, when the Qajar Shahs seized power. It retained its status in 1925, when they were usurped by Reza Shah Pahlavi, father of Shah Mohammed Reza whose authority was so dramatically overthrown by the Iranian Revolution of 1979. But the real revolution in the life of Tehran has not been one of religious or temporal power but a transformation in the economic life of a rapidly modernising nation. The growth of the Iranian oil industry accelerated a drift that is taking place in developing countries worldwide.

Today Tehran has a population of 7 million – five times as many as in the early 1960s. Under the police state run by the late shah, the vast majority were condemned to poverty, while his American-trained Savak secret police dealt out torture and assassination to those who opposed him.

The revolution may have helped to end the most glaring economic injustices, but the benefits it brought came at an appalling price in personal freedom. The religious reign of the Ayatollah Khomeini seemed to many to have taken Iran out of the authoritarian frying-pan and into the fire of religious purification. Today the rhetorical tone has softened; there have been diplomatic overtures to the West, and Iran's young people have been slowly and carefully pushing back the limits of permissible behaviour. Never one of the world's most beautiful cities, Tehran's true wealth has always lain in its human heritage. Once again Iranians are beginning to breathe life back into their country's capital.

***Overshadowed, overcast** The Elburz Mountains act not only as a towering backdrop, but also as a barrier to the movement of air. At times Tehran seems to be in danger of suffocating in its own microclimate of cloudy smog.*

Grim father of his country

The Ayatollah Khomeini was never really the 'mad mullah' of Western media folklore. That description does justice neither to his genuine idealism nor to the ruthless efficiency with which he pursued his political goals. A critic of the shah's American-backed regime, Khomeini was forced into exile in 1964. His Shiite Muslim message increasingly appealed as the bankruptcy of the monarchy became more clear. On his return in 1979 he was acclaimed a hero, but made more radical changes than the Iranians had bargained for. By the time he died in 1989 he had built a state as repressive in its religious puritanism as the shah's secular monarchy had ever been.

Jerusalem

1. Yad Vashem
A monument and museum to commemorate those killed in the Holocaust.

2. Billy Rose Sculpture Gardens Set out in 1960-5 by the Japanese-American sculptor Isamu Noguchi, these gardens are in the grounds of the Israel Museum. Israelis love to take their afternoon walks here.

3. The Knesset All strands of Israeli opinion are represented in the country's parliament.

4. Armed and ready Much of Jerusalem remains militarised, and many Israelis take their guns wherever they go.

5. The Damascus Gate According to tradition, the Prophet Muhammad appeared to Suleiman the Magnificent in a dream, bidding him to rebuild the walls around his beloved Jerusalem. The Ottoman emperor constructed new fortifications between 1536 and 1541. The Damascus Gate is one of the four main entrances to Suleiman's city.

6. Beyond the pale The old city is protected, but beyond its boundaries new construction schemes have been springing up to house new settlers.

7. Shopping mall No modern city is complete without its malls: this one is in West Jerusalem.

8. Apple Core, 1992 Claes Oldenburg's work is in the Billy Rose Sculpture Gardens.

9. St Mary Magdalen This Orthodox church stands west of the city on the Mount of Olives – a site sacred to Muslims too, but barred to them for several centuries.

In the heart of the holy of holies

Contested territory Both Jews and Arabs insist that Jerusalem is their capital; the city has been a persistent flashpoint.

There seems to have been a city where Jerusalem now stands as long ago as 3200 BC. A succession of early civilisations have left their traces in the archaeological record. But it was not until around 1000 BC that the site began to realise its sacred destiny, when King David of the Jews captured the city from the Jebusites. He made the city his capital, and his son Solomon built his temple here. Thus was the long and often agonising history of Jerusalem as a religious centre set in motion.

The city was sacred to the Jews – fought for to the death, and yearned for through generations in exile – long before Christ made the city holy for his followers. Six hundred years after Christ was crucified there, the city was sanctified anew when the Prophet Muhammad ascended to heaven from the Temple Mount.

This single place is, accordingly, sacred to no fewer than three of the world's great religions. Here are to be found some of the holiest sites of all three – the Wailing Wall, the Holy Sepulchre and the Dome of the Rock. To that heady theological brew have now been added the most intense of nationalistic emotions: Jerusalem stands now on the front line in the ongoing conflict between the Israelis and the Palestinians.

Competing traditions The Dome of the Rock (above) marks the spot from which Muhammad ascended to heaven. Here, too, Abraham offered to sacrifice his son.

The way of the cross Christians can retrace the last steps of Christ along the Via Dolorosa (left).

Living history This father and son on their donkey would not have been out of place in Biblical times.

Judaism's most sacred site Only this last great wall remains of Solomon's wondrous temple; the rest was deliberately destroyed by the Roman conquerors. Now, as the Western or 'Wailing' Wall it is a focus for Jewish religious observance, and memorial to a history of persecution and exile.

1. Western ('Wailing') Wall
2. Dome of the Rock
3. Al-Aqsa Mosque (the other great Muslim monument on the Haram ash-Sharif or Temple Mount)
4. Holy Sepulchre
5. St Anne's Church and Pool of Bethesda
6. Franciscan Friary of the Flagellation
7. Via Dolorosa
8. Arab Quarter
9. Damascus Gate
10. Christian Quarter
11. Jaffa Gate
12. David's Tower (Citadel)
13. Jewish Quarter
14. Hurva Synagogue
15. Armenian Quarter
16. Maghreb Gate
17. Mount of Olives and Church of the Ascension

'He is not here!' *The Holy Sepulchre was built by Emperor Constantine on the site where Christ was buried and is claimed to have risen from the dead. All strands of the Christian Church are represented here.*

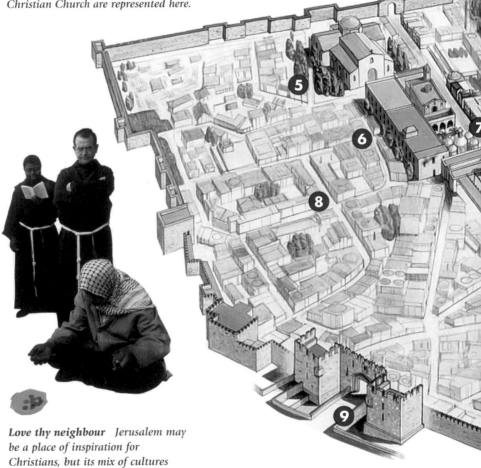

In the Arab quarter *Stallholders sell spices, sweetmeats, fruit and trinkets for the tourists.*

Love thy neighbour *Jerusalem may be a place of inspiration for Christians, but its mix of cultures demands tolerance of all.*

'The Pious' *Their black coats and hats mark out the Chassidim, most orthodox of the Jews.*

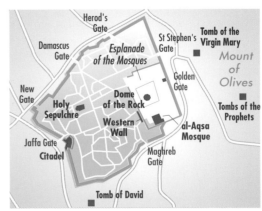

Jerusalem : The Old City
— wall of old city   500 m

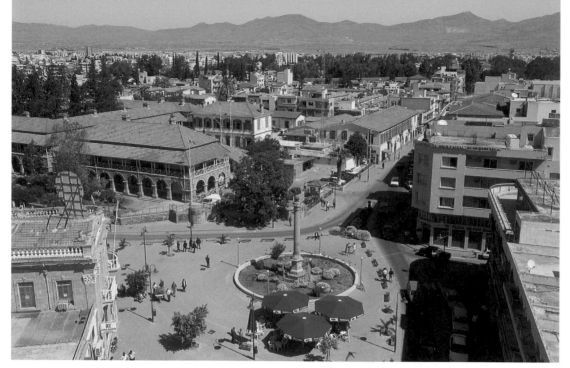

A place of prosperity Through 5000 years of history, Nicosia has learned to handle good times and bad times: invaders may come and go, it seems, but the business life of the city goes on forever. At once easy-going and hard-working, Cypriots are well equipped for success as traders and entrepreneurs; no other nation in the Middle East looks forward quite so expectantly to the rise of globalisation.

Nicosia, a city divided

At the very heart of an island torn apart by conflict stands a city severed right down the centre: one half of Nicosia is Greek, the other strictly Turkish.

At ease Despite its problems, Nicosia has managed to maintain an atmosphere of conviviality and calm.

Frescoes and mosaics adorn every wall and sprawl across the ceilings; every intervening space is picked out in gilt; a thousand halos glint and glisten in the twinkling light of the chandeliers, while incense smoke swirls headily between them. Inspired by a tour of Agios Ioannis, St John's Cathedral, many visitors cross the square to Nicosia's Byzantine Museum, which contains the ecclesiastical art of a thousand years, including a superb collection of religious icons. After the sublime interior of Agios Ioannis, its setting may seem somewhat muted, even dull – but there is still something irresistible about the museum. There may be many more impressive museums in the Middle East, but few haunt the visitor quite like this one.

Every picture tells a story
At the centre of the museum's collection are works looted from the Christian churches of northern Cyprus in the course of the Turkish invasion of 1974. They were bought back after their subsequent appearance on the international art market – although most of the loot disappeared into the collections of wealthy connoisseurs around the world. Up to 20 000 icons were stolen in the weeks of plunder that followed the first attack, as well as chalices, statues, crucifixes and Bibles. Mosaic flooring was torn up and frescoes hacked from the chapel walls. Nobody realistically expects these treasures to be seen again, but then nor do many Greek Cypriots expect to see any of the hundreds of relatives who 'disappeared' from the newly Turkish territory – if the churches were ransacked, so were the people's lives.

Through the looking glass
As for the 'enemy', they live only a stone's throw away and lead remarkably similar lives to their Greek-speaking neighbours. The visitor who completes the formalities and crosses over to the Turkish city will find it not much different. There are more mosques, and several old churches have been converted to other uses, but the crowded cafés and bustling market stalls are much the same. Hard as the authorities have worked to make it seem alien, 'Lefkosia' is still very recognisably Nicosia. The invasion gave Turkish Cypriots their own country, but in some ways they remain as much a minority as they were before. Ankara, in its eagerness to underline the true 'Turkishness' of Northern Cyprus, has colonised it with Turkish-born settlers. Thus has this beautiful island become a mournful looking-glass in which two communities with much in common have come to see and define themselves as one another's enemies.

The Green Line: a dismal history

In 1963 Cyprus was designated an independent country with bicommunal status, both Greek and Turkish. A British force sent to establish order created a fortified front line between the two communities, marked on the map by a green line (hence the border's name). A decade later this became a national boundary. In 1974 Turkish troops invaded northern Cyprus, ostensibly in defence of the Turkish community there, though it was the Greeks who were being driven southwards. The state they established, though supposedly independent, is clearly a colony of Turkey itself, whose settlers now outnumber the native-born Turkish Cypriots.

Line of hatred The Green Line runs through the heart of Nicosia.

6

7

8

9

Holy place *Muslims flock in their thousands each Friday to worship at the Al-Aqsa Mosque (left).*

Behind bars *Young Palestinians watch from a window in the Arab Quarter.*

Under surveillance *Israeli soldiers on the Damascus Gate (above) keep a close eye on the Arab Quarter.*

Palm Sunday *Christians celebrate the day that Christ rode into Jerusalem on a donkey 2000 years ago.*

Place of instruction *Many serious-minded young Jews come to Jerusalem to attend the yeshivas or religious schools of the Jewish Quarter.*

Cooling cup *Old and new come together incongruously in the equipment of a drinks vendor.*

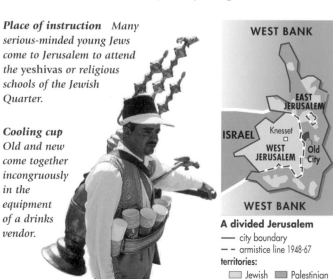

WEST BANK

EAST JERUSALEM

ISRAEL Knesset

WEST JERUSALEM Old City

WEST BANK

A divided Jerusalem
— city boundary
- - armistice line 1948-67
territories:
☐ Jewish ■ Palestinian

Sabbath celebrations *When the Sabbath starts the wailing at the Western Wall is turned to rejoicing.*

Twice a minority *Around 10 per cent of Palestinians are Christians. They have their own quarter in the Old City.*

Peace at last *This ancient Jewish cemetery lies just outside the city walls on the slopes of the Mount of Olives.*

To the glory of god *One of the most beautiful churches in the city is the Armenian cathedral of St James, built in the 11th century.*

78

A kaleidoscope of creeds Looking out over the old city you can see mosques, churches, synagogues and other religious buildings jumbled together.

Flying the flag Parts of east Jerusalem are festooned with Israeli flags (right), as Jewish settlers seek to consolidate their claim to a conquered territory.

Drive carefully The narrow, winding lanes of Old Jerusalem pose problems of access for modern vehicles.

The Citadel David's Tower, or the Citadel, has now been made into a stunning museum, its exhibits documenting the history of Jerusalem from its foundation to the present day.

Quiet Kabul

As Afghanistan's Taliban rulers became the first objective of the 2001 'War Against Terrorism', US military spokesmen pointed ruefully to the lack of what they called 'high-value targets'. Twenty years of war has left Kabul so badly damaged that there is hardly any of it left. Such infrastructure as was left intact after the overthrow of the ten-year pro-Soviet regime was largely demolished in the years of civil conflict that followed.

Claimed at one time or another by Arab, Persian, British and Russian rulers – not to mention by ever-changing factions from Afghanistan itself – Kabul has been bitterly fought over almost without interruption for several centuries. Yet, to the never-ending astonishment of outsiders, the city's own self-image is as a quiet contemplative centre and seat of learning; it takes great pride in its mosques, its museum, its university and colleges.

In the wars: Kabul and Baghdad

Baghdad has had a dismal time in recent years, yet no one doubts that it will rise again. As for Kabul, the miracle is that the city survives at all.

Baghdad for sale Under sanctions imposed after the 1991 Gulf War people were reduced to selling their possessions for money to buy food.

The 11th-century Arab scholar Yakut described Baghdad as 'a veritable city of palaces.' In his day, Baghdad was the greatest metropolis of the Islamic world. But such splendours were not to last; Baghdad stagnated until the oil boom of the 1970s, when it finally underwent something of a renaissance. The catch was that this took place on the terms of one man: the then Iraqi President, Saddam Hussein. His improvements gave Baghdad an up-to-the-minute infrastructure, from sewers to superhighways, modern apartment blocks and a new airport. But he also created some of the most hideous civic statuary ever seen. The 'Hands of Victory' arch, for instance, depicts the dictator's giant hands grasping twin swords. The blades of the swords were cast from the guns of Iraqi soldiers killed in the war against Iran in 1980-9. Saddam's main contribution to his country was war and terror. In 2003 US-led coalition army forces forceably ended his brutal regime.

Merchant city Baghdad's black market thrives despite great hardships, recalling the city's origins as a trading centre.

City of strife

By comparison, Kabul, the Afghan capital, has always been a bit of a backwater; no great civilisation ever had its headquarters here. Yet this citadel 6000 ft (1800 m) up in the mountains has always had a significance disproportionate to its size, as a vital staging post for the trading caravans plying back and forth across the Hindu Kush mountains between the Middle East and India. When, in the 18th century, the Durrani dynasty set about establishing a distinctly Afghan state, they took steps towards developing their capital as a modern Muslim city with housing, mosques, public baths and other amenities. Even then, though, Kabul's defensive situation proved as much a curse as a blessing, commanding as it did what became known as the 'North-west Frontier' of Britain's imperial domain of India. Throughout the 19th century the city would be a crucial piece in the 'great game' of military and diplomatic strategy played between Russia and Great Britain for the prize of imperial access to the stupendous resources of the subcontinent.

Amman, a city on seven hills

A meeting-point of cultures for nearly nine millennia, Amman was too often a place passed through by visitors on their way elsewhere. But there is plenty here to detain the more curious traveller.

Even in the Middle East, few places can point to a continuous history as long as Amman's. Nor could many match the beauty of its setting, on seven hills or *jabals*, each of which defines a neighbourhood in the modern city. Despite such assets, Amman has never enjoyed the prominence it deserves. Until recently, it seemed to be a city that had missed its chance. As long ago as 1321, the Arab traveller Abu al-Fida wrote that this 'very ancient town' had been 'ruined before the days of Islam'. Things went from bad to worse in the centuries that followed; by the end of the 18th century, Amman was a backwater. A visitor in 1806 found the city uninhabited, though local farmers were using some of its buildings for housing livestock and storing grain.

With their European dominions under threat, the Ottoman rulers attempted to consolidate their holdings nearer home; Circassian refugees dislodged from eastern Turkey by the wars with Russia were resettled here. In 1905 Amman had a population of 3000; by 1948 it had 25 000. At that point, the population rose abruptly in the aftermath of the first Arab-Israeli War, as Palestinians streamed across the border into Jordan. Though the poorer refugees remained in camps, the middle class came into Amman itself, adding a rich and vibrant stratum to its cultural life.

Still growing *Amman grew enormously during the 20th century, and its expansion shows no sign of abating.*

A place apart

Caught between the main belligerents in the 'Middle East problem', the Hashemite kings of Jordan have for the most part walked their diplomatic tightrope adeptly. Amman has thrived through the years of conflict, its rulers on the whole respected by both sides as honest brokers. The city's prosperity has soared, and the population, now at almost 2 million, looks set to keep growing. An unassuming city, Amman's haphazard layout offers no majestic vistas, no transporting sights, but it is full of treasures to enthral the more persevering tourist. Scattered about its higgledy-piggledy streets are relics from just about every phase of its lengthy history. A new generation of travellers has finally begun to appreciate this; at last, it seems, Amman is coming into its own.

A long history

Traces of occupation of its site date back to the Neolithic Age, 9000 years ago, but Rabbath-Ammon first came to prominence as a centre of the Semitic Ammonite civilisation around 1200 BC. Conquered by King David and the Jews, then by the Assyrians, Babylonians and Persians, Amman's fortunes did not revive until the 3rd century BC, when Ptolemy II rebuilt the city and renamed it Philadelphia. Its subsequent decline paralleled that of the Byzantine Empire. In the 7th century, Islamic invaders restored its Semitic title, Amman. When the centre of the Islamic empire moved from Damascus to Baghdad, the fortunes of this trading city were reversed. Only in recent decades has it found a new economic impetus.

City lights *A commercial centre even when it was only a desert caravanserai for Bedouin traders, Amman has embraced modern consumerism.*

Super-sheikdoms: the Gulf States

Along the western shore of the Gulf are strewn a series of states, small in area and minuscule in population. But the Gulf States have influence out of all proportion to their size, thanks to their enormous resources in natural gas and oil.

Artificial atoll *Thousands flock each weekend to the Green Island amusement park, Kuwait City.*

Desert princes in flowing robes stepping out of luxurious cars, oil wells stretching to the horizon – in the Gulf States, popular myth comes close to reality. Here nomadic chieftains have become oil moguls overnight, their tents replaced by cities, their camels by limousines and private jets. Little sheikdoms have become wealthy world-class petro-economies.

Life before oil

The cities of the Gulf owe their existence to the coastal traffic of a trading empire that extended from Indonesia and China in the east down the Swahili coast of Africa to Zanzibar and beyond. Dhows plied back and forth along the northern and western edges of the Indian Ocean more or less uninterrupted for 500 years. Luxuries such as myrrh and frankincense, Arab horses, prestige daggers, swords and other weaponry, embroidered textiles and woven carpets were exported from the Gulf, along with bulk goods such as dates, dried fruit, leather, coffee, rock salt and dried fish. These were exchanged for a range of products, including gold, copper and silver from East Africa; cotton textiles, gemstones and cereals from India; spices from the East Indies; precious porcelains, silks and teas from China.

The start of the 16th century saw a new power claim possession of the seas. 'In this year,' wrote an Arab chronicler in 1502-3, 'the vessels of the Frank appeared at sea en route for India, Hormuz, and those parts. They took about seven vessels, killing those on board and making some prisoners. This was their first action. May God curse them.' The Franks were in fact Portuguese, and their behaviour seems to have been every bit as brutal as the Muslim writer claimed. In the years that followed they pursued a policy of terrorising the Arab traders, hoping to confine them in the Gulf so that they themselves might have a monopoly of the most lucrative trades. For a time they succeeded, but the Ottoman Empire became a formidable sea power, and the hold of the Portuguese was weakened; by the 17th century it was broken altogether.

Britain's hold on the Indian Ocean grew throughout the 18th and 19th centuries, and the Arab merchants were again marginalised. The real money was being made by European traders shipping goods round the Cape of Good Hope from India. The supply of luxury goods unique to the region kept the Gulf trade alive, but well into the 20th century this was still a trading backwater.

Though technically British protectorates, these states were of limited interest to an empire that could command the wealth of India and much of Africa. Even when prospectors first struck oil in eastern Arabia in the 1920s, the effect on the Gulf States was initially underwhelming: the richest reserves appeared to lie some way to the north of the Gulf, well inland from the Persian shore.

Though exploitable deposits were discovered in Bahrain in 1932, there was no indication that the oil boom was beginning in earnest.

Map legend:
1 Kuwait
2 Manama
3 Doha
4 Abu Dhabi
5 Dubai
6 Sharjah

Institutional conservatism

In architectural and civil engineering terms, the modernisation of the Gulf States has been spectacular. Doha (left), in Qatar, is typical of the cities that have risen from the desert sand. The sheikhdoms' institutional structures have developed more slowly; large ruling families, and restriction of the franchise to native 'first-class' citizens, means that democratic rights come with strict conditions. The 40 members of the ruling council of Bahrain, the *Shura*, are elected not by the public but by the emir himself. However, the emir of Qatar, although his rule is absolute, holds informal assemblies or *majalis* where members of the public may raise any issue.

A torrent of wealth

By this time, the sheiks' hopes were increasingly pinned on oil, the bottom having fallen out of the pearl market. The big Western companies continued to regard their reserves with disdain, until the nationalisation of the Iranian oil industry in 1953 changed everything. Long happy to go on exploiting Iranian reserves on the advantageous terms allowed by a loyal shah, Western companies suddenly realised that for security's sake they needed to start diversifying their sources of supply.

In the mid 1950s, the long-awaited good times arrived. Britain's gradual disengagement after 1961, when Kuwait became independent, alarmed the region's rulers at first. Bahrain and Qatar had independence more or less thrust upon them in 1971, as did Abu Dhabi, Dubai and Sharjah, along with the other small sheikdoms that came together to form the United Arab Emirates. But events quickly conspired to ease the Gulf States' feelings of insecurity. The oil crises of the 1970s saw their stock soaring in economic terms, and their geopolitical importance increased

Petro-plenty

A series of shocks on the global market have shown that oil is not exempt from the normal ups and downs of economic life, but for the Gulf States it still remains a valuable commodity. In the late 1990s, the United Arab Emirates were making more than US$14 billion a year from oil exports, the lion's share going to Abu Dhabi and Dubai. Kuwait's current revenues are believed to stand at well over US$10 billion a year. Bahrain (right) has only small oil reserves, but shrewd investment in petrochemical and other industries has enabled it to take its full share in the bonanza its neighbours have enjoyed.

commensurately. With money rolling in as fast as they could pump their petroleum out, they began investing in roads and hospitals, schools and universities, showering services on their subjects.

The Gulf States have not taken their good fortune for granted; all have taken steps to prepare themselves for when the oil runs out. They have taken control of processing as well as production, building sizable petrochemical industries. Since the Gulf War of 1991, they have redoubled their efforts to diversify, seeking out and exploiting deposits of uranium, lead, zinc, sulphur, iron, copper, manganese and other minerals. They have also used their oil revenues to establish themselves as bankers, Kuwait in particular creating a thriving financial services industry.

Architects' playground
In Dubai (below), as in most of the Gulf States, oil revenues have funded some of the most spectacular architecture in the world.

God and mammon *A traditional minaret and an ultra-modern skyscraper stand side by side against the skyline of Abu Dhabi (above).*

CHAPTER 4
LIVING IN THE MIDDLE EAST

The Middle East is too often seen in the West as an undifferentiated Islamic empire, but in fact three great world religions have their spiritual and cultural roots here. The predominant faith is of course Islam, but there are significant communities of Christians to be found – as well, of course, as a whole nation of Jews. And Islam itself includes not only sects such as Sunnis and Shiites, but also a range of distinct ethnic groups. Arabs, Turks and Iranians – all these, and many others, have their own particular linguistic and cultural traditions. Some, like the Kurds and the Palestinians, are nations without a home – yet their identity is, if anything, all the stronger for their dispossession. Nowhere are these differences marked out more colourfully than in the various festivals celebrated in the Middle East. These provide vivid testimony to the region's rich diversity and ebullient energy.

The week-long market at al-Maaras, Yemen, is as much a social as a commercial affair.

The quest for a country

The Kurds and the Palestinians have no homelands they can call their own. The sympathy of the outside world, though sometimes genuine, has invariably proved fickle: the one thing on which these peoples can rely is their own undying hunger for what they see as justice.

Mountain men Kurdistan is mostly hill country, and the Kurds are used to hardship.

The famous lines of Ahmed-i-Khani's Kurdish epic of the 17th century, *Mem o Zin*, are known to every Kurd today: 'These Kurds who have gained glory by their swords, How is it that they are denied the empire of the world and are subject to others?' They sum up not only the pathos of the Kurds' position, but also its paradox. For, fierce warriors since time immemorial, the Kurds are not even a minority: after Arabs, Iranians and Turks, they are the fourth largest community in the Middle East. But for the most part

they have remained invisible. Only in the 20th century did they figure in the history books, blamed – unjustly – for the genocide of Turkey's Armenians. And in 1919 a revolt against British rule in north-west Iraq gave them the unhappy distinction of being the first ever victims of aerial bombardment.

Missed opportunities

In modern times, the Kurdish story has been a tale of missed opportunities. In the aftermath of the First World War, when the map of the Middle East was being redrawn, Turkey, Syria, Iraq and Iran all became independent nations. But Kurdistan was disregarded as a 'mountainous irrelevancy' and its people were divided up between the four surrounding states. The next let-down was after the Gulf War of 1991, when President Bush and the Western allies urged Kurds to rise up against Saddam Hussein's forces and help to sweep the dictator from power. Within days Washington policymakers had apparently changed their minds: Saddam's government was to be spared as a counterweight to Iranian power. The Kurds, having broken cover, were ruthlessly mopped up by Iraqi forces, while the Western powers did little to help them.

Between these betrayals, Kurdish guerrillas have fought an unavailing struggle against impossible odds. In Turkey, hundreds of Kurdish villages have been destroyed and their people deported. In Iraq, Saddam Hussein deployed chemical weapons against the Kurds in the 1980s, while Iran has dealt similarly brutally with Kurdish aspirations. With hindsight it can be seen that the Ottoman Empire accommodated a far greater religious and ethnic diversity than the modern nation-states created in its aftermath. Without any more positive *raison d'être*, these states had to define their nationality against somebody else's, hence the aggressive anti-Kurdish rhetoric and the actions of Turkey and Assad's Syria.

Fighting for survival In the remote valleys of the Kurdistan region, guerrillas continue their long military campaign against Turkish forces.

Exiled everywhere Their country spans four states, but they are welcome nowhere. For many Kurds the refugee camp (right) is their only homeland.

Linguistic oppression

Mustafa Kemal undertook the first campaign of aggression against the Kurds when he tried to silence them by depriving them of their language. In the 1920s and 30s, Kemal purged the Turkish language of Arabic and Persianisms, giving it a new and forward-looking Latin alphabet. The use of Kurdish was banned completely. Kemal was undoubtedly sincere in his belief that Kurdish nationalism was nothing more than wilfulness on the part of a backward people who should feel privileged to be allowed a part in building the new Turkey, just as he was of the view that Islam was no more than an obscurantist superstition and that the fez was an outmoded form of dress. But, however high-minded he may have been, his actions in dealing with these perceived obstacles to progress were every bit as brutal as those of his successors.

Squalid strip *Israeli statesman Yitzhak Rabin famously wished that the Gaza Strip would sink into the sea – and there must have been moments when its Palestinian inhabitants agreed with him. Overcrowded and inadequately serviced, it is an enclave of despair.*

The longest road

The tragedy of the Arab-Israeli conflict is that it resulted from such good intentions. First, the commitment of Britain, in its Balfour Declaration of 1917, to create a 'national home' for the Jews while protecting the rights of Palestine's existing Arab population; then, in the aftermath of the Nazi Holocaust, a guilty goodwill that brought about the establishment of the state of Israel. The Arab nations' promise to drive the interlopers into the sea did nothing to create a climate of cooperation or compromise; neither did the declaration of Israel's first Prime Minister David Ben Gurion that 'for the Arabs of the Land of Israel, there remains only one function, to flee.' Many did just that. Some 700 000 refugees left in the first weeks of the new state's existence – though the Israeli authorities denied that they had either been expelled by force or fled in fear, insisting instead that all had departed 'voluntarily'. Further waves of refugees followed Israel's victories over its Arab neighbours in the Six-Day War of 1967 and the Yom Kippur War of 1973.

Israel's claims of self-defence found a sympathetic hearing in the West, while Arab alliances with the Soviet Union prejudiced Western opinion. It was hard for the Western public to regard as 'victims' those who hijacked airliners and murdered civilians. Yasser Arafat and his Palestine Liberation Organization (PLO)

By force of arms *In Jerusalem Israeli soldiers make no bones about their status as an army of occupation, especially in the Arab quarters.*

were reviled as 'terrorists'. Though the continued Israeli presence on Palestinian lands seized in 1967 was acknowledged in the West as illegal, most Western leaders justified the occupation as a necessary security zone for Israel – and closed their eyes to Israeli oppression.

The 'War on Terrorism' of 2001 onwards has made any dialogue between the two sides even harder. On the one hand, in their eagerness to convince the Islamic world that they recognised its concerns, both President Bush and Prime Minister Tony Blair gave encouraging signs to the Palestinian cause. On the other, Israel found justification in the 'anti-terror' agenda for some of its most warlike actions yet against Arafat's Palestinian Authority. Palestinian suicide bombers and Israeli assasinations of Hamas leaders show that the *intifada* (popular resistance to Israeli occupation) rumbles on. However, a positive step may be the withdrawal of Israeli settlements and troops from the Gaza strip and parts of the West Bank planned for 2005.

Owner occupiers

The Gaza Strip is one of the most densely populated and deprived places in the world. More than a million Palestinians live alongside 6000 Jewish settlers who have been granted almost a quarter of the area. The Jews live in suburban comfort while the Palestinians are crammed into slums. For more than 30 years now the Palestinians have seen Jewish settlers nibbling away at what is supposed to be their land, under the protection of the Israeli state and with its tacit

Young protestor *Young Palestinians play a large part in the* intifada.

blessing. The agenda of the more militant settlers and their friends in government is to make these territories an integral part of Israel itself. If anything, the peace process has stiffened the hardliners' resolve. 'Everybody has to move, run and grab as many hilltops as they can to enlarge the settlements because everything we take now will stay ours. Everything we don't grab will go to them,' said the then Israeli Foreign Secretary Ariel Sharon in 1998.

The Kurds: Astride four states

87

Carrying the cross

We associate the Middle East so closely with Islam that it comes as a surprise to find that the region has a sizable minority of Christians, in some countries accounting for almost 10 per cent of the population.

Old believers *The Iranian Church is one of the oldest Christian traditions in the world.*

The Koran is unambiguous in its injunction that Muslims respect the religions of Christians and Jews: 'Do not argue with the followers of earlier revelation otherwise than in a most kindly manner – unless it be such of them as are bent on evildoing.' It is one thing to urge tolerance, but quite another to change human nature – and there was good reason to regard Christians in particular with suspicion. The Crusades convinced many Muslims that the 'Franks' were all 'bent on evildoing', and all they subsequently heard of Western ways confirmed this opinion. Europeans bathed only twice a year, it was said; their women went about practically naked and were permitted to dictate to their husbands and fathers in an outrageous manner.

The cultural differences and geographical separation between medieval East and West were so pronounced that there was little understanding between the two. Yet Christians were still living and worshipping in the Muslims' midst, and for the most part they were not badly treated. Along with Jews, Zoroastrians, Hindus, Buddhists and Sikhs, they were regarded as *dhimmis*, protected subjects. As long as they recognised Islamic sovereignty they could worship as they wished. A *jizyah* or poll tax was levied to provide for their military protection, for it was a condition of their contract with Islam that they could not bear arms. They were not allowed to hold public processions, for that smacked too much of proselytising, nor could they hold services outside their appointed chapels. These rules would have seemed very

The Armenians: tried in the fire

When Turkish Armenians refused to pay a poll tax to the Ottoman authorities in 1894, 50 000 men, women and children were killed in the ensuing pogroms. The massacres continued intermittently until, outraged at Armenian involvement on the side of Russia in the First World War, the Turkish government sought to expel the entire people; half a million died in the accompanying violence. Armenians are almost non-existent in Turkey today, but sizable communities in Lebanon, Syria and Iran honour the unique rite their ancestors followed for so many centuries.

At first glance the Armenian Church is the most Westernised of the Eastern Christianities. In the Middle Ages it united with Rome for a time – the Armenians make the sign of the cross in the Roman way and their bishops wear mitres like their Roman Catholic counterparts. In other respects the Armenians conform more closely to Orthodox traditions. Their prohibition of elaborate icons, however, gives their church interiors a certain simplicity that recalls the strict severities of Western Protestantism. Ultimately, though, this is an Eastern creed: whatever the superficialities of its presentation, it is based on a theology that is not accepted in any of the Western Churches.

A Christian community *For Lebanon's Maronites, churchgoing is not just a spiritual tradition but a social and political one too.*

Christian strongholds *During the Crusading period religious buildings were constructed like fortresses. This one (left) is the monastery of St George of Cosiba, in Israel.*

Sacred and sublime *The great icons of the Orthodox Church are perhaps the single most celebrated inheritance handed down to the world by the Byzantine Empire. They are still created in the Church today.*

An island in time

In the mountains north-east of Damascus lies the tiny village of Ma'lulu. Some of the earliest Christians found refuge from the Roman persecutions here. One who was not so lucky, St Sarkis (or Sergius) was put to death and is commemorated in the 4th-century chapel that bears his name. But the most important monument is the spoken language, for this is one of the last places where the Aramaic tongue survives.

restrictive to the Church in Western Europe, an institution that had grown in wealth and worldly power with each passing century. By the height of the Middle Ages the pope was practically an emperor, expecting as of right the submission of monarchs. In the countries of the Middle East an altogether quieter brand of Christianity had emerged – one that some would say was truer to the founding principles of Christ himself. Taking their cultural cue from the society around them, these communities were in no danger of slipping into Western ways; their women were as demure, their manners as good, as those of their Islamic neighbours.

Eastern unorthodox

Even before the Muslim conquest, there had been no single, monolithic Church here; no institutional giant to match Rome. Many in Syria were Melchites, who followed one version or other of the Byzantine rite, though after the rise of Islam they took Arabic, rather than Greek, as their liturgical language. The Nestorians of Syria, Iraq and Iran (where they are known as Assyrians) are named after the 5th-century bishop of Constantinople who first propounded their most controversial theological belief. The first of the so-called 'Monophysite' sects, they followed Nestorius in denying the Holy Trinity. Rather than a separate spiritual entity, they asserted, Christ was an extension of God himself – the mortal human body that Mary bore was a mere receptacle for God's divinity. This claim was denounced as heretical by both the Roman and Orthodox Churches, who were adamant that Jesus was at once 'true God and true man', but it found support among the Eastern sects.

For the Egyptian Copts and the Jacobites of Syria and Iraq, the Islamic conquest of the region must have come as something of a relief: better the indifference of the Muslims than the persecution of their fellow Christians. The Maronites of Lebanon and Syria, after half a millennium in the Monophysite wilderness, made their peace with Rome in 1182. They have retained a semi-autonomous status, with their own liturgy and organisation, and have traditionally enjoyed a disproportionate importance in Lebanese political life. Although very much a minority, they outnumber each of the country's different Muslim communities individually; and with Sunni, Shiite and Druse locked in opposition to one another, the

Maronites for a long time held the balance of power. In 1934 agreement was reached that the interests of peace and harmony would be best served by always having a Maronite as Lebanese president, and the formula seemed to work well for four decades. But the events of the civil war in the 1970s and the Israeli invasion of 1982 shattered the consensus irretrievably.

A dwindling influence

Throughout the region the Christian sects have felt themselves increasingly squeezed by the growing polarisation of East and West and the mounting militancy of Islam. Demographic forces play a part; quietly industrious and comparatively affluent, the region's largely middle-class Christians have in recent times tended to have smaller families than the Muslims around them. By the same token they have found it easier to move on when their countries' troubles have become too much to bear. There are communities of these eastern Christians now in several North American cities.

Neither Christian nor Muslim *The monotheistic Sabaeans had a strong influence on Muhammad's religious thought, but they recognise neither the authority of the Prophet nor the divinity of Christ. Exiled from their native Palestine to Yemen, and then to Iraq, they have, like other small sects, suffered persecution in modern times.*

See Mecca and die

The hadj, the pilgrimage to Mecca, is the goal of all Muslims. Once in a lifetime at least, each must make this most solemn of journeys. The tradition has taken on a new lease of life in the age of jet travel, as a global community finds a focus in its oldest, most sacred site.

Mecca was a holy city long before Muhammad's day. A black meteorite, said to have been hurled from heaven by the ancient deity Hubal, was exhibited at Kaaba, and thousands came to venerate it each year. In visiting the sacred stone, Muhammad was performing an ancient rite. In making the hadj today, pilgrims are following in the footsteps of their prophet and also reaffirming those older rites to which Muhammad himself did honour.

Adam and after

To some extent, Muhammad seems to have valued the Kaaba shrine simply because it was traditional to do so. Muslims claimed no special powers for the stone, still less any intrinsic divinity, but stories had accreted around it to explain its significance. It was said by Arabian Jews, for example, that Adam, in exile from Eden, had built the first shrine at Kaaba but that it was washed away in the great deluge that an angry God unleashed upon the world. Afterwards, Abraham rebuilt it with the assistance of Ishmael, his son by his concubine Hagar.

Born outside the 'legitimate' line from which the Jews claimed descent, Ishmael was revered by the Arabs, who regarded the patriarch's natural son as their ultimate ancestor. In the Genesis account, Hagar and her son were reluctantly rejected by Abraham, who drove them out into the wilderness together. The

Centre of the world *No place looms larger in the Islamic world than Mecca.*

Sacred stone *Draped with black silk and trimmed with gold brocade, the cube-shaped shrine of the Kaaba contains the stone itself.*

Arabian story that father and son worked together to reconstruct the Kaaba shrine was particularly significant in that it was supposed to have taken place some years *after* this original expulsion, when Abraham had tracked down Hagar and Ishmael in order to pay them a visit. It can thus be said to represent a rewriting of the Bible story, restoring to Ishmael and his line an endorsement they are refused in the 'official' version. How literally Muhammad believed this tale is not clear, but it certainly appealed to him, dignifying as it did his Arab ancestry. More important, it yoked together two traditions, old and new, providing a modern, monotheistic gloss for a pre-existing pagan ritual.

A spiritual journey

Today, most pilgrims to Mecca fly to Jeddah by jumbo jet before being whisked to the Holy City on an air-conditioned coach. To those used to more ascetic traditions this can seem inappropriate: where are the weeks on the road, the barefoot slog up a stony mountain? In fact, such questions miss the point: the Kaaba pilgrimage is no act of endurance. The Arabic word hadj ('tour' or 'walking around') does not refer to the journey to Mecca, as many assume, but to the sevenfold circumambulation of the stone at the site itself.

A place of danger

Two million people a year make the pilgrimage to Mecca. Most pilgrims find it an overwhelmingly rewarding spiritual experience. But the enormous numbers involved and the violent emotions of which the hadj is a focus have meant that the city has all too often been a scene of tragedy. Over a period of 20 years almost 3000 pilgrims have been killed.
1979 300 Egyptians and Yemenis attacked the Grand Mosque: 400 killed in confrontations with security forces.

1987 Conflicts between Iranian Shiite pilgrims and Saudi security forces: 400 killed, 300 of them Iranians.
1990 Stampede in a tunnel: 1410 killed.
1994 Panic at the subsidiary shrine of Mina: 270 killed.
1997 Fire in pilgrim camp: 343 killed, 1357 injured.
1998 Mecca stampede: 118 killed.

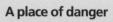

In the eyes of God *Pilgrims wear only a simple robe to signify the equality of all in Allah's eyes.*

Mecca, around 1900

Camp of the Syrian Pilgrims

Khadija's Tomb

Cemetery

Fort

Camp of the Bedouins

Muhammad's Birthplace

Kabah

Grand Mosque

Camp of the Bedouins

Fort

Camp of the Yemeni Pilgrims

500 m

The logistics of faith *What amounts to a second city with its own road system has sprung up outside modern Mecca. The difficulty of transporting and accommodating so many pilgrims and ensuring supplies to serve their needs has represented a real challenge to the authorities in Saudi Arabia.*

The steps of the hadj

The first ritual of the hadj is the circumambulation of the Kaaba: seven counterclockwise circuits of the holy shrine. Next, pilgrims must prostrate themselves twice at the 'Site of Abraham' and visit the nearby well that God revealed to Hagar and Ishmael. After this they must cross back and forth between the mountains of Safa and Marwa seven times, as Hagar had to do in her desperate quest for water. Then the pilgrims assemble at the foot of Mount Arafat at noon, remaining there until sunset in prayer and meditation. Next day, at Mina, they throw stones at three pillars or 'satans' representing the Devil. After that, animals are sacrificed and the meat distributed to the poor.

From the beginning, the journey to Mecca was a communal activity. Throughout the Middle Ages, camel caravans set out three times a year from Cairo, Damascus and Baghdad. The main route from Baghdad ran for almost 1000 miles (1600 km) across southern Iraq and the northern Nafud. It was known as the Way of Zubayda, after the wife of Caliph Harun al-Rashid, who ruled from 786 to 809. Work on the road seems to have been inaugurated by Harun's predecessor al-Mahdi, but it was completed by Zubayda. Journeying all the way to Mecca on foot, along with her husband, she benefited from al-Mahdi's improvements but realised how much still remained to be done. Accordingly she set up a series of caravanserai all along the route, at intervals of 15 miles (24 km) – a typical day's journey under desert conditions. Hydraulic engineers dug wells to tap shallow aquifers and constructed cisterns to conserve rainwater, rendering what had been a hazardous journey a great deal more comfortable and civilised. But these facilities must have been taxed to the limit by the sheer volume of traffic on the route. Along with the pilgrims came the personal bodyguards and servants of the better-off; large caravans comprised hundreds, even thousands, of travellers.

Four corners *Pilgrims flock to Mecca from as far afield as China and South America.*

Every caravan had its organisers and guides, as well as soldiers to protect it from attack by nomads along the way. There were also merchants selling food and clothing, moneylenders and bankers – an entire economy of the road. An English merchant who accompanied the caravan from Cairo in the second half of the 16th century estimated that the total number travelling was about 200 000. As early as 1184, the Arab scholar Ibn Jubayr wrote: 'Who has not seen with his own eyes this Iraqi caravan has not experienced one of the genuine marvels of the world.' But so huge a crowd could also be quite alarming, he noted, observing the 'pain and fright' of those caught up in its mass momentum. That this fear could be all too justified has been underlined by a number of tragic stampedes. There is also the problem of terrorism – which has a surprisingly long history. Islam's most sacred site, Mecca has also been its most hotly disputed, the rival strands of the religion contesting one another's rights to proprietorship and access. As long ago as 930 the Kaaba shrine was raided and the sacred stone abducted by a sect of dissidents. Mecca has lost none of its importance – or its capacity to cause controversy – in the intervening period.

The politics of oppression

With the notable exceptions of Cyprus and Israel – and, to a lesser extent, Turkey – no Middle Eastern country enjoys a democracy. Those in which absolute monarchies have been overthrown have for the most part become strict one-party states: 'liberation' has brought only alternative forms of servitude.

Born to rule   *The government of Saudi Arabia remains very much a family concern in the hands of the al-Sauds (above).*

At a meeting in 1979, Iraqi president Saddam Hussein told his audience: 'Politics is when you say you are going to do one thing while you intend to do another. Then you do neither what you said nor what you intended.' Unpredictability has been the one thing the Iraqi people could depend on in a dictator who once shot a general dead for disagreeing with him. The Middle East as a whole is governed by degrees of authoritarianism. The Middle East files of Amnesty International and other human rights groups bulge with cases of abuse; no government, not even Israel's, is excepted. Arbitrary arrest and torture are the norm, the one continuity between the shah's Iran and the ayatollahs'; the one thing that religious Saudi Arabia and secular Turkey share.

The second sex

The Ayatollah Khomeini said in 1979: 'We owe our revolution to women.' But he repaid them by confining them to their homes, to venture out only under the strictest conditions and 'protected' by the veil. The Taliban regime that ruled in Afghanistan from 1997 to 2001 was if anything more unyielding in its attitudes. Such extremes of discrimination only exaggerate a more general plight of women in a region where democratic rule is a rare commodity and where sexist traditions mean that the majority of women are doubly disenfranchised.

In the family

The region's monarchies see themselves as stable families, *in loco parentis* over their people. What need for representative government when the emir can give them everything they need? And why would humble voters expect to know better than the sultan or the shah? How well this ancient attitude has weathered has depended on just how discontented the electorate has been; pride and dignity have often been as important as material conditions.

The abuses of the Iranian monarchy were many and varied, but what really seems to have outraged the people was their perception that Iran had been reduced to the status of American dependency. The rulers of the Arabian Peninsula have fared better, although the timely arrival of oil revenues smoothed what might otherwise have been a turbulent half-century. In theory, at least, those Gulf emirates that were once under British protection, such as Bahrain, Qatar and Kuwait, have constitutions that guarantee freedom of the press and religious tolerance. But in the context of an absolute monarchy, such functions inevitably atrophy and the business of state is conducted more or less entirely on the ruler's say-so. The fact that Arab society has always been organised into large family groups has also helped, ensuring that a considerable proportion of the population feels it has a real interest in the fortunes of the monarchy. It is significant that the first real signs of discontent in the Gulf states have come, not from native subjects, but from the large

By the people   *In Turkey (left), a resurgent Islam is proving a headache for the inheritors of Kemal's secular state. Democracy in Jordan (below) provides representation, but some observers doubt the validity of the polls.*

Father figure *The image of the Ayatollah Khomeini (left) remains ubiquitous in Iran, although the regime has – to the relief of many – been softening its attitude in recent years.*

Free speech *The Israeli Knesset is one of the few real parliaments in the Middle East.*

immigrant populations brought in to service the oil boom. Rulers have shown little inclination to give these people a political stake in the running of society – a policy that may well prove shortsighted in the longer term.

Even before the rise of modern fundamentalism, Islam insisted on its place in every sphere of human existence. The separation of Church and state in which the Western democracies have taken such pride is seen in the Islamic world as a failing, not a virtue. Like Muhammad himself, the caliphs who succeeded the Prophet were both temporal and spiritual leaders, and their mantle has to a large extent been passed down to individual chiefs and monarchs at a more local level in the centuries since.

Nowhere is this more true than in Arabia, where one family, the al-Sauds, has reigned for almost 250 years with only a brief interruption in the early 20th century. The only threat to absolute Saudi power has originated with the country's clerics, who have sometimes looked askance at Arabia's economic accommodations with the Western oil-consuming countries. In so far as there can be such a thing as 'popular opinion' in such a society, it seems to favour greater rigidity, not relaxation; the country's exiled dissidents have often appalled Western interviewers with their hardline views.

The fear that 'people power' might be a force for reaction has been evident in several countries in the Islamic world in recent years. The Algerian military coup in 1992, when elections which gave a majority to the fundamentalist Islamic opposition were deemed to have produced the 'wrong' result, caused mixed feelings

Late lamented *President Hafez al-Assad ruled Syria with an iron hand, but his death in 2000 seemed to be sincerely mourned by his people.*

among Western governments equally apprehensive about the rise of fundamentalism. No such blatant act of interference has taken place in the Middle East recently, although eyebrows were raised at the alterations made by King Hussein of Jordan in his country's electoral laws in 1993. In two elections since, Islamic radicals have been forced to the political margins; how long they will be content to remain there remains to be seen.

A hollow shell of freedom

The idea that either a monarch or a mullah should hold absolute power seems wrong to many among the Middle Eastern intelligentsia. Those educated in Western ways have attempted to establish Western forms of government, with varying degrees of failure but never any real success. The temptation has always been to try to force 'freedom' on the people – not recognising that a liberation imposed from above is no liberation at all.

Under the French mandate in the 1920s and 30s, a true democracy was tentatively established in Syria, but it could not endure the climate of Arab nationalism that accompanied the rise of Gamal Abdul Nasser in Egypt in the 1950s. As ideological messages go, the secular socialist rhetoric of the Ba'ath parties of Syria and Iraq seems less alien to many Western ears than the feudalism or religious fanaticism of certain other governments of the Middle East. The Ba'ath contribution to the region has, however, been the regimes of Hafez al-Assad and Saddam Hussein – not the best advertisements for a modern political philosophy.

The extended family

In the Islamic Middle East the family sits at the heart of society. Ties of kinship bind hundreds or thousands together.

Age and authority
Druse chieftains are community leaders.

Royal family *Abdullah (centre), the young king of Jordan, belongs to the Hashemite family, which claims descent from the Prophet Muhammad himself.*

In the Islamic Middle East in particular, the nuclear family is just the beginning of a tribal structure that embraces hundreds, even thousands, in a common kinship. A British journalist who asked a young Palestinian boy how many there were in his family was amazed when he answered: 'Oh, around two thousand'. In the most traditional Arab cultures, the individual can scarcely be said to exist at all; the family is both defined more widely and felt more intensely than it is in the West.

Several households are likely to be included in an Arab's immediate family, including all male first cousins on his father's side along with their wives and children. Typically, such groups will live in close proximity to one another, and cement their relationship with regular meetings and meals. The ultimate authority resides with the oldest competent male. On his death, his son takes over, inheriting authority over his own mother, for power is very much the preserve of males.

The family group can be particularly enormous when a man has the four wives permitted by Islamic law, though in practice polygamy has been declining in recent decades. Loyalty within the group is fierce and far-reaching, encompassing every area of life. Arab families look askance at a Western culture in which the elderly are regarded as a burden, the sick and needy the responsibility of strangers paid for by an impersonal state.

For better and for worse

Whatever benefits it confers, the extended family also exacts obligations from the individual that would astonish and appal the average Westerner. The Western wife who cannot wait for her in-laws' visit to be over; the husband who resents the demands made on his wife by her siblings – both would be horrified at the degree to which the Middle Eastern code made them responsible for the welfare of their wider family. If the Middle Eastern family is a benevolent institution, offering help and support when needed, it can also be a force for violence and hatred. A slight to one family member is regarded as a slight to all; in some societies the honour of the clan will be defended to the death. Such aggressive tribalism underlies a range of evils from minor nepotism to murderous blood feud. Despite his leadership of the high-minded pan-Arabist Ba'ath party, the Iraqi leader Saddam Hussein surrounded himself with members of his own al-Bejat clan – men from his home town of Tikrit were the only people he really trusted.

Strong as its ties may be, the tribal structure is in certain ways unstable, making conflict as intrinsic to family life as loyalty. 'Myself and my brother against my cousin; myself and my cousin against the world,' runs an Arab proverb. It highlights the capacity for tensions and splits to complicate what at first glance is the impregnable structure of the tribe. Relations may be allies or enemies, while the father who would die for his children might deny them if called on to do so by his duties to the clan.

A point of honour

Its curved blade ribbed at the centre, its handle often richly ornamented, the *jambiya* is found throughout the Arab world. In Yemen this ceremonial dagger has a special place; it is, as one Yemeni put it, his country's 'equivalent of the suit and tie'. No self-respecting Yemeni man would ever be seen in public without it. Handed down from father to son, the *jambiya* represents continuity with the past and kinship with the clan; it is a symbol of membership in a close-knit society.

Daggers drawn *The* jambiya *is more a badge of belonging than a weapon.*

The souk, bustling heart of the city

From Istanbul's Grand Bazaar and the al-Hamidiyeh of Damascus to the tiny trading posts of the Arabian desert or the Afghan mountains, in the Islamic Middle East every urban settlement has its souk, a busy commercial and social centre.

Meeting-place The souk is a place for chatting with friends and acquaintances, the gregarious heart of Middle Eastern city life.

Market value

The riotous profusion of the souk, the *ad hoc* haggling by which sales are made – the Western visitor is easily left with an impression of commercial anarchy. Nothing could be further from the truth: the business of the souk has always been strictly policed, by an inspectorate of *muhtasibs* in whom the authority of Allah and the state are joined. The Koran is strict about business ethics: 'And the sky devised scales so you may not cheat. Give true weight, and never tamper with the scales.' In traditionalist societies such as Afghanistan, a prayer is still offered over the scales before each sale, to ask Allah to referee the contract between seller and buyer. The merchant mumbles a formula in which God's help in all previous such sales is acknowledged, before a final blessing is added on completion of the deal.

Family firm Stalls – and skills – often remain in the same families for generations.

The Italian traveller Edmondo de Amicis recalled his first visit to the Grand Bazaar of Istanbul in 1878. 'It is not an edifice but a labyrinth,' he wrote. 'At every turn, by the side doors, are seen perspectives of arches and pilasters, long corridors, narrow alleys, a long confused perspect of bazaar, and everywhere shops, merchandise piled up or hanging from wall and ceiling, busy merchants, loaded porters, groups of veiled women, coming and going, a perpetual noise of people and things enough to make one dizzy.'

Order in the chaos

The older cities of the Middle East may seem haphazard and sprawling, but a logic underlies the chaos. In the centre, beside the defensive citadel and the grand mosque that dedicates the city to God, was their commercial centre, the souk. Like the modern shopping mall of the Western city, it was covered by roofs to protect strollers and traders from rain and the scorching sun. Its arcades or lanes

The business of life There is no more important function than commerce in the Islamic world. It embraces social and cultural contacts of every kind.

were interconnected to encourage circulation, and each specialised in a different commodity or trade, with separate streets for spices, foods, textiles, metalwork, jewellery or other goods. Generally speaking, the dirtier the trade, the farther its designated street lay from the centre of the souk – booksellers and jewellers were in the middle, while butchers and tanners were on the periphery. Moneychangers had their own sections, as did a range of restaurants and cafés – some 12 000 chefs served food for shoppers in Cairo's enormous souk. Out of sight of the public there was a courtyard where camels could be unloaded, with space for warehousing and accommodation for merchants away from home.

Today's bazaar is a sanitised shadow of its former self; the smell of camel-dung is gone, the babel of languages reduced to a handful. But it retains an exotic mix of modern goods and traditional artefacts. The shopper can still find silks and satins, carpets and costumes, and metalwork in copper, silver and gold. Gemstones adorn everything from decorative daggers to costume jewellery. Ancient scents of perfumes and leathers, tobaccos and coffee still assail the nostrils.

Fasts, feasts and festivals

Jews, Christians and Muslims in the Middle East celebrate a range of different feasts, testimony to the cultural and ethnic variety embraced by the three great religions. But the roots of these festivities lie in the pagan past, when nomads and farmers felt themselves at the mercy of an often unyielding natural world.

For the first farmers of the Fertile Crescent, the cycle of the seasons was the rhythm of life. That summer's heat should give way to autumn was as inevitable as that rest should follow work, or night should succeed to day. But the onset of winter was always a shock. What if winter stayed for ever, the earth abandoned by its divine protectors, barrenness the permanent condition of a dying land? Precisely this anxiety seems to have haunted the ancient Hittites, whose mythology returned again and again to the subject, though only a few tales have come down to us complete in their fragmentary inscriptions.

One such is the story of the sun-god's abduction by an envious sea-god, who resented the heat and light cast upon the airy realm of his bitter rival Teshub, god of sky and storms. Catching the sun-god in an enormous net, the sea-god placed him in a giant jar and sealed it with a stopper. The effects upon the earth were dramatic

Mud mourning Shiite Muslims in Iran daub themselves in mud – a traditional sign of mourning – in memory of the martyrdom of Hussein, Muhammad's son and their first imam.

and immediate: in the absence of the sun's warmth, frost ranged freely across the fields; sown seed lay infertile, while livestock fell dead in barren pastures. Soon mortal men and women were dying too, as famine tightened its grip; a frantic Teshub seemed utterly helpless against frost's ravages. One by one his sons and brother set out to do battle with the frost and one by one they were humiliated. The storm-god was forced to acknowledge that winter was all-powerful.

Tantalisingly, the tablet on which this story is inscribed has crumbled away at just this point, but another fragment seems to take up the tale at its conclusion. A sacrifice seems to have been made as the ransom for the sun's return – an offering thenceforth to be renewed by the Hittites themselves with each passing year. 'If you, oh Sun, grant your assistance to a man, let that man sacrifice nine animals to you; let the poor man at least make an offering of a single sheep.'

From darkness into light

Since the Hittites, countless civilisations have devised rituals to appease the wrath of winter, or to offer thanks for the return of spring. All three monotheistic religions have winter festivals, each with its own individual story, but each serving a similar social function of providing light and cheer at this darkest time of year. The winter festival of Christmas commemorates the birth of Jesus, the 'light of the world', though many Middle Eastern Christians prefer to celebrate the baptism, held to have taken place on January 6, a date associated in the West with the Epiphany, the visit of the Three Wise Men.

The Jewish and Muslim faiths both follow the lunar rather than the solar calendar, so their religious timetables do not conform

Rite of passage The bar mitzvah, the rite of puberty, marks the time when the Jewish boy becomes a man and takes his place in the wider religious community.

Calendar chaos

For the Jew and the Muslim, it is a different month and even a different year. Based not on solar but on lunar months, the Muslim year is 11 days shorter than the West's, with the result that key fasts and festivals give the impression of 'migrating' across the calendar. The month of Ramadan, for instance, may as easily fall in summer as in winter; it takes 33 years to come

full circle through the Western year. The Jewish calendar is also based on lunar cycles, though tradition ordains a series of complicated adjustments that ensure it never deviates too drastically from the solar year. Important religious festivals may 'move' against the standard secular calendar, but they will nevertheless remain at roughly the same time of year.

Feast of the Tabernacles During this festival the Jews commemorate their ancestors' journey in the wilderness of the Sinai Desert.

with those of Western Christians. But the Jewish Feast of Lights, Chanukkah, recognisably springs from the same human impulse as the Christmas festival. It marks the recapture of the Temple of Antiochus from Seleucid invaders by the warrior Judas Maccabeus and his followers in 165 BC, and the miracle supposed to have attended its rededication. When the Maccabees came to relight the sacred lamp that was supposed to be tended for all time, they found they had only enough oil for a single day. In the event, however, the flame burned for eight full days – the duration of the Feast of Lights from that time forward.

The Muslim festival of Eid al-Fitr marks the end of Ramadan, the holy month, and the regime of fasting stipulated by Islamic tradition. Throughout the ninth month of the lunar year, the *sawm* or fast begins at dawn and does not end until sunset; no food, drink, smoking or sexual activity is permitted in that time. The arrival of the new moon is the signal for an outburst of joyous festivities – clearly analogous to the winter feasts of the other great religions.

The deliverance of spring

The arrival of spring was marked by festivals of thanksgiving in the ancient world, as men and women celebrated their survival through another winter. They offered sacrifices to the gods who had seen them safely through the months of cold and darkness, and indulged themselves, feasting on the earth's new plenty. The 40-day fast of Lent and the Easter festival that follows can clearly be seen as symbolically replaying the death of winter

A shared feast   The tradition of sharing is strong in Islam, constantly emphasised by the Koran and reinforced by many aspects of social custom.

His and hers   After a wedding in Yemen, it is the social custom for men and women to celebrate with their own separate parties, the men outside in the street, the women safely inside the home.

and the rebirth of spring – reflected also in the springtide remembrance of Christ's crucifixion and resurrection.

The Jewish feast of Passover, which is celebrated at around the same time, marks the delivery of the Israelites from their enslavement at the hands of the pharaohs of Egypt. On the night that the Israelites are believed to have begun their escape from captivity, each Jewish family sacrificed a lamb for a feast, carefully marking their doorpost with its blood. The Angel of Death 'passed over' all the houses he found thus marked, but he killed the first-born sons of the Egyptian families. In the ensuing chaos, the Israelites escaped across the Red Sea – and they have celebrated the festival every year since that time.

With a new lamb as its centrepiece and its powerful theme of delivery from death, the roots of the Passover in pagan spring ritual are easy enough to see. The same goes for Eid al-Adha, the great feast of the Muslim year, at which, again, animals are sacrificed in thanks for man's deliverance. In this case, the event commemorated is God's sparing of Abraham's son Isaac – a story known and cherished by Christians and Jews too. As a test of his piety, God asked the patriarch to sacrifice his son to him; when it became clear that he was prepared to do so, an angel showed Abraham a ram caught by its horns in a nearby thicket, to offer as the sacrifice in place of Isaac.

The scapegoat

The ram that stood in for Isaac found a striking echo in later Jewish tradition in the culminating ritual of the Day of Atonement, or Yom Kippur. The original inspiration for the Muslim Ramadan, the regime of prayer and abstinence goes on for ten days, beginning with the Jewish New Year, the Day of Creation and of Judgment, Rosh Hashanah. During that time, pious Jews refrain from a wide range of activities considered unclean, including everything from food, drink and sexual relations to the wearing of leather shoes. In grief and lamentation, they recall the destruction of Solomon's Temple by Nebuchadnezzar's armies in 586 BC and the long generations of what was called the Babylonian Captivity. That Yahweh should have permitted the wanton sacking of his sacred shrine, and the re-enslavement of the people he had saved from the pharaohs, was regarded by the Jews as the ultimate abandonment.

In the rites of this holy week, however, they acknowledge their own responsibility for God's rejection, the part played by their behaviour in the alienation of their protector. But if the New Year begins in the recollection of despair, Yom Kippur allows optimism to return, recalling the moment when the 'scapegoat' was ceremonially saddled with all their sins. The chief priest, by tradition,

New traditions Young people dance in a nightspot in Istanbul (above). Similar scenes can be found in Tel Aviv, and to a lesser extent in other cities in the region. Beirut (left) has always been famous for cabaret.

symbolically placed the people's guilt on to a goat, which was then driven out of the city into the desert. Thus unburdened, the Jews could go on to face the main part of their religious year feeling that Yahweh was, once more, their loving father. The inauguration of a second temple after the destruction of the first amounted to a re-creation of the whole Jewish world, hence the yoking together of Yom Kippur with the start of the New Year and the Day of the Creation.

A comparable process of contemplation and atonement is observed weekly during the Sabbath, which begins at dusk on Friday and lasts until Saturday nightfall. Like the Christian Sunday, the seventh day on which God is supposed to have rested after the creation of the world, it allows the believer time and space for spiritual re-creation. It goes without saying that shops and offices will

Man and wife All marriages, whether Jewish, Christian (as here, in Iran) or Muslim are religious.

A Cypriot wedding

Aphrodite, Greek goddess of love, is said to have been born in Cyprus. It is a tradition that the island's tourist industry has not been slow to recognise, or to use in their publicity material. In recent years a significant package trade has emerged, catering to couples from northern Europe who want something a bit special for their wedding. Mediterranean sunshine and sand with a dash of antique exoticism – the Cypriot recipe can make a potent cocktail.

But it would be an enterprising couple who could outdo the Cypriots themselves. The Greek community in particular has a history of riotously noisy, colourful weddings. Rites recalling those of Dionysus, the ancient Greek god of drunkenness and licence, continue to flourish under the aegis of the Orthodox Church. Music, dance and raucous chanting accompany the bride and groom, who are publicly bathed before being escorted to the nuptial chamber. There, far from being left in peace, the uproar goes on, the guests dancing round the bed, where offerings are laid. They proceed downstairs for a rich banquet, before more music and dancing and a final triumphal tour by the bride and groom. Friends and relations pin banknotes to their garments as the couple make their way upstairs at last.

close on the Sabbath, but in Orthodox homes a long list of carefully specified activities must also be avoided, including everything from lighting a fire (and therefore cooking) to writing or any sort of needlework. Not only are these acts themselves to be avoided, but so is anything that might potentially lead somebody else into Sabbath-breaking. No hot baths are allowed, therefore, lest someone should have to heat the water. The playing of music is likewise prohibited, in case it should lead somebody into the labour of making an instrument. To many, more reformist Jews, such rules seem quaint in the extreme; the Orthodox are proud to obey them as a way of affirming their unique identity.

Life goes on Conditions in the Gaza Strip may be difficult, but that is all the more reason to celebrate life's joys.

Women's rites

The Koran insists on the indivisible closeness of Muslim spouses: 'They are your garments and you are their garments,' it says. But how do men and women meet in cultures that keep the sexes firmly apart? The arranged marriage is more a match between two families than a romantic contract between bride and groom, but in a society in which the family comes first this is not necessarily regarded as a bad thing. However different Islamic understanding of the institution may be from Christian, weddings are celebrated every bit as enthusiastically as in the Western world. Alcohol is forbidden for observant Muslims, but the revelry is fuelled by wonderful food and by the excitement everyone feels at such an auspicious occasion. In some cultures the segregation of the sexes extends even to the wedding feast, with men and women having separate parties. The ceremony is legal rather than religious; a man learned in Muslim law, a mullah, officiates, his main purpose being to ascertain from the bride's representative that she accepts the groom's proposal and the gift he bears, which may be anything from a house to an item of jewellery. Around this basic procedure various rituals have taken form, their details varying from country to country. A Palestinian mother, for example, gives her daughter a jug of sugared water to signify sweetness in life – she herself was given the same jug on her wedding day. She also gives her a rose: the green leaves represent life and the red petals are a symbol of love and happiness.

A special day Omani village life is always colourful, as women still wear their traditional costumes; for weddings, though, they make a special effort.

At home in the Middle East

An air of desertion and dilapidation can prevail in even the liveliest of the older Middle Eastern cities, traditional houses turning high, blank, mud-brick walls to the outside world. Climatic conditions and religious rules combine to make a Muslim home a retreat of coolness, calm and privacy.

Framed *Windows make a perfect perch for children to watch the world go by.*

No Middle Eastern tradition is as strong as that of providing generous hospitality – except valuing one's own privacy and respecting that of others. 'Do not,' commands the Koran, 'enter the dwellings of other men, until you have sought their permission and wished them peace.'

The importance of domestic privacy is obvious in the architecture of the traditional house. The residential districts of the old Muslim cities appear to be on the point of exploding, so tightly are the houses packed together. But closer inspection reveals that each home is a little island unto itself, an oasis of ordered calm amid the clutter and chaos. Typically square in construction, the house turns an unfriendly face to the street, with no windows at a low level to interrupt an often crumbling mud-brick façade. Inside it opens out on to a tiled patio or courtyard, with pot plants and sometimes a tree or fountain. The *diwan*, or reception room, lies just inside the house; even trusted visitors do

High rise *Traditional tower houses in San'a can be anything up to eight storeys high.*

Art nouveau – or Islamic?

From Barcelona to Glasgow, from Paris to New York, art nouveau was the last word in sophisticated interior design in the late 19th century. But its swirling, florid forms and its scorn for representation clearly owed much to earlier Muslim decorative styles.

Sugarloaf city   These extraordinary houses of mud and straw are in northern Syria, not far from Aleppo.

not get far into the innermost recesses. The harem, or women's quarters, are set well away from street and the *diwan* so that even welcome guests cannot see the women of the house.

San'a skyscrapers

Houses of a basic, box-like construction are found across much of the Arab Middle East, but other forms have evolved to suit particular conditions. In the mountainous terrain of Yemen, for example, fertile land is so scarce that every available plot was brought under cultivation. The people were forced to huddle together in the little space that was left, and their solution was to build upwards, like a medieval Manhattan. Many old houses still standing today are up to eight storeys in height – a remarkable achievement, given their mud-brick construction.

Typically, the ground floor walls were built in stone to ensure a solid base for the towering edifice. This area was used for livestock. Separated off from the stable area were granaries, pantries and storerooms, and in some cases accommodation for family servants.

The first floor was sometimes set aside for storage, the family inhabiting the storey above. The main focus of the family quarters was the *diwan* and the kitchen. Around and above these rooms the extended family would arrange itself,

Old Arabia The prevailing architectural style in Jeddah is 20th-century glass and concrete, but some buildings survive from an older time.

the women being the farthest removed from the public areas.

In most respects, despite the obvious differences, these towers recognisably follow the form of the standard Arab house, but the *mafraj*, or 'room with a view', is unique to Yemen. A room specifically for men to meet and chew kat in the afternoons, the *mafraj* is always on one of the house's more prestigious upper storeys. Sometimes, rather than an integrated room, the master has a separate *manzar* – a sort of penthouse on the roof in which he can entertain his friends.

The Marsh Arabs

While Yemenis reach for the sky, the Marsh Arabs hug the earth – or they would if solid ground could be found in the swamps of the Lower Euphrates. Here, since the days of Sumer, they have lived among wetlands in light but practical shelters made of reeds. In the absence of suitable sites, they heap up bundles of vegetation to create artificial islands. On these they raise their houses, which look rather like thatched Nissen huts; they make cramped but adequate accommodation. Hanging screens of reeds allow a degree of partitioning in the one-room *bayt* or larger *raba*; at the least, livestock can be sectioned off from the family. For safety, the cooking fire or *tanur* is kept away from the house, often on a separate island. At the centre of the village there may be a larger house for the sheik; this *mudhif* also acts as a guesthouse for visitors. With care, a house may last for 25 years. What it lacks in permanence it makes up for in portability when waters are high – a medium-sized *raba* can be dismantled and reassembled on a new site in hours.

Tragically, after 5000 years, this way of life is facing extinction. The Marsh Arabs are marked out from their fellow Iraqis not only by lifestyle but by religion. As Shiites, they were regarded with suspicion by Saddam Hussein's regime and the Ba'ath government made little secret of the true purpose of its policy of 'land reclamation' – a programme that was intensified in the 1990s in the wake of the Iran-Iraq War. Over the course of 25 years, 90 per cent of the southern marshes were drained and the Marsh Arab population fell from around 250,000 to 40,000. In the process the largest wetlands ecosystem in the Middle East was destroyed.

Draining away The Marsh Arabs of Iraq have lived this way for 5000 years; now their culture faces extinction within a generation.

Waterfront palaces

Well into the days of the Turkish Republic, the retired official Edhem Bey is reputed to have kept Ottoman hospitality alive, keeping open house for guests of every description. One day, so the story goes, he leaned over to his wife and said: 'I do not recognise that young man at the end of the table.' 'Neither do I,' she replied, 'but he has been with us for a fortnight.' Unconcerned, the couple continued with their meal. Such nonchalant generosity is possible when you have a palace at your disposal – and that is basically what grandees of the empire had in their waterfront *yali*. Built on stone foundations, sometimes with pillars taken from Turkey's ancient ruins, these astonishing wooden constructions dominate several stretches of the Bosporus shore. They are often approachable by boat from the seaward side as well as by road: their raised verandahs offer safe mooring for visiting vessels. Outside, the *yali* were richly painted, while inside they were sumptuously appointed in an extravagant blend of Western and oriental styles – the last word in opulence and luxury.

Seaside splendour The yali of the Bosporus coast are remarkable for their range of colours.

101

A complex cuisine

The Middle East has a spicy and fragrant cuisine in which all the influences of a complex history come together. Arab armies brought back foods from North Africa and Spain, while Mongols, Turks and Crusaders introduced other innovations. With many different ethnic groups established here, the evolution of a wonderfully varied cuisine was assured.

Cooking on board *Fresh fish plays a vital part in the cuisines of coastal regions.*

Oily fruit *Originating in Syria, the olive is used throughout the region.*

Up on the Bam-i-Dunya, at 13 000 ft (4000 m), a Kyrgyz caravan makes its way against the rigours of a mountain winter. A real no-man's-land, wild and empty, this slender panhandle of north-eastern Afghanistan insinuates itself between the borders of Uzbekistan, Pakistan and western China. This is not a time of abundance, nor can a well-appointed kitchen be carried on the road, but a nourishing diet can make the difference between life and death. The nomads' favourite dish, *qurut*, is very simple. As a pot of water simmers on a fire fuelled by dried yak dung, a rock-hard chunk of curdled-milk cheese is crumbled into it and slowly stirred. A little fat adds flavour, while bits of bread lend body to the stew. To drink, there is a brew of tea – so precious a commodity that each man carries his own leaves in an embroidered bag

Sweet and sticky *Pastries are soaked in syrup or honey.*

Communal dining *Traditionally, food is eaten with the fingers from a common dish.*

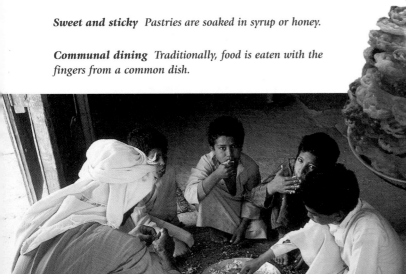

around his neck. There is no sugar, so it is taken with salt instead. An austere fare, perhaps, but the nomads are fortified against the gruelling terrain, the altitude and the fierce cold.

A simple but varied diet

Over the centuries nomadic herdsmen such as these have helped give rise to a cuisine characterised first and foremost by its variety. The sailors of the Arab dhows contributed, too: their diet was also necessarily constrained, even though at sea fish could be caught, and livestock carried.

In the fabled feasts of the Ottoman emperors, the Persian shahs and the Arab sheiks, the flavours and aromas of an Islamic world that stretched from Morocco to Malaysia and from Greece to Zanzibar were combined. But this sumptuous cuisine was based on the simpler recipes developed through thousands of years by farmers and nomadic herdsmen who had to struggle to survive, their staples being cereals, vegetables, yoghurt and cheese. Greek and Roman conquest, the Islamic expansionism that took Arab armies east to Persia and west to the Atlantic; a series of Western Crusades; the colonial influences from more modern times – all these historical influences have contributed to a cuisine of endless variety.

Middle Eastern cookery strikes a balance between purity and combination. Its flavours come from good ingredients, straightforwardly prepared. The first pressings of olive oil; the tang of goat's cheese; the plumpness and moisture of a muscat raisin – these are as much a part of the culinary experience as the more exotic delights of yoghurt-marinated kid with saffron, honey, apricots and lightly toasted almonds. Such sophisticated dishes take to extremes an impulse found in Middle Eastern cooking at every level to mix contrasting flavours. Thus the sharpness of lemon juice or vinegar sets off the nutty stodginess of cracked wheat couscous, chickpea hummus or boiled rice with vegetables, while these in turn bring out the blandness of a basic yoghurt. Cheese, pickled vine leaves, onions and sweet tomatoes combine to perfection in a 'Greek' salad, whose popularity extends throughout Turkey and beyond. Unleavened pitta bread makes the perfect foil to the flavour of a lamb kebab.

Throughout the Arab Middle East, vine leaves and olives (pickled or fresh), onions, cucumber, radish, spinach, mint and parsley are eaten as mezze, appetisers served as an accompaniment to cooling drinks before the main meal, recalling the tapas (Moorish in origin) of modern Spain. Contrast, again, is the key – complexity and subtlety in the juxtaposition of flavours.

A sweet tooth

Contrary to what many outsiders assume, the Prophet placed no strict prohibition on wine. The Koran ranks alcohol alongside gambling as a sin, although it is not explicitly forbidden like eating pork. Over time, however, temperence hardened into something close to taboo; drunkenness was one of the degradations the Muslims most despised in the Crusaders. But though most Muslims shun alcohol – and indeed a wariness of the consumption of alcohol is a feature of other cultures of the region as well – they do not necessarily avoid all culinary treats. In one indulgence in particular, Middle Easterners leave their Western counterparts standing: that is, in their sweets.

Lokum, cubes of flavoured gelatin with a dusting of sugar, are famed throughout the world as Turkish delight. But Turkey, and the rest of the region, has many other delights: baklava, honeyed pastries stuffed with pine nuts and pistachios; pancakes with soft cheese and golden syrup; rice or semolina cakes sprinkled with sesame seeds; *muhallabia* milk puddings made from tapioca or semolina flour not to mention sweetened fruit drinks and dried and candied fruits.

Pick and mix *Mezze may equally be a way of eking out scarcity or showing off abundance.*

Her Majesty's favourite

When French Empress Eugénie visited Sultan Abdulaziz's Istanbul court in the 1870s, she was famously delighted by the creamed aubergine she was served at dinner. The dish has ever since been known as *hunkar begendi* ('Her Majesty's favourite') in her honour, and she asked the sultan's chef to give her own retainers the recipe. He was amazed to find them asking him for precise weights and cooking times. 'When one is preparing food for a king,' he said, 'one has to be able to trust one's own senses.'

Forbidden foods

The variety of Middle Eastern cuisine is remarkable given the lengthy lists of ingredients proscribed under the dietary laws of its religious creeds. *Kashrut*, the law of what is clean or 'kosher', prohibits pork and its by-products to all Jews – a commandment echoed in the Koran's code of halal. Shellfish and crustaceans – indeed any seafood without both 'fins and scales' – are banned for Jews by the laws of Leviticus. Birds of prey, as well as carnivorous and scavenging animals in general, are considered unclean by both traditions. Both insist that even permitted animals must be killed in a special way, the blood drained completely during slaughtering. These basic prohibitions may of course be interpreted either freely or strictly. Orthodox Judaism adds stipulations about everything from storage conditions to cooking utensils and cutlery. The Middle East's Christians, by and large, are comparatively relaxed in their dietary restrictions, at most avoiding meat and eggs during Lent (the fast before Easter), and perhaps on Fridays.

Our daily bread *Every culture in the region has its distinctive bread, and its traditional methods of preparing it.*

The veils of Islam

The veil is older than Islam, dating back to ancient Assyria and perhaps beyond. Modest, well-born women of all creeds have been covered for much of Middle Eastern history. Today the veil has become a hotly contested symbol, said by Western critics to represent the Islamic world's oppression of its women.

Traditional costume

Modesty was only one factor in the original formulation of the Islamic dress code. Long, loose-fitting robes and enfolding headgear make sense in the climate of the Middle East. The distinctive chequered *kaffiyeh* is still widely worn by men, in part because it proclaims its owner's Arab identity; PLO leader Yasser Arafat and the late King Hussein of Jordan have made it familiar on the international stage. It is also practical, providing effective protection against the sun. With cloth to spare, the *kaffiyeh* can be unwound and used to shield the face against a desert sandstorm. National and regional variations enable Arabs to tell one another apart. For example, Palestinian *kaffiyehs* are black and white, while the Jordanian version is red and white.

The tradition that women should cover their heads in places of worship has died out in Christian churches of the West, but many Orthodox Jewish women still wear veils or wigs in accordance with the rule. The all-enveloping habits still worn by conservative Roman Catholic nuns were common to all well-born Western women in the Middle Ages, but in the modern world the practice of veiling or *hijab* is seen as a peculiarly Muslim practice.

Oppression or freedom?

The *chador*, the long cloth that covers head and shoulders – and in many cases all except the eyes – seems alien to Westerners, who see it as an indication that Islam is inherently misogynistic. But many Muslim women would disagree; the Prophet ordained the veil for their protection, not (as St Paul did) as a mask of uncleanness or inferiority. 'O Prophet!' bids the Koran, 'Tell thy wives and thy daughters and the women of believers to draw their cloaks close about them… so that they may be recognised and not annoyed.'

Some would argue that the veil assures a woman's dignity, even liberates her as an individual in a society that would otherwise enslave her in the servitude of sexual objectification. Where, Muslim feminists ask, is the 'freedom' in being coerced by culture into wearing revealing clothes, the female body becoming the property of male scrutiny? Reverence for women is written into Islamic tradition; what Westerners regard as oppression should rather be seen as solicitude and respect. 'Women are above men in many things,' the Arab scholar al-Jahiz wrote in the 9th century. 'It is they who are wooed, wished for, loved, and desired, and it is they for whom sacrifices are made and who are protected.'

Supporters of the *chador* point to the freedom it has given them to develop academically and professionally, allowing them to participate in society to the full without fear of unwelcome male attentions. Historically, Islam has often been better than the West at allowing women educational opportunities; the veil can be said to have freed them to fulfil their potential. Other women say they would rather do without a protection that, in placing them on a pedestal, subjects them to male control – and as for harassment, is it not the responsibility of men to police their own behaviour? The debate seems set to continue.

Unveiled Traditionally, Bedouin women (above) have never had their faces veiled.

Changing times The Thermos for tea may be new, but traditional costume remains the choice of many Muslim men.

Coffee and the café culture

Originating in north-east Africa, coffee was introduced to the Arab world through Yemen. Since then it has gone on to conquer the world, but it still has a special place in Middle Eastern civilisation, both in its own right and as the heart of a thriving café culture.

Waiting game   *In the unhurried atmosphere of the maqha, or café, Palestinian boys acquire the chess skills of strategy and patience.*

It has been said that the wonderful properties of coffee were discovered in Ethiopia just over a thousand years ago, when goatherds noticed that animals browsing on the beans became unusually lively. Tribesmen subsequently dipped the beans in fat and chewed them on hunting expeditions to promote alertness and endurance. The Arabic name *qahwah* – literally,

Game of chance   *Lotteries are particularly popular in Turkey.*

The smoke that soothes

A distinctive aroma of downtown Damascus is apple tobacco, which is smoked in the traditional hubble-bubble pipe or *nargileh* – a strange contraption standing up to 4 ft (1.2 m) tall. Tobacco mixed with apple blossom is heated by glowing charcoal in a dish at the top, then smoke is drawn down through a chamber at the bottom, where it is cooled with water. It then goes up a flexible tube to the mouth of the smoker, yielding a refreshing taste that is mildly narcotic. Aficionados insist that it is the most soothing of smokes.

'that which enables one to do without' – suggests it lent an extra edge to those suffering from food and sleep deprivation.

Inconclusive archaeological evidence suggests that coffee may actually have been under cultivation in Yemen as early as 200 BC. Until more definitive evidence emerges, however, there seems little reason to doubt the traditional story that coffee came to the Arab world across the Bab al Mandab strait separating the Red Sea coast of Arabia from Eritrea and Djibouti. The name of the port of Mokha, long linked with the African trade in coffee, is now forever associated with that of the finest Arabica coffee beans. The drink was taken up enthusiastically by the Sufis, the Islamic mystics of the Middle Ages. Thanks to its stimulant powers, they were able to prolong their vigils, performing ever more epic feats of ecstatic devotion. It was said that coffee, the 'wine of Islam,' gave the true Muslim visions of Paradise.

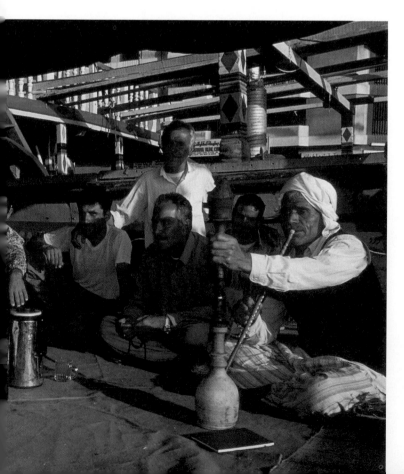

A cup of controversy

Soon coffee was being enjoyed as a recreational drink in secular society. The first-ever designated establishment for drinking coffee, called *qahwah* in honour of the drink, is said to have opened in Mecca at the start of the 15th century – but, again, it is difficult to be sure of the precise chronology. One date that does seem to be certain is 1511, when the governor of Mecca, Kair Bey, issued an official decree prohibiting coffee-drinking. He was rapidly overruled by the sultan of Cairo, but his concern was shared by several subsequent rulers, as well as by those moral puritans who, unimpressed by coffee's religious credentials, saw it as a spur to disorder and immorality. The problem was that the *qahwahs* were fast becoming unofficial forums for the exchange of information and opinions that were not necessarily welcomed by those in authority.

Coffee-drinking and intellectualism have always gone together in the West, uniting everyone from London's 18th-century satirists to the Left Bank radicals of 20th-century Paris. The connection was made much earlier, though, in the *qahwahs* of the Middle East, where its continuing significance should not be underestimated. Primarily a place for relaxation, the café is also a rendezvous where individuals and ideas can come together.

105

A medley of tongues

The peoples of the Middle East use many different languages. Some, like Syriac and Aramaic, are up to 3000 years old, while Arabic and Turkish have been much modernised. Others are a legacy of colonisation: English established itself through military conquest, but has stayed on as the lingua franca of globalisation.

Hebrew is both the oldest and the youngest language in the Middle East. When, towards the end of the 19th century, Jewish pioneers set about realising the Zionist dream in the deserts of Palestine, many felt that, despite their longed-for homecoming, they remained linguistically in exile. The German-based Yiddish they generally spoke was the language of the East European ghetto, learned through generations of exclusion and humiliation. The answer, they decided, was to revive the Old Testament tongue of Hebrew – despite the fact that it had not been in everyday use as a spoken language for well over 2000 years. Not since the days of the Babylonian Captivity had Jew talked to Jew in Hebrew; a subject people, they had adopted the language of their masters, speaking Aramaic, like others in the Babylonian and Persian empires. This, the language of Christ, still survives in some places in the Middle East, spoken by small Christian communities.

Hebrew would have disappeared completely had it not endured in the scriptural context of the Bible and the Torah. To all intents and purposes a dead language, like classical Greek or Latin, it could hardly be employed as a living tongue. A radical overhaul was required, and this was led by Eliezer ben Yehuda, a Lithuanian-born scholar who contributed no fewer than 4000 modernising coinages. Since 1948 the official language of Israel, Hebrew is today a contemporary medium of communication, as much at home with advanced software systems as with ancient prophecies.

An early start   One way of reconciling an ancient tongue with modern needs is to embrace a wholesale policy of bilingualism: Omani children (right) learn English at primary school.

*Young and old
The sons of Orthodox Jews learn Biblical Hebrew at religious schools, or yeshivas, to enable them to study the laws and scriptures of their people.*

Ancient and modern

The reinvention of Hebrew is one of several modernisation stories in the Middle East, as nations have attempted to adapt ancient languages to their changing needs. The experience has not always been a happy one. Kemal's romanisation of Turkish script formed part of a wider programme of language reform

*Education en masse
It is a long-standing demographic truth that the poorest countries have the highest birthrates, with the consequent problem of overcrowded schools. Many Middle Eastern children are taught in classes of 50 or more.*

106

LIVING IN THE MIDDLE EAST

The Sephardic tongue

If the first Zionists had not thought of reviving Hebrew, there would have been other options available to them. As well as Yiddish, which many of them had grown up speaking, another language existed – and is indeed still spoken by some 150 000 Jews worldwide. *Judezmo*, as it is called, is the language of those Sephardic Jews who were expelled from Catholic Spain in the 15th century. Also known as *Ladino*, after its Western (Latin) origins, *Judezmo* is an archaic version of Spanish – now almost unrecognisable and rendered that much more exotic by being written in the Hebrew alphabet. The language has survived in several places in the Middle East, and is still used by significant communities in Turkey and, of course, in Israel.

that included the updating of vocabulary to accommodate modern social, political and technological circumstances. But Kemal did not stop there: he embarked on a more ambitious project whose ultimate aim was what today might be described as 'linguistic cleansing'. The *raison d'être* of the Turkish Republic has been the attempt to forge a centralised nation-state, as the Armenians, Kurds and other minorities have found to their cost. Ankara has always seen homogeneity as the price of admission to the modern world, regarding what we might see as linguistic richness as a mark of economic underdevelopment and cultural backwardness.

The problem of reconciling a venerable ancient language with the demands of modern communication has been managed rather better in the Arab world. Unlike Hebrew, the language of the Koran thrived both in written word and in speech; far from being forgotten, indeed, its use was exported far and wide with Islam.

But the Arabic as spoken in 6th-century Mecca could hardly be expected to take in its stride the linguistic challenges of modern society. Its scriptural sanctity was if anything a brake on evolution and adaptation. Nonetheless, the crisis that might have been predicted never came; instead, the passage of time saw a progressive divergence between a formal, 'classical' Arabic and a vernacular version used in everyday speech. In addition to being the language of scripture and ritual, therefore, Arabic has remained the written medium of government, law and literature, while surviving as the spoken language

Facing facts   The vernacular Arabic used to teach modern scientific truths (here, a physics class in Oman) exists alongside formal, classical Arabic.

of intra-regional diplomacy and commerce. Meanwhile, localised forms have also developed. Swahili, spoken in East Africa, is the best-known of several hybrid languages in which Arabic and local speech have been synthesised into a single common tongue. But the same thing has happened in countries from West Africa to Central Asia, all along the fringes of the old Islamic empire. Arabic has thus preserved its classical form, yet also adapted to modern needs.

Past glory   Before the Gulf War, Baghdad University was one of the most prestigious in the Arab world.

A national academy

There have been three separate attempts at establishing a national academy for the Persian language in 20th-century Iran. The idea was first mooted at the start of the century, and the first Iranian Academy was founded in 1935 by Reza Shah Pahlavi. It aimed, like Kemal's modernisation, to find Persian equivalents for modern, foreign terms, and to promote national coherence. The shah's son Muhammad refounded the academy in 1970, underlining how far the requirements of the regime had changed in 35 years. The last shah was schizophrenic in his view of Iranian cultural identity: on the one hand he wanted a united Persian people to rally round his throne; on the other, he and his American allies were eager for them to adopt the values of Western consumer culture. This produced an odd arrangement under which national TV bombarded its audiences with sex and violence, while the print media were strictly censored by the secret police. The relaunched Academy was supposed to give authority to these contradictions.

Despite clearer and more coherent aims, the third Iranian Academy of Persian Language and Literature (Farhangestan) has foundered every bit as badly as its predecessors. Established in 1991 by the country's revolutionary regime, it has been driven by a passionate devotion to a strict Islamic culture far more fervent than the Persian patriotism that underpinned its predecessors. Even so, as English has strengthened its position as the international language, the academy's task has become more hopeless with every year.

107

CHAPTER 5

5 A WORLD OUTDOORS

The thunder of hoofs in the desert, the swish of a falcon's wings – ancient sounds of the hunt still stir the imagination. In the modern Middle East, traditional outdoor pursuits retain their place – even if the snort of the dromedary has been replaced by the growl of the 4 x 4. Arab horses are as prized as ever, and hawking remains a major sport. But such pastimes do have their modern rivals: a mass following shares the global fascination with football, while track and field athletics have attracted increasing interest. Other outdoor activities remain for the most part the preserve of tourists, who can go camel-trekking, climbing or walking here to their heart's content – as well as yachting in the Mediterranean, windsurfing in the Gulf of Aqaba and diving among the Red Sea's coral reefs.

Horse-breeding and racing are a long-stnading passion in the Middle East, as here in Beirut.

Hunting with birds

Falconry, or hawking, is the art of hunting using birds of prey. Bas-reliefs from ancient Mesopotamia suggest that it emerged as a sport as long ago as the age of the first cities.

Teamwork *An Arab falconer with his partner.*

The long history of falconry is amply attested to by carvings and inscriptions from the ancient world. A bas-relief from the days of Sargon II's Akkadian Empire of the 8th century BC shows a falcon on a man's wrist, its feet held by short leather thongs. A still older carving from Anatolia in Turkey, believed to date from 3500 years ago, appears to show not only the hawk and its master, but also the hare that the raptor has caught. But even these ancient falconers may have been comparative newcomers to the scene. Archaeologists have identified animal remains found at the earliest settlements, dating back to 10 000 BC, as the bones of birds of prey. Speculation continues as to whether they were killed for food, or offered in sacrifice. Keith Dobney, a research fellow in the University of York's Environmental Archaeology Unit, proposes a more daring theory: circumstantial evidence, he suggests, supports the idea that falconry may have been practised as long ago as the end of the last Ice Age, hawks being used to hunt alongside the first domesticated dogs.

A noble art

In the form in which it was taken back to medieval Europe by the returning Crusaders, falconry was very much the sport of kings and their courtiers. A strict code, recorded in the English *Boke of St Albans* (1486), allocated birds of prey to different ranks, ranging from 'an eagle for an emperor' and 'a gyrfalcon for a king' all the way down the social scale to the common 'kestrel for a knave'. It could take months of patient training to persuade a bird caught in the wild to come to the lure, a scrap of leather swung around on a length of cord; only then could its master be confident that it would return to his arm. The expense of training and maintaining these temperamental birds meant that falconry was in many cases an aristocratic sport in the Middle East, too – and in the Gulf States in particular it remains so to this day. The most prized of desert hunters, a fine female saker, may change hands at well over US$300 000. The tradition of subsistence hawking still endures, however, among desert nomads such as the Bedouin, for whom the catch provides a welcome supplement to a monotonous, largely meat-free diet.

But the real purpose of falconry is not the securing of a good meal; still less is it the acquisition of a status symbol. Falconry is about the patient partnership between man and bird, the long struggle to soothe the nerves and gain the trust of what is – and always remains – a wild animal. The unique excitement of hawking is that it allows man a participatory role in a purely natural contest of speed, strength and courage.

At ease *Hooded, and attached by leather jesses to its perch, the falcon waits quietly its chance to hunt.*

Modern falconers *A customised 4 x 4 transports an ancient art into the 21st century. For the most part, though, falconry remains unchanged.*

Frederick's falcons

Holy Roman Emperor Frederick II of Hohenstaufen led a Crusade in 1228-9 and had himself crowned King of Jerusalem. Given the name *Stupor mundi* (The Wonder of the World) by an admiring age, he was an enlightened ruler, tolerant towards Jews and Muslims and liberal in his attitude to his own people. He brought back many birds, with their trainers, from the Middle East, and spent 30 years writing his classic *De arte venandi cum avibus* (*The Art of Hunting with Birds*). On one campaign, it is said, he failed to capture an enemy fortress because he abandoned the siege to go hunting with his hawks.

A passion for pigeons

Noah's dove may be the first instance of a bird being used as a messenger in Middle Eastern history, but the tradition continued for thousands of years. Communications are carried by other means now, but pigeons retain their importance as a popular and competitive hobby throughout the region.

Pigeon city *Huge dovecotes produce fertiliser.*

Timur Leng – or Tamerlane, as he is more commonly known – is remembered in the annals of history for his fearful massacres. Few people realise that the 'scourge of God' who chastised the peoples of the Middle East so severely was also a persecutor of pigeons on a massive scale. When he conquered Iraq in 1400, one of the Mongol leader's first acts was to destroy the caliph's beloved birds. But what may seem a cruel and irrational act would have had a similar effect in medieval times as an air strike on a command and communications centre today.

The imperial pigeon post was in fact one of the glories of the Abbasid Empire. A large bureaucracy of pigeon-keepers and clerks administered an elaborate system by which information could be transmitted at astonishing speed across the entire Middle East. Dispatches from the war front; reports on harvests and the docking of ships; government memos for circulation through a civil service with centres in cities from Baghdad to Cairo – all could be carried by the imperial flock. The breeding and training of the tens of thousands of birds was a considerable industry in itself.

Game birds

The carrier pigeon is at least as old as the Book of Genesis, in which the dove is sent out by Noah to look for landfall for his Ark at the end of the deluge. The dove brought back its message in the form of an olive twig, suggesting that dry land was at last emerging above the waves. The origins of the pigeon post must be almost as ancient as the Bible story, and it remained in use well into modern

Messengers of love

Pigeons were traditionally used in the Middle East to carry amorous messages. These were conventionally unsigned, but the sender was identified by a perfume dabbed on the letter. Soot was smeared on the pigeon's plumage when it carried bad tidings – so bad news could be seen coming a long way off!

Releasing the pigeons *Pigeon fanciers in Damascus pit their birds against one another in ruthless competition.*

Divine messengers *White doves flock in the esplanade of the mosque at Mazar i-Sharif, Afghanistan.*

times. In 1815 the banker Mayer Rothschild managed to double his fortune thanks to advance news of the outcome of the Battle of Waterloo brought by this method.

Ever since pigeon post was superseded by other means of communication, pigeons have been kept for their meat, and for sentiment. But, fond as Middle Eastern pigeon fanciers may be of their birds, there is a distinct competitive edge to their affections. At dusk in the old towns of Damascus and Beirut and other cities of Lebanon and Syria, the air resounds with the noise of thousands of wings. The sky is darkened by flocks of wheeling, banking birds, which circle above their watching owners on every rooftop. Every loft has been opened for the evening's exercise; they will not be closed until the wanderers have returned – or until it is clear that they have been hijacked by another fancier. For each enthusiast hopes his pigeons will disrupt his neighbours' flights, and, above all, that they will pair off and bring home valuable pedigree birds from which to breed. The owners can be seen comparing the previous evening's tallies each afternoon in the souk.

The world's finest horses

When Abraham and his son Ishmael completed their work on Mecca's Kaaba shrine, Allah bade the boy climb a nearby mountain and call for his reward. He had scarcely opened his mouth when all the wild horses assembled on the plain beneath him, enrolled in the service of his Arab descendants by divine command.

Cup of gold *The Dubai World Cup is the world's most lucrative horse race.*

Flaring nostrils, pounding hoofs, streaming mane and flowing tail – there can be few more thrilling sights than a galloping pure-bred Arab horse. It is a living alliance of grace and speed, of strength and beauty. The privilege of riding such a creature is given to very few foreigners, but those who have enjoyed the experience would agree with the old Arabian proverb: 'The air of heaven is that which blows between a horse's ears.'

The myth and the history

According to one Middle Eastern tradition, the Arab horse was created from the swift south wind on the orders of Allah. The new animal, Allah ordained, would be able to fly without the use of wings and strike fear into the hearts of the infidel with its neighing. Blessing the beast above all others, Allah tied success and good fortune to its forelock: those who rode it would triumph over their enemies. Many such myths testify to the importance of the horse in the region, but shed little light on its actual origins.

Heaven on horseback *Riding a pure-bred is a memorable experience.*

Perfect lines *The arched neck, short back and high-borne tail are the marks of a pure-bred Arab horse.*

If anyone gained a military edge from possession of the horse, it was the first nomadic raiders who burst in upon the settled areas of the Fertile Crescent. But any status the horse may have had as a 'secret weapon' could hardly have lasted very long, given the rapid diffusion of the animal through much of Eurasia. What we would now call a 'technological gap' did exist for a time – around 1700 BC it helped the Hyksos horsemen of Syria to overwhelm what had seemed to be an impregnable Egyptian Middle Kingdom. To all intents and purposes, though, throughout the documented history of the Middle East, the horse was the property of all.

The pure-bred Arab

Others might have horses, but the Arabs alone had possession of the pure-bred Arab. This unique animal surely did give them an advantage over their awestruck neighbours in North Africa and the Middle East. Helped by the speed and strength of their mounts, Muhammad's followers were able to build a mighty empire in a matter of years. Its qualities were further underlined when, pitted against the mounts of the Crusading knights, it made its Western counterpart look clodhopping and clumsy. Whether the horse or its rider was the key to this success is impossible to say – the Arab's horsemanship was matched by the Mongol's and the Turk's – but all seemed to agree that the Arab horse was something special. It was not simply a matter of strength

Desert cavalcade There are few more stirring sights in the world than a troop of Arab cavalry.

but also just about every other saddle breed has been enhanced by the contribution of Arab ancestors.

Extreme polo

A traditional saying of Central Asia poses the rhetorical question 'When the Tartar is separated from his horse, what can he do but die?' Among the nomads of northern Afghanistan the old ways have persisted into our own age; these men are marked out not just by the old horsemanship but by the old Tartar toughness and ferocity. The spirit that brought the world Attila the Hun and Genghis Khan is alive and well in the *boz-kashi*, a sort of polo played with the headless carcass of a goat or calf. Whips are wielded freely in the rucks and scrums, and it is not unknown for players to be killed. The spectators, also mounted, are themselves in danger if they get caught between a determined set of players and the ring of quicklime that represents the 'goal'. Yet this is a game of great beauty and skill as well as violence – an extraordinary spectacle and a fascinating fragment of ancient tradition.

or stamina – despite a comparatively small stature, the Arab horse has both – courage, intelligence and, above all, gentleness were just as important. The Bedouins wanted their most valuable possessions with them at all times, even sleeping in their tents, so it was essential that these spirited horses should also be tractable.

The Arabs were in no doubt as to their horses' superiority, guarding their genetic purity jealously, almost fanatical in their concern to prevent outside contamination. The illiterate culture of the nomads prevented the keeping of formal studbooks, but records were handed down orally from father to son through many generations. There are five main strains of Arab horse, but all share certain characteristics, notably the wide forehead on which the blessings of Allah are borne. Other hallmarks include a tail carried high with pride, and that unusually short, strong back that results from the horse's spine having one vertebra fewer than other breeds.

Spanish horses bred out of Arabs (taken to Spain by the Moors) were sought-after throughout Western Europe in medieval times. Crusaders in the Holy Land, impressed with the Arab's virtues, took care to bring stallions back with them to enhance their native bloodstock. Not only the thoroughbred racehorse of modern times,

Afghan polo The boz-kashi *game is as exhilarating as it is dangerous.*

Desert queens

If there is anyone who loves horses as passionately as the desert nomad does, it is aristocratic English women. In the 19th century some adventurous women took their love of horses to extremes, going off to live among the tribespeople of the Middle East. A niece of Prime Minister William Pitt the Younger, Lady Hester Stanhope (1776-1839), found British gentility too tame, and in 1810 went off to Lebanon in search of excitement. She found it with the Bedouin, among whom she commanded respect for her pride, her courage and her horsemanship. She finally married a local chieftain. Lady Jane Digby (1807-81) had had affairs with King Ludwig of Bavaria, an Albanian bandit and several other notables before she went out to the Middle East at the age of 50. There she fell in love with and

married a nomad prince who was 20 years her junior. They lived happily together until her death at 74. She, too, was a marvellous horsewoman, often in the saddle for 14 hours at a time through the desert night; she impressed her new compatriots with her skills as a camel rider in particular. The romantic life of Lady Anne Blunt (1837-1917) seems pallid by comparison: she remained happily married to her husband, the writer and orientalist Wilfrid Scawen Blunt, but she too loved the Middle East, and experienced it as a famously intrepid rider through the wildest reaches of Arabia and northern Iraq. Her unique contribution, however, was to establish England's first stud for Arab pure-breds – to which many modern commentators attribute the survival of the breed through the 20th century.

The ship of the desert

Domesticated 5000 years ago in the Arabian Peninsula, the camel still has a capacity to amaze; recent research has revealed just how strange its evolutionary odyssey has been.

Pampered pets In the Gulf States pick-ups are the favoured means of getting about – even transporting the camels that they have replaced. Camels are now painstakingly bred and trained for racing.

The heavily laden camel train plodding slowly through the desert is one of the eternal images of the Middle East. Now largely replaced by the articulated lorry, the camel nevertheless remains an important symbol of an ancient heritage. And despite its surly manner, it is popular with the people, being regarded with the indulgence accorded to a grumpy old relative.

The 'camel' of the cliché is strictly speaking a dromedary; the shorter, stockier, woollier, two-humped bactrian camel is found towards the region's north-eastern edge, in the nomad caravans working the high-altitude route between Afghanistan and China.

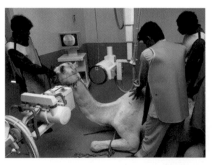

State of the art Dubai's high-tech industry is revealing much that was previously unknown about the camel.

Facts and figures of a freak

For all its apparent freakishness, few creatures are so perfectly adapted to their environment as the camel. It has two separate sets of eyelids and nostrils that can be sealed against the wind-blown desert sand. It can go for a fortnight without drinking at all, then take on a third of its body weight in water in 10 minutes, coping with levels of salt and toxicity that would kill any other mammal. It hardly needs to urinate at all, because its body screens out the toxins, enabling it to keep back almost all the absorbed water to resist dehydration. The camel even retains water vapour when it breathes out: around 60 per cent of exhaled moisture is immediately reclaimed by its open nostrils.

The fat stored in the camel's hump can keep it going over several weeks, though by the end of a long trek the hump may be looking droopy. It can endure a weight loss of 25 per cent in a week without being unduly troubled or suffering any ill effects in the longer term. The camel's resilience extends to changes in temperature, too – essential in an environment in which temperatures can reach 50°C (122°F) or more by noon and then plunge below zero overnight. A metabolic process allows the camel's body temperature to vary by as much as 11 degrees over a single day, taking variations in external temperature in its stride. And as if all these amazing quirks were not enough, the camel has an aptitude for swimming.

Camel racing

What sounds like a stunt for tourists is in fact a serious business in the Arab Middle East: a racing dromedary can fetch up to US$1m. Although not as fast as a racehorse, with a top speed only just nudging 40 mph (65 km/h), it can cruise at 20 mph (32 km/h) for some distance. A big race at Dubai's Nad al Sheba racetrack may have up to 50 runners. For the sake of lightness, the jockeys are generally young boys, but concern about their safety has led to the stricter policing of official events. Dubai now insists on a minimum rider weight of 100 lb (45 kg). Given the sums of money involved, the Bedouin who owns a winner may be set up for life if he can sell it to a watching sheik. The actual prizes are not great, however, nor does much betting take place: without actually forbidding it, the Koran certainly frowns upon gambling. The big players take part for the prestige and honour, and to celebrate their ancient inheritance. The al-Maktoum family of Dubai is said to have a herd of 10000 camels; scientists and vets have been brought from all over the world (many making the transition from the field of horse racing) to help to maintain their welfare and improve their bloodlines for the future.

Traditional wrestling

In Turkey and Iran, folk forms of wrestling have found a new lease of life, not just as spectator sports but as affirmations of ancestral tradition in an age of change.

Duel *Turkish wrestling is both a sporting and a cultural spectacle.*

Some 700 years ago, as the Ottoman Turks consolidated their hold around Byzantium, Suleiman Pasha was camped out with his forces west of the city near Edirne. In breaks between the fighting, his 40-strong bodyguard amused themselves – and their lord – with bouts of wrestling: two brothers, Ali and Selim, were par-

The Persian powerhouse

The name of the Turkish wrestler, *Pehlivan*, comes from the old Persian word for 'hero'. This type of wrestling is Persian in origin and a similar form endures in Iran, where it is known as *zurkhane*, 'house of power', after the designated 'gym' in which it took place. A series of physical exercises in which weightlifting and acrobatics are combined, the activities take place to the rhythm of drums. Some 1300 years ago these routines were performed underground in the secret cellars and far-flung caves of Persia as patriots prepared themselves to offer resistance to Arab invaders.

House of power *The* zurkhane *calls upon qualities both of personal endurance and of national pride.*

ticularly well matched. They tussled for a whole day, without either finding an advantage; all night, and all the next day, the struggle continued. In the end they both died still locked in combat and were buried together beneath a fig tree. When their comrades returned from battle, they found a fountain springing from their grave. In the days and weeks that followed, other bodyguards lost their lives in the thick of the fighting and a spring rose spontaneously for each one who fell. In the end, all had been lost of this heroic company. The place has been known as Kirkpinar ('forty fountains') ever since.

A future in the past

Turkey's resolutely modernist rulers have had to make their peace with the past in recent years; it is, after all, among their country's most priceless assets as a tourist centre. And if foreigners for the most part come to see a country fixed firmly in the 19th century – if not before – the same has turned out to be true for a surprising number of Turks. More than 100 000 people, both visitors and natives, come to Kirkpinar every year for a three-day wrestling tournament that is the focus for a wider festival of Turkish culture. Their bodies slick with olive oil, and dressed in a *kispet* – a pair of tightly fitting leather pants – the wrestlers clap as they advance upon their opponents in a line. With several bouts taking place simultaneously, side by side, and the contestants following strictly ritualised steps, it can seem more like a dance than a combat. But once the pairs have engaged, the determination of the participants can hardly be doubted as they battle back and forth. The fights used to go on for several hours but they are now stopped after 30 minutes.

As in other forms of wrestling, the object of the exercise is to force one's opponent off his balance, sweep him down and then pin his body to the floor for a set period of time. Music, drumming and chanting accompany the action, building suspense as contestants fall by the wayside and the field is steadily narrowed down. The final is a fitting climax, an extraordinary fusion of prize fight and cultural event. The ceremonial may date back centuries, the language of the chants may be irrevocably archaic, but it all helps to complete a thrilling spectacle in the present.

115

Yemeni excursions

Opened up by the peace that has finally come after years of civil conflict, Yemen has been rendered accessible, too, by modern vehicles. In a land gripped by a fever of development and modernisation, the country looks set to lose its status as one of the world's wildest, least-known lands.

The empty quarter *The sands of the Rub al-Khali present no problem for tourists in their off-road vehicles.*

Yemen is a country of heights and inspiring names. San'a, the capital, dominates the Djebel Nougoum (the Mountain of the Stars). The road westwards towards the port of Hodeida winds through an elevated landscape of black basalt and huge fields of *qat*. For thousands of years, the villages have been built on the heights to maximise the available arable land. The steep slopes are chiselled into terraces or rock-cut basins to collect rainwater.

After Djebel Kawkaban (the Mountain of the Two Planets), the road straightens out. Soon Djebel Shahara comes into view, famous as a refuge from the Ottomans. The way becomes impassable, even for off-road vehicles. Travellers have to continue on foot to experience the breathtaking view and cross the dizzying Bridge of Shahara, thrown over the abyss in the 17th century. Here a Yemeni proverb seems to fit: 'Happiness lies at the foot of the clouds.'

A thousand and one sights

The country is a traveller's paradise, accessible but unspoilt, with sublime scenery and a fascinating heritage. Here ancient tribes really do live as they have for centuries. The social rituals are not staged for tourists, but living history; you can buy a native dagger here and know it was not mass-produced in China. The people have not yet been enlisted into the service of a mass tourist industry. Their friendliness is unforced and their hospitality sincere. In a 4 x 4, tourists can strike high into the mountains or drive deep into the empty desert of the Rub al-Khali, the 'deserted quarter'.

But the old city of San'a is already under pressure from modern developers. Neither the ancient streets of the capital nor the vertiginous tracks of Yemen's mountains were built for motor vehicles. And as growing numbers of tourists arrive, the strain on scant water resources will become unbearable. The challenge for Yemen, as for other states in the Middle East, is to reconcile the rival claims of development and heritage.

Hunting the ibex

The famous Wadi Hadramawt runs from west to east across the desert uplands of southern Yemen, a band of green fertility through some of the most unforgiving country in the world. Hemmed in on both sides by mountains, it has something of the atmosphere of a lost world – a feeling that is strengthened by the ruins of several ancient cities. Frescoes dating back 2000 years commemorate what were clearly the sacred rites of the ibex hunt, and the animal's head can be found adorning temple walls. A type of wild goat that is remarkable for the graceful, curving sweep of its horns, the ibex is now regarded as an endangered species. The tribesmen of the Wadi Hadramawt have always hunted the ibex, causing concern to conservationists, who recognise the significance of what is still very clearly a ritual event. In recent years, however, they have been alarmed at the intervention of the tourist industry, which seems to encourage both broadening the participation and upping the kill. Though the traditional ceremonies are still observed, the event is becoming unrecognisable, as sportsmen, largely from within the Arab world, come in increasing numbers to join the hunt. The resulting carnage represents an uncomfortable compromise between reverent sacrament and indiscriminate shooting spree.

High living *Situated at well over 3000 ft (1000 m), many villages in Yemen can be reached only on foot – and even then the trip is hardly one for the faint-hearted.*

Rock bound *In Yemen it can be hard to tell where the rock leaves off and the village begins, a strategy not only for defence, but for saving every patch of fertile land for cultivation.*

Football women For a generation of Iranian women, support for the national football team has been a matter of personal liberation, despite opposition from government conservatives.

Internationals In the Middle East, as elsewhere, boys dream of being football stars. The game is both loved and feared as an instrument of globalisation.

Political football

At once a focus for the fiercest patriotism and the ultimate globalised game, football expresses the hopes – and encapsulates the dilemmas – of Middle Eastern nations.

Every state in the Middle East recognises the importance of football. In the modern world, participation in the sport makes a contribution to the nation's international image. Most Middle Eastern countries have therefore shown no compunction about employing top-quality international coaches for their national teams; the game is growing rapidly in the region as a result. In Turkey, football reigns even in the hallways and streets, without regard to passers-by. Major clubs have signed rights deals with local television stations for sums of money that are astronomical in a country where the average white-collar worker earns less than US$400 a month.

The queen abdicates

The decision of Ghada Shouaa to retire from athletics saddened all in the Arab world when it was announced in 2001. Five years previously the Syrian had returned from the Atlanta Olympics a heroine after taking the gold medal in the heptathlon. Her victory in such a demanding event struck a mighty blow for Arab sporting pride in general, but its significance was especially great for women in what is still for the most part an oppressively patriarchal culture. This was, alas, to be her finest hour: a major injury in 1997 saw her miss two full seasons at what should have been the peak of her career.

Further injuries spoiled the Sydney Olympics for her and she lost her title to Britain's Denise Lewis. But for Arab women her glory would always be assured.

Role model *Ghada Shouaa has been an inspiration to Middle Eastern women.*

Popular goals

The sport's most visible impact, though, has perhaps been in conservative Iran. Football's history as a major sport in Iran is short. The country's league was established in 1960 and the game remains largely an amateur affair. Iran's first major international success came in the 1978 World Cup finals in Argentina, where the team held Scotland to a 1–1 draw. In the years of the Iran–Iraq War a generation of potential players died, but a team emerged to win the Asia Cup in 1990. The high point came in 1998, when at the World Cup finals in Paris an army of Iranians – both male and female – went to cheer their team. Iran's win against the USA caused delirium among the supporters. Since then football has been a true social phenomenon, bringing huge crowds out on to the streets. The many women fans often provide the most vocal and enthusiastic support, removing their headscarves, dancing and singing in open defiance of conservative Islamic values. 'It's the main thing in Iranian society,' said one young fan. 'It's a good excuse for boys and girls to mix, and in a way it's political, because it's a demand for social change.'

Welcome to hell...

The fatal stabbing of two Leeds supporters in April 2000 after their team's match against Galatasaray in Istanbul highlighted the fearsome reputation of the Turkish fans. Clashes with supporters of rival Fenerbahce had claimed casualties in the past, but there had previously been little violence towards foreign fans. Intimidation is a different matter, though. The Galatasaray fans know their ground can be a terrifying place; placards at the Galatasaray end bid visitors a 'welcome to hell', while the frenzied drumming and chanting can unsettle the most confident opposition.

The Red Sea in all its colours

The Red Sea is a flooded geological fault. It reaches oceanic depths just a short way out, but heat from hydrothermal vents in the floor keeps it warm at every level. Perfect for corals and other marine life, it also attracts increasing numbers of holidaymakers.

Safe playground *Ashore it may be extraordinarily arid, but the Gulf of Aqaba is the perfect haven for water sports. The Red Sea is sheltered on either side here by the mountains of Sinai and Arabia.*

At the height of the great share mania that engulfed London at the end of the 18th century, credulous investors fell over one another in their eagerness to sink their savings in the most unlikely schemes. None could have been more improbable – though it attracted a frenzy of interest – than the company created to drain the Red Sea and recover the treasures of the lost Egyptian army of the Bible. Potential investors would all have been familiar from childhood with the story of how Moses led the Israelites to safety between standing walls of water, while the pursuing forces of the pharaoh were lost beneath the waves behind them. With the new technological confidence of the industrial revolution added to the age-old allure of easy money, the investors' willingness to be deceived is not difficult to understand.

True treasures

Unfortunately for those would-be venture capitalists, no trace of the pharaonic armies has ever been found. The Red Sea, though narrow, is extremely deep. Following the line of an immense geological fault that runs down the Jordan Valley through the Dead Sea, continuing south to form the Great Rift Valley of East Africa, its bed falls steeply away from either shore to depths of almost 10 000 ft (3000 m). The name 'Red Sea' was given to it by the ancient Greeks, apparently as a translation of an earlier Semitic name, and was adopted by the Romans. The reasons for the title remain obscure. Explanations range from the appearance of floating micro-organisms to the colours of the surrounding mountains in the setting sun. The sea certainly has its treasures, though, in the form of one of the most exciting ecosystems in the world and some of the planet's most spectacular coral reefs.

The key to the astonishing biodiversity of the Red Sea is, in the first place, its enormous depth. This allows deep-sea species to flourish close to the shore. Another factor is the hydrothermal vents associated with the geological fault, which release deep-earth heat to maintain a balmy temperature at every level. So it is that gigantic hammerhead sharks share these waters with dolphins and dugong turtles, parrotfish and gorgeous coral groupers. Gliding manta rays, meanwhile, cast their shadows over reefs enamelled with all the sparkling colours of corals, sponges and the most exquisite anemones.

Divers' paradise *Divers come from all over the world to experience for themselves the Red Sea's spectacular coral reefs – still for the most part miraculously intact despite the bustle of shipping back and forth through the Suez Canal.*

Contradictions *Beneath the blue waters of the Red Sea the ocean seems to be afire with the vibrant colours of corals and sponges, sea anemones and a multitude of exotic fishes.*

Diversity in danger

Thanks to the unique conditions of the Red Sea, where rich reefs may begin just yards offshore, many thousands of tourists have been able to enjoy the splendours of its underwater world. But the Red Sea ecosystem is also delicately balanced and very vulnerable. Corals are tiny carnivorous animals that feed on the micro-organisms washed over them by the tides and currents. As generations live and die, their hard external skeletons become encrusted one upon another; in this way, over thousands of years, a coral reef grows. What takes centuries to build up may be damaged in seconds by a souvenir-hunting diver, a carelessly cast anchor – or over a longer period by pollution or excessive dredging. So far there has been relatively little damage, despite development along both coasts and the busy traffic of shipping to and fro between the Gulf of Aden and the Suez Canal. Established only relatively recently, the tourist industry that has sprung up along both Egyptian and Arabian shores has in general been careful to protect its vital heritage. But now there are fears that factors beyond its control may already be undermining the careful work of decades. Naturalists, officials and entrepreneurs are currently watching rising water temperatures with mounting concern; global warming could jeopardise the entire ecosystem of the Red Sea.

The dolphins of Eilat

Having fun in Eilat can seem like hard work. First there are the elaborate rituals of Israeli airport security in a state that has, with some reason, felt itself under siege from terrorism for many years. Then there is the blazing summer heat, which makes even the few steps to an air-conditioned taxi feel like a mini-marathon. After that there are the crowds; Eilat is Israel's one tiny toehold in the Red Sea, so it has to do service as a vital ocean-going port as well as a beach resort for pleasure-seekers, which does not leave a great deal of room for sunbathing. The sea itself is very congested: giant container vessels inch slowly up and down the busy shipping lane that links the Eilat docks with the Indian Ocean, while yachts and dinghies dodge and weave in between. Closer inshore, speedboats buzz and water-skiers

spume, while windsurfers scud across the satin surface of what is just about the perfect paradise for water sports. Swimmers, for their part, have to watch out amid all this traffic: the pressure on every bit of bathing space is almost too great to be enjoyable.

But Eilat's famous Dolphin Reef is different, for while the waves here are just as crowded, the throng is of bottle-nosed dolphins joyfully romping with delighted bathers. Can such intelligent creatures really be said to be 'playing' with human 'friends'? The scientist might be a little sceptical, but it is hard to reach any other conclusion, given how close the dolphins come to their human audience, the freedom with which they frolic and the clicking and singing with which they seem to signal their own enjoyment.

A sort of safari park of the sea, the reef is enclosed at its outer edges, but within these confines the semi-wild dolphins are allowed to come and go as they please. Several were born in the reserve and they are particularly at home with humans. Thanks to the ministrations of a well-organised team of staff geared up to assist non-swimmers and handicapped children, visitors of all kinds can enjoy the experience.

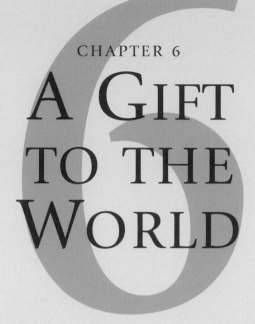

CHAPTER 6

A GIFT TO THE WORLD

Every region of the world has its own heritage, but the Middle East has given the world a unique inheritance. Here it was that the Mesopotamians put in place the foundations for 5000 years of culture, intellectual enquiry and technology. As empires rose and fell, three great world religions evolved: all have left their traces in the region today. Some of these are as tangible as the stones of Petra, Palmyra or Ephesus; others are less concrete but even more influential, such as profound and complex moral systems or ancient languages that have lived on into the modern world. The stunning symmetries of a carpet, the swirling calligraphy of a Koranic verse, the rhythm of a dance, the vault of a dome; uncounted generations of human history still speak to the visitor in signs like these. Nowhere in the world does the past address us with so clear a voice, or resonate so deeply for all humanity.

Once the Nabataean civilisation had its home here at Petra, Jordan; now it is a world heritage site.

Eternal cities

From Palmyra to Persepolis, from Byblos to Babylon, the Middle East abounds in ruined cities. Some are little more than memories, others are awesome in their complexity and scale, but all stir the spirit as the portals of our past.

Rise and fall *Itself now an ancient monument, an Arab citadel dominates the Roman city of Palmyra on the Syrian plain. In the Middle East a succession of civilisations have each left their own distinctive mark.*

The wind and rain of three millennia have washed away the mud-brick majesty that was Babylon; its monuments have been pillaged for building stone. In the 19th century, the overenthusiastic practitioners of the new discipline of archaeology swept down upon the city from the West to complete the depredation that Middle Eastern armies and migrating steppe nomads had begun much earlier. Now Babylon's greatest memorials are in the museums of Berlin, Paris, London and New York. The large stone statue of a lion is the grandest sight available to visitors to the site, but even this is sufficient to spur the imagination: this was once the most glorious city in the world.

Palmyra, Roman no more

'The fabulous golden-ochre colonnades, the Temple of the Sun with its pillared court, the great field of ruins like a garden of broken daffodils…' Palmyra, wrote Rose Macaulay, 'has excited… a more startled ecstasy in beholders than almost any other of the world's wrecked cities.' She was right; the literature on this vast complex of Roman ruins in the Syrian desert resonates with reverence and awe. But the site left another English writer, Vita Sackville-West, in more mischievous mood. 'I like Palmyra,' she

volunteered: 'It is very feminine; it is gay, whimsical, and a little meretricious. It seems to have drunk the desert sun, and to have granted free passage to all the desert winds with a wanton insouciance. Palmyra is a Bedouin girl laughing because she is dressed up as a Roman lady.'

Such levity may seem perverse in the presence of one of the most impressive monuments to Roman architecture, sculpture and city planning. Yet the author does put her finger on a feature common to all the great Graeco-Roman ruins of the Middle East: the fact that they share a distinctive, pre-Roman identity. The Romans were not just great conquerors, but great standardisers. Wherever they went, they built idealised Romes, with the same street plans, temples and amphitheatres. But in the Middle East they seem to have met their cultural match. Long before even the Greeks had set one stone upon another, civilisations had been rising, thriving and falling here. When the Romans

East meets West *The Temple of Hadrian, at Ephesus, Turkey, expresses the emperor's love for his Asian realms.*

were gone, their traces were reabsorbed into the region's culture. We never have the sense here, as we might in a city farther west, that the Roman ruins, however fragmentary, were the foundation for all subsequent historical development. Here, the Romans were no more than another wave of conquerors, building on an older, already rich tradition.

Forever Ephesus

At Ephesus, the Greek-built Temple of Artemis was one of the wonders of the ancient world, and the Roman ruins have endured as a wonder of our own. But even here, the clear lines of the classical colony seem to have a certain oriental feel, the Greek and Latin spoken with an Anatolian accent. Appearances are deceptive, though: if the capital of the province of Asia has an apparently Asiatic character, this is largely because Roman severities collided here with the luxuriant lines of late-Greek Hellenic architecture. Whatever the precise configuration of cultures and styles brought together at Ephesus, the overall effect is quite staggering.

Persepolis, Persia's pride – and its fall

The ancient Persian capital, Persepolis, was constructed by divine command, according to an inscription discovered on a section of its foundation. 'And Ahura Mazda was of such a mind, together with the other gods, that this fortress should be built. And so I built it… secure and beautiful, and adequate.' It seems to have been Emperor Darius I who first heeded the will of the god of wisdom, but he and his successors made sure that the completed capital would reflect gloriously on both the deity and the Achaemenid dynasty. Dug out of the desert at Takht-i Jamshid, 400 miles (640 km) south of the country's modern capital, Tehran, the ancient capital awes the visitor, even in its ruined state. A number of imposing buildings once stood upon an extensive terrace of stone, including the imperial palace and the emperor's *apadana*, or audience hall. Several of this building's

Persian glory The ruins of Persepolis leave no visitor unmoved. This is the apadana, *with (inset) one of its reliefs.*

Babylonian captivity

Built by Nebuchadnezzar II in the 6th century BC, the Ishtar Gate was one of eight ceremonial entrances to Babylon. It was named after the high goddess of the empire's pantheon. The gateway was unearthed during excavations at the end of the 19th century; the structure of the gateway itself had more or less disintegrated, but the blue-glazed bricks with which it had been faced were still intact. Archaeologists were subsequently able to assemble the remains... in the Pergamon Museum of Berlin.

mighty columns still stand, and archaeologists have been able to reconstruct the remains of the astonishing double staircase down which Darius and his heirs must have swept in state with their attendants to receive important envoys and state officials. The grandeur of the imperial court can be surmised from the scale of the remains, but hints are also offered by some of the stone reliefs discovered round the hall. Depicting various sacred ceremonies, they confirm the staggering pomp of a place that considered itself the world's most powerful city.

In the event, though undoubtedly as beautiful as its builder had claimed and a marvel of the age in which he built it, Persepolis was to remain secure for only some 250 years. Alexander the Great sacked and burnt the city after his defeat of Darius III in 330 BC. He used 20 000 mules and 5000 camels to take away his plunder, according to the Greek historian Plutarch. At least Persepolis could

Empire rebuilders

The men who rediscovered ancient Assyria in the mid 19th century were as much adventurers as archaeologists, but they were patriots and imperialists first and foremost. Both France and Britain had embarked on expansionist programmes of conquest at the time, and the race between French diplomat Paulo Emilio Botta and Englishman Austen Henry Layard to find the secrets of one of the world's most ancient empires was a contest to decide which of two modern states could claim Assyria's role as seat of civilisation. It was Layard who won in the end, as French diplomacy met with several setbacks and Botta lost his support.

claim to have exacted a revenge of sorts; Alexander fell ill and died here on his homeward journey. There was little cause for Persian satisfaction, however, because the Macedonian conqueror had left the city gutted, the burnt-out palace subsiding into its own ashes. It remained undisturbed until the 17th century, when its site was identified by European antiquarians; serious excavations were not undertaken until the middle of the 20th century. The work is still going on, but enough has already been uncovered to give the visitor a real sense of the splendour of ancient Persia.

Dramatic entrance
The approach to Petra is made through a narrow natural fissure known as the Siq (above). On emerging, the visitor is confronted with the awesome sight of the city carved from rock.

Petra, a city in stone

Of all the magnificent monuments in the Middle East, there can be no doubt that for sheer visual impact, the most striking are those in the south Jordanian desert at the city of Petra. Here the classical columns and porticoes have been carved straight out of the living stone, the strata lending a natural feel to the architecture. The prevailing idiom is Graeco-Roman, as in many respects is the layout of the city, but Petra (the name itself is Greek for 'stone') was established by the Nabataeans, a seminomadic tribe of traders who seem to have been indigenous to Jordan.

The Nabataeans built up their wealth by controlling the traffic in incense and myrrh (the aromatic resin of the Arabian myrtle) up from Arabia via the Red Sea to the eastern Mediterranean. This was a lucrative trade at a time when both were used in religious

Burckhardt the Bedouin

Johann Ludwig Burckhardt was born in 1784 in Lausanne, Switzerland. He might have become a merchant like his father, but hankered after a more adventurous life. He went to London to seek his fortune as an explorer and met the naturalist Sir Joseph Banks, who recruited him into a scheme to follow the old caravan routes across the desert and find the source of the River Niger. Burckhardt's expedition was a fiasco, at least in the sense that he never got near the West African river. He did, however, win quite a consolation prize. Stumbling upon the most remarkable lost city in the middle of the Jordanian desert, he was the first Westerner to see Petra for 600 years.

ceremonies. By the 1st century AD Nabataean traders were moving between 200 and 300 tonnes of incense a year, and had an effective monopoly on the trade in myrrh. They enjoyed a monopoly in several rare minerals, too, including a natural bitumen from the Dead Sea that was widely used in embalming the dead. With the open-minded attitudes – and the contacts – that one might expect in a mercantile society, the Nabataeans created a hybrid culture. The Graeco-Roman element is evident even to the casual visitor – the classical form of the buildings could hardly be clearer – but experts point to the presence of other influences, too. There are significant Egyptian features in their architecture, as well as what seem to be native Nabataean strands that draw upon the common Semitic inheritance of the Jordan Valley.

But no amount of historical background can prepare the visitor for the stunning sight of a city that appears to emerge out of the hillside before one's eyes. There may be other ruins in the region more historically important, but none is quite as spectacular as Petra, nor has any caught the imagination of the world's tourists in quite the same way. The undoubted jewel in Jordan's cultural crown, the city has become the pre-eminent destination for visitors to the country.

City of the Book

Byblos (modern Arabic Jbail) is one of the oldest continuously inhabited towns in the world. It was called Byblos by the Greeks because the Phoenicians made the port a centre for trade in papyrus (*byblos* in Greek) from Egypt to the Aegean. The town has other connections with writing, too. The inscription round the burial casket of King Ahiram, buried here in 1200 BC, is the earliest known example of the Phoenician alphabet – the ancestor of our own.

Persia's genius for ceramics

The Middle Eastern skill with ceramics is shown not just in jars and vases, but in massive Mesopotamian gateways and modern mosques. The art reached its zenith in 17th-century Persia, where it expressed the spiritual, aesthetic and mercantile values of the Safavid shahs.

Abbas I, 'the Great', of the Safavid dynasty, ruled Persia from 1587 to 1629. Safavid defeats at the hands of the Ottomans in the preceding 60 years had gravely weakened Persia's influence, and Abbas embarked on a programme of economic reforms and building projects aimed at projecting Persian culture throughout the Islamic world. He made Isfahan his capital, and was determined to create a mosque there that would provide an image of Paradise on earth. Abbas's mosque, the construction of which began in 1611 and continued until 1637, was not the first of its type – but when it was finished it was unquestionably the most magnificent of its age.

The elegance of its four minarets – or 'candles of stone' – and the soaring height of its dome made visitors quickly forget that its construction had taken over 25 years. Even the vast size of the mosque was hardly noticeable beneath its dazzling interplay of subtle colours and the extraordinary finesse of its decorative detail. Apart from the plinths of marble, every square inch of the royal mosque was covered with a shimmering mosaic of brilliant ceramic tiles.

The ceramic state

Abbas's mosque enabled Persian craftsmen to bring to undreamt-of heights the ceramic arts that Muslims had been perfecting through the previous centuries. No medium better represented the outward-looking artistic atti-

Shimmering façade   The mausoleum in Mazar-i-Sharif, Afghanistan, is a fine monument to the art of ceramics.

tudes of Abbas's reign, drawing as it did both on Western influences and those of Chinese porcelain. The Royal Mosque at Isfahan was the most spectacular of a series of monuments in which the techniques of ceramics were given full rein.

Western ideas of 'mere' ornamentation are challenged by this set of architectural masterworks that match the Sistine Chapel in resourcefulness and ambition. Islamic rules against representation were clearly no restriction to the imagination of these anonymous workers: simple abstract shapes seem to tumble one over another in perpetual motion; hard geometric forms find infinite fluidity; the brittle glaze takes on the warmth and softness of silk.

The awesome scale on which the decorative patterns in these buildings are conceived is matched only by the astounding attention to detail. This attention began with the manufacture of the tiles themselves, made by a double-firing process called *mina'i*, first introduced by the Seljuk Turks in the 12th century but brought to new levels of refinement under Abbas. Pigments were applied in two separate steps: first the stronger, clearer colours; then, after an initial firing of the tiles, more subtle, translucent tones. The technique permitted a much wider and more sophisticated palette than ever before.

Islamic artists have retained their genius for ceramics ever since, developing this and other techniques over the centuries, but the works of Abbas's craftsmen have never been bettered.

Abstract patterns   Flat geometric forms recur in endless repetition; the Islamic aesthetic shuns Western ideals, but can be captivatingly beautiful.

Vision of Paradise   In the Royal Mosque of Isfahan, with the juxtaposition of symmetry, colour and water, the art of ceramics reaches its apotheosis.

Museums, houses of history

In the museums of the Middle East are many of the world's most precious relics – objects and writings that record the turning points of human development. From early cuneiform inscriptions to the artefacts of the Ottoman court, they span the whole of human history.

Noble aim   A Hittite archer looses an arrow in this ancient bas-relief.

The shouts of men in combat, the crash of falling masonry; the cries of women and children – in AD 70 the Citadel of Jerusalem finally proved inadequate to protect the Jewish zealots who had risen up against Roman rule. The building is quieter today: the main disturbance comes from excited children, for the Citadel has been made into a museum of Jerusalem's history. Lights flash as children push buttons; a cartoon chronicle of the city gets a noisy response; Solomon's Temple looms – the Holy of Holies in hologram. Orthodox Jews may object to this modern depiction of the sacred Temple, but the Citadel museum is opening up the history of an ancient city to its youngest citizens.

The shrine of the Book

Those offended by the style of the Citadel's display may be better off crossing town to the Israel Museum, where an incongruously ultramodern complex houses exhibitions organised along more traditional lines. The entrance is through the Billy Rose Sculpture Garden, with its collection of challenging modern artworks, but inside the museum itself the visitor can wander through gallery after gallery of contemplation and quiet.

The archaeological collection includes objects of staggering antiquity: a female figurine found in the Golan Heights and dated to around 300 000 BC is the world's oldest artwork. Youthful by comparison, yet still for most visitors the highlight of the exhibition, are the scriptures to be seen in the 'Shrine of the Book'. Here, under carefully controlled conditions, is the Book of Isaiah, believed to be the oldest

Old and new   In Jerusalem's Israel Museum ancient manuscripts contrast with contemporary architecture.

Biblical manuscript in existence. Here also are ancient copies of the Psalms, the Law and other books. The same gallery also displays the famous Dead Sea Scrolls, believed to have been written around the time of Christ by the Jewish religious sect known as the Essenes. The scrolls were found by Bedouin shepherds in the 1940s and 1950s in a cluster of caves at Qumran in the Jordan Valley.

From the alphabet to Avicenna

For ancient writings, however, the National Archaeological Museum of Damascus has an even better collection, with several tablets originating in the court of Ugarit in the 14th century BC. This northern coastal city-state was the centre of a trading network that stretched from Crete through Anatolia to Mesopotamia. It is from the last, perhaps, that the Ugarit civilisation ultimately derived a written script which, though often loosely referred to as 'cuneiform', was in fact an exciting new development. Where the Sumerians, like the Egyptians, had used cuneiform characters as hieroglyphs (simple pictures) for whole words, this script seems to use them to represent sounds – in other words, the Ugarites had developed the first alphabet.

Even without the Ugarit Tablets, the museum would still be a remarkable place. Its Manuscript Room includes priceless writings by Ibn Sina (980-1037). 'Avicenna', as he is often known, was one of the fathers of European thought: his (Arabic) writings were a conduit for the wisdom of Aristotle, lost in the Europe of the Dark Ages. In addition, his medical works – which drew not only on classical but also on Asian scholarship – laid the foundations for 'Western' medicine.

Treasure house
The National
Archaeological
Museum in
Damascus (left)
is itself one of
the treasures of
the Middle East.

Reverence
An idol from the
Museum of
Anatolian
Civilisations
embodies Atatürk's
determination that
Turks should find a
national heritage
predating both their
Arab-Islamic and
their Greek-
Byzantine past.

Archaeology at work   Traces of the earliest civilisations
are still being deciphered in Turkey's museums.

The people's palace

A recent guidebook to Istanbul suggests setting aside 4 hours for a visit to the Topkapi Palace – but one could wander here for weeks without seeing all of its fabulous treasures. What the visitor can see clearly in an instant, however, is the stupendous scale of the place, the astounding wealth and influence the Ottoman Empire could once command. The seat of the sultans for 400 years, the Topkapi Sarayi was begun around 1461 by Mehmed II and finally abandoned in the mid 19th century when Abdulmecid built the Dolmabahce Palace. Restored by Atatürk in 1924, the palace was redesignated as a museum, a place for all: the symbolic reclamation of a monarchical heritage by a confident young republic. The expense involved was colossal and Atatürk seems to have proceeded with a degree of sensitivity he did not necessarily display in all his cultural policies. The result is a national monument of stunning magnificence and a rich repository of art from every phase of the empire's long and fascinating history.

Built around a series of four courtyards, each more secluded than the last, the Topkapi was home to a monarchy that took its public duties seriously but was protective of its privacy. The first court, the 'Square of Ceremonies', was the point at which the palace came into contact with the outside world; here the janissaries paraded and mustered for their campaigns. Ancillary services were also centred upon this area: the imperial mint was here, and the palace bakery – even a firewood store. A Byzantine church that happened to be here when Mehmed II first walled the area in and started building was absorbed as the palace arsenal. It is now a military museum and concert hall.

The second court was the centre of government. Here were the Divan, or council chamber, and the Inner Treasury (where nowadays arms and armour are displayed). Beyond the Gate of Felicity lay the third court, where an enormous imperial household lived and worked. The Imperial Treasury was also here, but the

court's most crucial building was the one in which their most prized spiritual possessions were installed. In the Apartment of Felicity lay the banner, sword and mantle of Muhammad himself. Captured by Selim I in Cairo in 1517, these were of particular importance in underpinning the sultans' claims to be caliphs of all Islam.

Grouped irregularly around the fourth court are pavilions where the household could relax in luxury and splendour. Around 400 women lived in the Harem, set away beyond the buildings of the second courtyard. Here, in addition to the spartan cells of the eunuchs, are rooms of the utmost opulence – the salons and chambers where the Sultan entertained his favourite wives and concubines. Throughout the Topkapi, indeed, the sumptuousness of the grand design is counterpointed by perfection in its details. Thus, in the 18th-century dining-room of Ahmed III, the overwhelming impression initially is of an explosion of gold leaf; only slowly do the exquisitely painted flowers and geometric patterns find resolution. The glory of the palace museum resides not only in the magnitude and magnificence of the complex as a whole, but also in the accumulated care that has been lavished upon its component parts. Every jewelled diadem or dagger; every embroidered footstool; every medieval map is a masterpiece. Taken in its totality, the Topkapi is breathtaking monument to the Ottoman world.

National monument   Istanbul's Topkapi Palace ranks among the most
magnificent museums in the world, but its appeal lies as much in the variety
and subtlety of its detail as in its grandeur.

A crossroads of creeds

Three great world religions have their origins in the Middle East, and all have left their architectural mark upon the region. Those synagogues, mosques and churches that survive are a haunting record of humanity's highest aspirations and most bitter conflicts.

Dome of the Rock *A dome now soars skyward at the spot from which Muhammad traditionally took flight.*

In AD 532, the Roman emperor Justinian assembled in his capital Byzantium the choicest bits of masonry and ceramic ornamentation from all the various monuments of his extensive empire. We might regard such pillage as an act of vandalism, but Justinian had an important ideological aim: the new church of Haghia Sophia into which he planned to incorporate these fragments was intended to reassert Byzantine power over an increasingly fractious realm. The Nika Revolt of January that year had come close to costing Justinian his throne, and it had taken a massacre of 30 000 rebels to put it down. Before their bloody suppression, the mob had burned down the second Haghia Sophia church, inaugurated by Theodosius II in 415 after the first (which dated from 360) was destroyed in similar disturbances. The reconstruction of Byzantium's greatest church was, accordingly, a defiant signal of 'business as usual' on Justinian's part, the sanctioned looting that began an assertion of his power. We may disapprove of the plundering of pagan sites as far afield as Ephesus and Athens, Delphi and Egypt, but few would dispute the stupendous glory of the monument that Justinian assembled out of all these odds and ends.

Holy Sepulchre *A church (right) now stands upon the tomb in Jerusalem in which Christ is reputed to have been buried.*

A composite faith

Justinian's recycling programme can be seen as being very much in the Middle Eastern spirit, a solid representation of an uninhibited traffic in ideas and influences between the region's different cultural communities. Just as Judaism drew on earlier paganism, and Christianity clearly derived its underlying tenets from the Jewish faith, Muhammad took both for the foundations of Islam. This process took concrete form when the Ottoman conquerors converted Haghia Sophia into a mosque in 1453 (in 1932 Atatürk made it a museum, a shrine of secular humanism).

The Umayyad Mosque in Damascus has had an even longer spiritual odyssey. The Aramaic temple here was co-opted by the Romans for the worship of Jupiter and Venus. The site then did service as a church before the great mosque was built in the 8th century. It still has significance for Christians, despite being the fourth most sacred site in the Muslim world; the head of John the

---

Lost generations

In his later years the Russian-born painter Marc Chagall turned to the medium of stained glass. Some of his finest work is at the synagogue of Jerusalem's Hadassah-Hebrew University Medical Centre, in 12 windows – one for each of the Biblical Tribes of Israel. 'My modest gift to the Jewish people,' the artist called his masterpieces of modern art. 'All the time I was working, I felt my father and my mother were looking over my shoulder, and behind them were Jews, millions of other vanished Jews of yesterday and a thousand years ago.'

The Umayyad Mosque *Aramaic and Roman deities were worshipped for centuries on this site in Damascus before a Byzantine church was built. Some of that church's features have survived in the Umayyad Mosque seen here.*

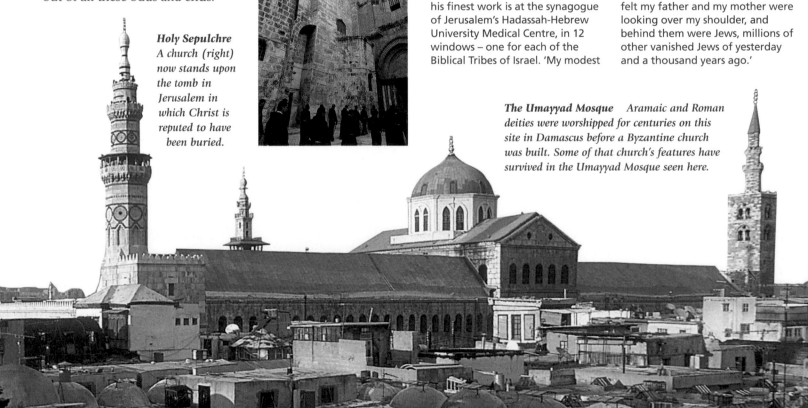

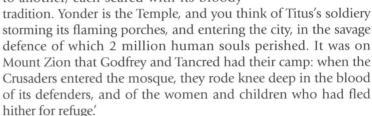

Conversion   *Saint Sophia's cathedral, Nicosia (left), was converted into a mosque by the Ottoman emperor Selim II in the 16th century.*

The divine dome   *Beloved of both Christian and Muslim traditions, the dome gives earthly form to the heavenly qualities of airiness and light. This one tops the Royal Mosque at Isfahan, Iran.*

'There is not a spot at which you look but some violent deed has been done there,' he observed. 'You go from one gloomy place to another, each seared with its bloody tradition. Yonder is the Temple, and you think of Titus's soldiery storming its flaming porches, and entering the city, in the savage defence of which 2 million human souls perished. It was on Mount Zion that Godfrey and Tancred had their camp: when the Crusaders entered the mosque, they rode knee deep in the blood of its defenders, and of the women and children who had fled hither for refuge.'

Thackeray may have grossly exaggerated the number of victims of the Roman assault that smashed the Temple in AD 70, but his account of the gory triumph of the First Crusade in 1099 is a lot less overblown than it might appear. The soldiers of Christ are believed to have slaughtered well over 30 000 people, both Saracens and Jews, as they swept through the captured city – including 10 000 who had climbed the roof of the Al-Aqsa Mosque to escape.

But Jerusalem owes its unique identity to such agonies as these. A lot of glass and stone had to be broken up for its marvellous architectural mosaic to be put together. For Constantine's Basilica of the Holy Sepulchre to be built in the 4th century, a 200-year-old Roman Temple of Venus had first to be demolished – and Golgotha, 'the place of the skull', may well have had a religious significance locally long before the death of Christ. Even the Holy Sepulchre is something of a hotchpotch, an entire medieval church having been grafted on to the existing complex by the victorious Crusaders, with further accretions added by later generations of pious pilgrims.

Uniformity of style is not one of the aesthetic virtues one should seek in a place of worship in the Middle East. This is a part of the world in which the different cultural influences have flowed thick and fast and in which creativity has often been built upon violent foundations. Even a purely Christian monument like the Holy Sepulchre has a strong element of hybridity about it, for just as they have been compelled to share their Holy City with Jews and Muslims, Christians of different types have had to share this most sacred shrine with each other. The results have undoubtedly at times been less than seemly, with a long-standing conflict between Roman Catholic and Orthodox Churches running throughout the early modern period, to be exploited gleefully by Jerusalem's Ottoman rulers. Even today, there is friction between the Christian communities here. But the tensions and the conflicts have served again to contribute to that extravagant sense of pluralism that is one of the great architectural hallmarks of the Middle East.

Spiral sanctity   *Inspired by the ancient ziggurats, the Great Mosque at Samarra, Iraq, dates from 848-52.*

Baptist is believed to be held in a reliquary here. Discovered by the workmen of Caliph Khaled al-Walid as they set about building the mosque on the church's old foundations, it was preserved faithfully by pious Muslims who, while they may have been enemies of the Christians, were nevertheless 'People of the Book'.

The prize for the longest spiritual pedigree of any place of worship in the region perhaps belongs to the Great Mosque at Samarra in central Iraq, a monument that dates from the 9th century. Around its enormous minaret a giant ramp spirals upwards, clearly recalling those ziggurat pyramids constructed by the ancient Mesopotamians 3000 years before.

Culture shocks

The destruction that built Haghia Sophia is a reminder that cultural 'influence' may often be a violent business. The exchange of artistic and cultural ideas has often been anything but harmonious. No area of endeavour brings different communities into closer contact than that of war, and the architectural history of the Holy Land has been written in blood and suffering.

Visiting Jerusalem in 1844, the English novelist W.M. Thackeray was both inspired and appalled:

A tradition of music and dance

Among the most important aspects of Middle Eastern culture, but at the same time the least immediately accessible to outsiders, music and dance derive from a long and highly sophisticated tradition.

Labour of love *The lute, central to musical ensembles in the Islamic world, is still made by hand.*

The American writer Bill Bryson likened popular Turkish music to 'a man having a vasectomy without anaesthetic to the sound of frantic sitar-playing'. Middle Eastern music sounds discordant to Westerners because polyphonic harmony, a key element in our music, is rare in that of the Middle East. Instead, complex and subtle refinement of a single melodic line is the aim, using wide rhythmic variety and an extensive range of microtones unrecognised in traditional European music.

What outsiders see as primitivism is simply their own lack of familiarity; music is one of the Islamic world's most sophisticated and highly theorised forms of art. As in other aspects of Muslim culture, the word of Allah is deemed pre-eminent, and for a long time musical instruments were reserved for providing accompaniments to Koranic verses. More dogmatic interpreters of the scripture continue to insist on the sinfulness of anything but strictly religious music, but more secular strands developed at the courts of the Umayyads in Damascus before being taken further by the Abbassid

rulers in Baghdad. Ancestral Arabic traditions were by now being supplemented by influences from Syria, Mesopotamia, Byzantium and Persia. Music grew both in richness and in complexity. Those same scholars who translated Aristotle, Plato and Pythagoras into Arabic were finding ancient Greek music treatises a source of enduring fascination; the theories they imported then have remained influential to this day.

East meets West

By the time Abul-Faraj al-Isfahani wrote his *Kitab al-aghani* (*Book of Songs*) towards the middle of the 10th century, music was already one of the great loves of the Islamic world. Western influences were welcomed, coming first through Muslim Spain, then with the Crusades of the 11th to 13th centuries. Influences came from the East as well, brought from Central Asia by successive waves of nomadic invaders and established in particular by the rulers of the Ottoman Empire, at whose splendid courts a wide range of music flourished. The military bands of the sultan's janissaries were famous, with their *kös* (copper kettledrums) and oboe-like *shawms*; their sound was celebrated by Mozart in his *Rondo à la Turque*.

Many other Western composers felt the attraction of an Orient that was being opened up by European travel writers through the 19th century. Nikolai Rimsky-Korsakov's orchestral suite *Sheherazade* (1888) shimmered with the exquisite exoticism of the *Arabian Nights*. Five years later, Maurice Ravel wrote a song cycle on the same theme.

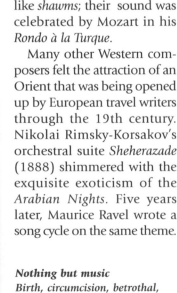

Nothing but music
Birth, circumcision, betrothal, marriage... any occasion will do for a musical celebration. When live music is not available, there is always the radio or stereo; many Middle Easterners like to surround themselves with music throughout the day.

Middle Eastern instruments

The *oud*, (the word literally means 'wood'), the short-necked, fretless Arabic ancestor of the European lute, still plays a central part in the music of the Middle East. Its four or five double strings are strummed with a plectrum, and its pear-shaped body provides the perfect chamber for resonation. A Turkish variant, the *saz*, has adjustable frets to guide the player's fingers. Iranian in origin, the *tanbura* is a long-necked, four-stringed lute. Today it is most often found in Turkey, where it is known as the *tanbur*; a three-stringed form, called the *buzuq*, is used in the classical music of Syria. A relation of the European psaltery or zither, the *qanun* can best be described as a sort of laptop harp, its strings resonating over a shallow wooden box. The Iranian *santur* is similar, although the manner of performance is completely different, the strings not being plucked but struck with little hammers like a Western dulcimer. A fretless, three-stringed lute, the *kemence* is bowed like the violin, which is increasingly shouldering it aside in Middle Eastern music. Although still played in Turkey, it would appear to be living on borrowed time: the Western fiddle has adapted remarkably well to the region's repertoire. The most popular wind instruments are the *nay*, a type of flute, and various relations of the Western oboe, such as the *zurna*. The raucous *mismar*, a sort of double-barrelled clarinet, is much used for festive revelry, with plenty of accompanying din from the *tabla* drum and *daff* tambourine.

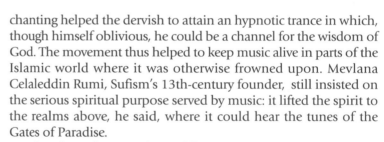

Divine dance *The loss of self-consciousness in the whirling ecstasy of the dervish dance is, say the followers of Rumi, the way to heavenly wisdom.*

Folk festival *A musician performs at the Babylon Festival, Iraq (left).*

Both these works are significant achievements of Western music, but neither has much to do with real Middle Eastern music. As time went on, though, European composers began to engage more seriously with Eastern traditions for their own sake. The German Paul Hindemith and Hungary's Béla Bartók both attended the Congress of Arab Music held in Cairo in 1932. For modernist musicians feeling increasingly restricted by Western tradition, the Arabic alternative exercised an appeal that went far beyond mere exoticism.

The dervish and the dance

Like the tribal shamans still found among remote peoples from Siberia to the Amazon, the whirling dervish of the Sufis makes his own body the medium of communication between heaven and earth. For any mystic, true wisdom is found through complete detachment from all that is worldly. The dervish finds this in the ecstatic trance that steals over his swiftly spinning body. The repetitive, rhythmic music and

Pop culture *Young people like these in Istanbul and their counterparts from Ankara to Tel Aviv are often more interested in Western popular music than their own traditions.*

chanting helped the dervish to attain an hypnotic trance in which, though himself oblivious, he could be a channel for the wisdom of God. The movement thus helped to keep music alive in parts of the Islamic world where it was otherwise frowned upon. Mevlana Celaleddin Rumi, Sufism's 13th-century founder, still insisted on the serious spiritual purpose served by music: it lifted the spirit to the realms above, he said, where it could hear the tunes of the Gates of Paradise.

Other dance forms in the Middle East are anything but religious in origin. *Rakkase* or belly-dancing was developed in the Turkish harem and was purely for entertainment. It is often performed as part of a serious programme of music, in which virtuosi of the *oud* (fretless lute), *nay* (flute), *qanun* (zither) or violin provide accompaniment alone or in combination. Musicians and dancer extemporise freely, with rhythmic breaks on the *tabla* (Arab drum) between melodic sections.

Folk traditions persist too, strongest among those least touched by modernisation: the Bedouin, for example, or the Afghan nomads. In Yemen, Oman and other countries, dancing tribesmen still perform what were once rites of fertility or war; there are dances, too, for social events of every conceivable description. Dance is seen as a fitting way to give thanks to Allah – and to have fun.

Escape into a world of words

Poetry has been one of the passions of the Middle East ever since the time of Gilgamesh. The world of the imagination opened up by literature has been especially prized in modern times in a region where political freedoms could not be taken for granted.

For generations of English readers, the Middle East meant Omar Khayyam (*c.*1050-1123), as revealed in the translations of Edward Fitzgerald.

> Think, in this batter'd Caravanserai
> Whose Portals are alternate Night and Day,
> How Sultan after Sultan with his Pomp
> Abode his destined Hour, and went his way...
>
> Ah, my Beloved, fill the Cup that clears
> Today of past Regrets and Future Fears:
> *Tomorrow!* – Why, Tomorrow I may be
> Myself with Yesterday's Sev'n thousand years.

Fitzgerald (1809-83) was a deskbound scholar who had hardly fared any farther east than his native Suffolk. But through his work an 11th-century Persian poet seemed to speak directly to another age. Today's scholars may cavil at the wayward freedom of Fitzgerald's translations, but what better escape could any reader have found from the restrictions and routines of a buttoned-up Victorian Britain? A great English poem – however dubious its relation to the Persian – Fitzgerald's *Rubaiyat* has largely been forgotten now, but its legacy lives on in our continuing sense of the Middle East as an intrinsically poetic place, home of a lyrical mysticism we feel is unavailable to us.

The golden age

That quality can certainly be found in the work of Omar Khayyam and other great Persian poets of the medieval period, such as Nizami (d.1209) and Jalal al-Din Rumi (d.1273). However, romantic fatalism was only one aspect of a multifaceted poetic tradition; one of the most important of these poetic mystics, Saadi (d.1292) is remarkable, too, for his wit and humour. Read in its wider cultural context, the full sophistication of Omar Khayyam's writing may be clearly seen. Like all the Persian poets, he was the beneficiary of a long literary tradition established in earlier centuries by the Arabs.

A nomadic race of warriors, the first followers of Muhammad passed their heroic epics from generation to generation through the oral tradition. As conquerors, however, they were able to settle down and enjoy the finer things of life. In Umayyad Damascus the artistic explosion that Islam had triggered found literary form. And it was not all religious; in the writings of al-Farazdaq (d.728) and Jarir (d.728) there were stinging satires, tender love lyrics and

Reading matters   Pioneers in paper-making, Middle Easterners were ahead of the West when it came to widespread reading. Even now, literature is discussed with an eagerness and intensity reserved in most of the world for football.

Public figure   Syrian-born 'Adonis' is one of the Middle East's most celebrated contemporary poets.

haunting elegies. Baghdad took up the challenge when, under the Abbassids, it became the imperial capital. Poets such as Bashshar ibn Burd (d.*c.*784) and Abu Nuwas (d.*c.*813) wrote works of considerable erotic power. Even wine was not banned from the poet's bill of fare – all these early Islamic writers wrote enthusiastic celebrations of its intoxicating joys.

In its heyday from the 16th to 18th centuries, the Ottoman court did much to revitalise verse in Arabic, poets such as Baqi (1526-1600), Khayali (d.1556) and Nadim (d.1730) taking old forms to unprecedented levels of sophistication and ornate extravagance.

Rebel writer Although of Kurdish descent, Yasar Kemal has consistently celebrated the history and culture of Turkey – yet he was still tried in 1995 for describing the Kurdish separatists as 'guerrillas' instead of 'terrorists'.

The women poets

Born around AD 575 into the influential Sharid clan of central Arabia, Tumadir bint 'Amr was a leading poet of the pre-Islamic period, or *Jahiliyya*. Khansa, as she was known, took on the task of chronicling and mourning her menfolk who were killed in battle – it seems likely that this was a well-established role among Arab women in those times. The work of Laila Akhyaliyya, who wrote a generation later in Umayyad times, is similarly elegiac in tone, although she seems to have ranged more widely in her subject matter. Rabi'a al-'Adawiyya (d.801), who lived in Abbassid Basra, was one of the first great Sufi poets. A freed slave, she lived ascetically alone and wrote with passionate beauty of her love of Allah. Conscious of such precedents, the generation of women poets presently writing in the Islamic world have always insisted that they represent a continuity rather than a departure. Even so, the work of women poets such as Saudi Arabia's Fawziyya Abu-Khalid and Syria's 'Aisha Arnaout can be seen as adding a new and more outspoken edge to a long-standing tradition that has been comparatively discreet until now.

A feast for the senses
Designed to be read aloud, and exquisitely illustrated, Saadi's Gulistan *(The Rose Garden) appeals to the eyes and ears simultaneously.*

Through the 19th century, however, the established conventions proved increasingly inadequate to a rapidly modernising Islamic world. In the face of dramatic political and social change, the temptation was to hold more tightly to traditional values, a beleaguered literary community falling back on its own resources.

The sense that the poet should sing not of himself but of his heritage has been heightened in recent decades by the all-consuming problem of the Palestinians and the perceived need for solidarity. Born in 1941, Mahmoud Darwish has been a bard for the Palestinians in their dispossession; Iraqi Saadi Youssef (b.1934) has also been strongly engaged politically. In a recent article, however, the Syrian-born Ali Ahmad Said, or 'Adonis' (b.1930), attacked the assumption that poets should write not for themselves but for their people. The result of such obedient solidarity, he claimed, had been stagnation in poetic sensibility and techniques over several decades. This was a damning and dramatic claim coming from the Arab world's most distinguished contemporary poet (and a man not afraid on occasion to make political interventions of his own). The

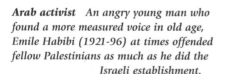

Arab activist   An angry young man who found a more measured voice in old age, Emile Habibi (1921-96) at times offended fellow Palestinians as much as he did the Israeli establishment.

truly creative artist, he insisted, must be an intrepid breaker of tribal taboos and crosser of conventional boundaries, answerable only to himself.

Novel solutions

If the Arab writer may feel oppressed by tradition, the Israeli has the opposite problem, that of working in a linguistic medium that has been in existence for only a hundred years. It is no surprise to find leading Israeli writers working in such relatively modern, Western genres as the novel: Amos Oz (b.1939) and A.B. Yehoshua (b.1936) have been among the most successful in this area.

In its own way a new nation – at least one built on reinvented cultural foundations – modern Turkey has also proved a fertile breeding ground for fiction. In the hands of a master like Orhan Pamuk (b.1952), however, the Turkish novel has (perhaps not unnaturally) looked westward to its European homeland. Pamuk's has been a troubling genius for Turkish officialdom to come to terms with.

The secrets of calligraphy

The divine truth is central to Islamic culture, words a vital medium of artistic expression – and not just for the sounds they produce or the images they suggest, but for the consummate beauty of their calligraphic forms.

The Jews and Christians say 'In the beginning was the Word', but for Muslims the Word is the beginning and the end of everything. Their Prophet deprecated representational art; pictures of earthly beauties could only seduce a believer who needed to have his mind on the high, heavenly wisdom that transcended the physical forms of the world below.

Instead, artists found beauty in the plenitude and order of Allah's creation, exemplified in intricate patterns and symmetries of abstract shapes, in the riotous explosion of lines and colours that – by divine mystery – came together in a poised perfection. Most of all, though, they were transfixed by the beauty of the words of the Koran itself. Many of the first Muslims admitted that they had been won to the faith by the power of its spoken poetry.

As the Islamic empire expanded and nomads put down roots in a settled civilisation, what had been an oral message became predominantly a written one. Its poetic beauty was just as profound, and its hold over believers every bit as firm. The art of calligraphy was the tribute paid to that inspiring scripture. Such writing does not merely transmit religious wisdom; in its own inscribed form it actually embodies all the unity, the beauty and the power of a divinely ordered Universe.

Reading from right to left, the simple 28 letter Arabic alphabet can vary enormously in its calligraphic presentation. Symbols can be large or small, curved or angular, tightly packed or teased out over a large area. With the traditional reed pen – or *qalam* – a huge range of subtleties can be

Medium and message
Islamic script does not merely communicate: it embodies the wisdom of God's Word.

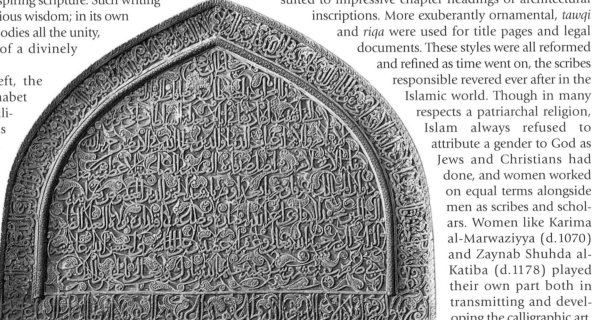

A living art

Modernity called into question the fundamental values of Arabic calligraphy. After Atatürk's Latinisation of the Turkish alphabet, an art that had flourished under the Ottomans was driven underground. In recent decades, the rise of Islamic consciousness has seen a calligraphic renaissance, with Middle Eastern artists increasingly incorporating written forms into painting and other visual arts. In Iraq, in the work of calligraphers such as Hassan Massoudi and Ghani Alani and painters such as Jawad Selim and Shakir Hassan al-Said, two traditions, Eastern and Western, have come together. Meanwhile the paintings of Lebanon's Etel Adnan – and perhaps most of all Morteza Momayez's stunning film posters in Iran – take the fusion to triumphant levels of complexity and richness.

achieved. By the 10th century, six clearly distinguishable scripts (with almost infinite variations) had evolved out of the original *kufic* style. *Naskh* was used for sacred manuscripts, the grander *muhaqqaq* and *rayhan* for large Korans; stately *thuluth* was best suited to impressive chapter headings or architectural inscriptions. More exuberantly ornamental, *tawqi* and *riqa* were used for title pages and legal documents. These styles were all reformed and refined as time went on, the scribes responsible revered ever after in the Islamic world. Though in many respects a patriarchal religion, Islam always refused to attribute a gender to God as Jews and Christians had done, and women worked on equal terms alongside men as scribes and scholars. Women like Karima al-Marwaziyya (d.1070) and Zaynab Shuhda al-Katiba (d.1178) played their own part both in transmitting and developing the calligraphic art.

Painting the future   In recent years the Middle East has taken with enormous enthusiasm to a Western art form. This Tehran student is participating in a discreet Iranian revolution.

A revolution in painting

Painting came to the Middle East as an alien, European art form. But in modern times it has established itself as an important – and authentically native – medium of expression.

One of the most important forms for Western art throughout modern history, painting was for many centuries almost unknown in the Middle East. Islam rejected the representational spirit that was its prime motivation. Only in the religious icons of the region's comparatively small Christian communities was a significant tradition of painting to be found, and even there the similarities with Western work were only superficial. With their stiff and stylised forms, these images showed little concern for 'life' or movement; mystic luminosity was the quality that was really sought after. This concern with the manifestation of divinity through the subtle play of multicoloured light makes the iconographer artistic kin to the Byzantine mosaicist or the Muslim architect with his kaleidoscope of tiles.

Shock wave The work of Chafic Abboud exemplifies a new approach in Lebanese painting.

French Impressionists

The renaissance in European art that began in Florence in the 14th century had little to offer a region in which its motivating principles were simply not recognised. It was not until the latter part of the 19th century that a Western artistic culture, whose centre had by now shifted westward to Paris, began to impinge on a Lebanon falling increasingly under French influence. To begin with the paintings produced here were frankly derivative – Beirut became 'the Paris of the East'. But in the 20th century, Lebanon began to emerge as an artistic centre, creating original works in the Western idiom rather than impersonations of French styles.

Today artists such as Chafic Abboud and Saliba Douaihy stand at the forefront of international art

– they are, indeed, consciously international in their outlook. Others, such as Etel Adnan (who is also a poet) and Maliheh Afnan have harked back to older, indigenous artistic traditions, incorporating Islamic and even ancient Phoenician forms and motifs into their creative work.

Since the 1950s, Baghdad has emerged to rival Beirut as a centre for Middle Eastern art – though many leading artists are now obliged to live in exile. Dia Azzawi is perhaps the most distinguished heir to the tradition established in Iraq by Jawad Selim and Shakir Hassan al-Said, in which Arab antiquity and Western modernity unite to great effect. An art that explores the cultural continuities between ancient Mesopotamia and today's Iraq might have been expected to find favour with Baghdad's Ba'ath regime, but Saddam Hussein has proved as impatient with artistic freedom as with freedom of any other sort.

Calligraphy and colour   Islamic heritage and a Western palette of colour come together in this relief by the Iraqi artist Dia Azzawi.

Behind the cameras

Despite censorship and conflict, some of the world's most exciting films are being made in the Middle East. Together they tell the story of a region in transition.

Eternal dilemma *Amos Gitaï's* Sacred *(1999) dramatises a struggle between love and religious duty that goes to the very heart of Israeli society.*

One day in 1974, a policeman stood on a Tehran street gazing after a beautiful young woman. On some pretext or other she had stopped him every day for a week or more. Suddenly, out of nowhere, he was attacked and stabbed by a teenage assailant. He was forced to fire off a shot to defend himself. The youth, a 17-year-old Islamic agitator, had been hoping to steal the officer's gun to wage his own armed struggle against the shah; instead he took a bullet for his pains. The pair went their separate ways – the youth to the shah's torture chambers, the policeman to hospital. For 20 years the policeman remembered the mysterious young woman. It was only when he showed up to audition for an extra's part in a new film by Iran's most distinguished film-maker Mohsen Makhmalbaf that this poignant little narrative found its resolution. Makhmalbaf turned out to be his former attacker, and the young woman another young radical who had acted as decoy. But the ironies were only just beginning. Getting the policeman to play his own older self as an ageing radical, while he took on the part of the officer in the original attack, Makhmalbaf made the story the theme of his 1994 film *A Moment of Innocence*.

Censorship and creativity

Makhmalbaf's story illustrates the remarkable capacity of Middle Eastern film-makers to turn their region's uncompromising politics into film art. With directors like Abbas Kiarostami and Jafar Panahi as well as Makhmalbaf, Iran is widely held to have one of the world's most important national cinemas in artistic terms. State censorship has if anything been a stimulus to creativity here, as in many ways it has been

in Turkey, too; the country's greatest film-maker, Yilmaz Güney, directed his most important films from prison. The shooting scripts were worked out by their Kurdish originator in his cell, and then realised by his collaborators in the world outside. But Güney escaped to Switzerland in time to work with his assisant Serif Goren on post-production for his most famous film, *Yol* (*The Way*, 1982).

Kippur (2000) by the Israeli Amos Gitaï has been described as *Saving Private Ryan* without the sentimentality – the sort of film that can only be made in a country that has experienced the reality of war. In Palestine, Michel Khleifi's *Wedding in Galilee* (1987) brought the Israeli occupation of the West Bank before the eyes of the world in what was far more than a mere protest movie. Rashid Mashrawi's *Curfew* (1994), the first-ever feature film to be made in occupied Gaza, represents a newer wave of films by younger Palestinian directors, while exciting new work is also emerging in Lebanon and – despite the best efforts of the censors – in Syria.

The heir apparent

Samira Makhmalbaf, the daughter of Mohsen, made the internationally acclaimed *The Apple* in 1998; two years later *Blackboards* won her the prestigious Jury Prize at Cannes at the age of 20. With cinema very much the family business, Samira is not short of expert advice, but as these two bleakly beautiful movies show, she has a genius all her own.

Made in prison *The Turkish public were forbidden to see the films of Yilmaz Güney. Before his death in 1984, it was an offence even to write about works like* Yol, *which won the Palme d'Or in Cannes in 1982.*

On suffrance *The Israeli authorities may be uncomfortable with the growth of Palestinian cinema, but they could not ban Michel Khleifi's* Wedding in Galilee *(1987).*

Drying time   Newly printed silk is left out in the sun.

Ancient industry   A Damascus silk factory (inset).

A taste for textiles

In a cuneiform letter dating from around 2000 BC, an Assyrian woman bids her merchant husband to bring back some wool with him, for 'wool in the city is costly'. The trade in textiles was old even then; archaeologists have found evidence of wool-weaving in Anatolia dating back to 6000 BC. Cotton textiles are almost certainly as ancient in their origins, while in China silk-making probably dates back just as far. Spun from the fine, fibrous cocoon lining of the mulberry silkworm, silk was for many centuries a jealously guarded Chinese monopoly, but it was imported at great expense by Middle Eastern merchants trading along the famous Silk Road of Central Asia. The story goes that in the 6th century the Byzantine emperor Justinian sent a pair of monks to steal several silkworms, which enabled the Middle East to establish an industry of its own. No commodity is more highly prized in the Islamic world than silk, for it is of this fabric, the Koran promises, that the garments of the godly will be made in Paradise.

Silk and steel

From finest silks to weapons of war, the Middle East has for centuries excelled in all kinds of crafts. In one city in particular the most skilled artisans can be found: Damascus, craft capital of the region.

Transformation   The craft of marquetry allows simple wooden objects such as boxes to be turned into beautiful treasures.

Damask silk, damascene metalwork – these well-known terms acknowledge the consummate skills of Syrian artisans. They conjure up shimmering fabrics and steel blades filigreed with silver and gold; the richest materials exploited by the highest human ingenuity – and even cunning, for Damascan craftsmanship conceals a certain sleight of hand.

Damascene deception

It was the Prophet who started it all by inveighing against conspicuous consumption. When served a drink in a golden cup, he hurled it in fury at his startled host. 'Do not drink in silver or golden vessels, and do not eat in plates of such metals,' he commanded, 'for such things are for the unbelievers in this worldly life and for us in the Here-after.' Human nature being what it is, his words were taken as a challenge, craftsmen competing with one another to turn the most commonplace materials into treasures by all sorts of artistic alchemy. What need was there of gemstones when a wooden box could be transformed into a jewel by marquetry?

With mother-of-pearl, ivory and hardwoods – and a little skill and imagination – the possibilities were endless. A steel blade subtly etched with silver tracery was a much finer thing than a sword of solid metal, however precious. Beautiful musical instruments could be fashioned from a few scraps of wood: the finest lutes in the world were made by glueing strips together with invisible joints. Glass (made from sand – a humbler raw material is hard to imagine) made by Damascan craftsmen taken back by the Crusaders led to the rise of Venetian glass during the Renaissance.

In textiles, too, simple materials were turned into precious products. Damask weaving exploited the innate properties of plain silk and linen thread. Playing off the warp (the vertical threads held taut in weaving) against the weft (those worked under and over), so that the light caught the fabric differently from different sides, the most subtle of designs were coaxed out of apparently unassuming cloth – another discreet miracle of the Damascan worker's art.

Metalwork   This splendid scabbard conceals a sword made of the toughest Damascus steel.

Carpets, an art for every day

From nomad tents to the palaces of Baghdad and Istanbul – and from there to the plush interiors of the West – the carpets of the Middle East have travelled far in their long history, accommodating changes in fashion and function without losing their stylistic integrity.

The legend woven into the famous Ardabil carpet from 16th-century Persia reads: 'Except for thy heaven there is no refuge for me in this world. Other than here, I have no place to rest my head.' The message is a moving one, evoking as it does not only man's metaphysical destiny as wanderer in the world, but also the more down-to-earth concerns that remain a part of the cultural heritage of the Middle East.

Lowly beginnings

A Byzantine deputation of 917 claimed to have seen 22 000 carpets in the Abbassid palace of Baghdad, and the products of Persia's Safavid court and Turkey's Ottoman Empire were legendary. But carpet-weaving started out as a craft of impoverished nomads, and never entirely left behind this lowly ancestry. Rugs were the ordinary furnishings that went with the nomads wherever they roamed. They were woven from wool gathered from the flocks of sheep and goats that provided their milk and meat. Hung from the walls of the nomad tents, carpets added an extra layer of insulation to keep out the wind on the freezing steppe.

Natural colours Hanks of wool or silk are plunged into vats of vegetable dye, mixed according to ancient – and strictly secret – recipes.

Repair shop Great skill is required in handling antique carpets or kilims.

A continuous thread

In the far north-east of Afghanistan, a fracas breaks out between Turkmen tribesmen in the doorway of a tent, as a visiting group steals a rolled-up carpet. No more than a mock struggle, the incident forms part of the preparatory ritual to a wedding: symbolically, they are stealing the bride from her father's household. In fact she will go with his blessing, and with several rugs and carpets that she has made herself; weaving is the main occupation of unmarried women among the nomads. Techniques, motifs and entire designs are handed down from mother to daughter. Some patterns, such as charms for fertility or good luck, derive from pre-Islamic paganism; others may represent the babbling brooks and luscious gardens of the Koranic Paradise.

Groups of women (often including girls as young as ten) may collaborate on larger carpets. The women work at

Aftercare Once a year, carpets are taken outside to be beaten and aired in the sun before being returned, refreshed, to the house.

Frozen in time

The secrets of making a perfect Persian or Turkish carpet have been handed down from generation to generation, the same tribal traditions maintained over centuries. Because they are made from the finest natural materials – pure wool and silk – and coloured with organic dyes mixed from roots, bark, leaves and even insects, the carpets do not last forever. Although quite resilient, they are perishable and with time will fade and fall apart. Hence the fascination of the Pazyryk rug, dating from the 5th century BC, discovered in 1949 by Russian archaeologists excavating a burial mound high up in the Altai Mountains of central Siberia. An opening made by grave robbers had allowed water to pour into the burial chamber. The rug, wrapped round the chieftain's body, was disregarded by the raiders and became frozen in the resulting flood, its rich red colour and its beautiful patterning preserved in perfect freshness. Deer trot round an inner border, while Persian horsemen parade around an outer one; in both design and technique its resemblance to modern carpets is striking.

around 30 knots a minute, and while their hands are busy there is plenty of chat and laughter.

Lighter, pileless mats or *kilims* are not knotted but woven smooth, using a technique similar to that employed in Western tapestry. For a long time *kilims* were retained for domestic use by Persian and Anatolian nomad families, while the knotted carpets were traded for livestock and household necessities – and, increasingly, for money. But in recent years the exchange value of *kilims* has soared as they have become sought-after artefacts.

Country versus court

Carpets made by the nomads are crude in comparison with the more sophisticated city-produced carpets, but what they lack in refinement they make up for in authenticity. Attempts at industrialisation in the mid 19th century yielded such an inferior product that traditionally produced carpets continued to be valued, with the result that stylistic and technical differences between communities survived to a large extent unaltered. Even today, the carpet connoisseur can pinpoint the provenance of a particular weave, and Western consumers can feel the satisfaction of buying a genuine piece of nomad culture.

Marvellous court carpets were made under all the great Islamic empires. The decorative repertoire of the Ottoman court was awesome; its artisans had an astonishing ability to conjure life and dynamism out of the most formalised designs. In the Ardabil carpet, dragons writhe, lions leap and horses gallop, while fountains play and flowers burst into bloom. It is rare for a carpet produced in a workshop today to match the meticulous construction and inspirational design of those of the old imperial courts, but the specialist skills available in the cities means that greater regularity can be attained than in homemade carpets. And there is real creativity, too; woven to carefully delineated geometric, floral and other conventional patterns, the best of these works combine respect for tradition with imagination, flair and artistic enterprise.

The export trade in 'court' *kilims* has a long history, too. As long ago as the early 17th century, sophisticated tapestry rugs embroidered with silk were being exported to the wealthiest buyers of the European market.

For the most part, though, the *kilim* is valued for the folk connotations that once dictated its low prestige; this is an aspect of their design and production in which urban workshops have found themselves increasingly having to follow the villages' lead. Carpets have even become an object of academic investigation. Their history and signficance are studied at degree level in Turkish and Iranian universities.

Only the best *The finest carpets in Iran are sold in Tehran's Grand Bazaar.*

Long-term employment *Even in a workshop, a large carpet (left) may take many months to make.*

139

MAPS, FACTS AND FIGURES

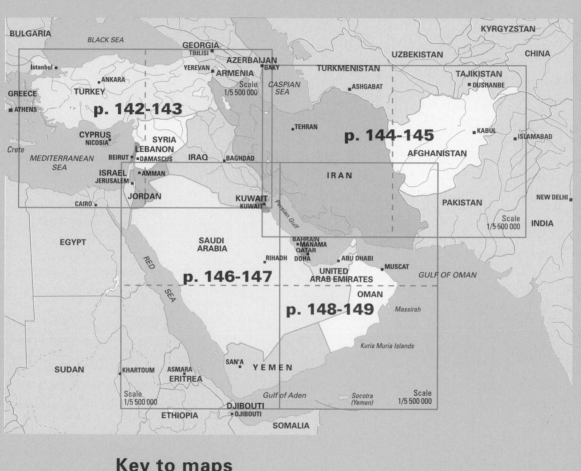

BULGARIA · BLACK SEA · GEORGIA · TBILISI · AZERBAIJAN · KYRGYZSTAN
Istanbul · ANKARA · YEREVAN · BAKY · UZBEKISTAN · CHINA
ARMENIA · TURKMENISTAN · TAJIKISTAN
GREECE · TURKEY · Scale 1/5 500 000 · CASPIAN SEA · ASHGABAT · DUSHANBE
ATHENS · **p. 142-143** · TEHRAN · **p. 144-145** · KABUL · ISLAMABAD
CYPRUS · SYRIA · AFGHANISTAN
Crete · NICOSIA · LEBANON · IRAN
MEDITERRANEAN SEA · BEIRUT · DAMASCUS · IRAQ · BAGHDAD
ISRAEL · AMMAN · PAKISTAN · NEW DELHI
JERUSALEM · KUWAIT · INDIA
JORDAN · KUWAIT · Scale 1/5 500 000
CAIRO · Persian Gulf
EGYPT · SAUDI ARABIA · BAHRAIN · MANAMA · QATAR
RIHADH · DOHA · ABU DHABI · MUSCAT · GULF OF OMAN
p. 146-147 · UNITED ARAB EMIRATES
RED SEA · OMAN
p. 148-149 · Massirah
SUDAN · KHARTOUM · ASMARA · SAN'A · YEMEN · Kuria Muria Islands
ERITREA
Scale 1/5 500 000 · Socotra (Yemen) · Scale 1/5 500 000
ETHIOPIA · DJIBOUTI · Gulf of Aden
DJIBOUTI · SOMALIA

Key to maps

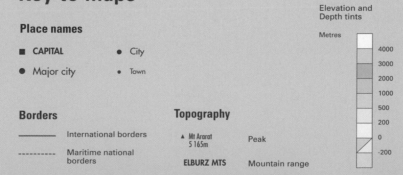

Place names

■ CAPITAL   ● City

● Major city   • Town

Borders

— International borders

---- Maritime national borders

Topography

▲ Mt Ararat 5 165m   Peak

ELBURZ MTS   Mountain range

Elevation and Depth tints

Metres

4000
3000
2000
1000
500
200
0
-200

BULGARIA

Malko Turnovo

Paranésti Svilengrad Edirne (Andrianople) Kirklareli

Drama Xanthi Babaeski Lüleburgaz

Kavala GREECE Komotini Uzunköprü Çorlu

Feres Alexandroúpoli Enez Tekirdag TURKEY

THASSOS Athos Samothraki Gelibolu (Gallipoli) Istanbul Üsküdar Sile Agva

Imroz Eceabat Çanakkale Erdek SEA OF MARMARA Kartal Izmit (Nicomedia)

LIMNOS Moudhros GOKCEADA Dardanelles Biga Bandirma Kapidagi Yarimadasi Karamursel Iznik

BOZCAADA Geyikli Karacabey Gemlik Iznik Gölü

Mithimna Ayvacik Edremit Kus Gölü Bursa Ulubat Gölü Inegol

LESBOS Bergama Balikesir Bozüyük

Mitilini Akhisar Demirci Gediz Eskisehir

AEGEAN SEA Yenifoca Manisa Simav Tavsanli Kütahya

PSARA Chios Cesme Turgutlu Salihli Kula Alasehir Afyon Anatolia

Izmir (Smyrna) Odemis Aksehir Gölü

Torbali Ephesus Egridir Gölü

Neo Karlovasi Samos Aydin Nazilli Sarayköy Isparta

ANDROS Söke Çine Denizli Burdur Aksu

TINOS Kale Boz Dag 2 421 m Seydisehir

CYCLADES Mugla Gok Tepe 2 407 m Köprü

NAXOS Bodrum

AMORGOS KOS Akdag 3 086 m Antalya Manavgat Alanya TAURUS MTS

LEROS Simi Fethiye Gulf of Antalya Gazipasa

DODÉCANESE Rodos Kalkan Kas Finike Yardimci Burnu Kaledıran Anamur Incekum Burnu

TILOS Lindos RHODES

KÁRPATHOS

Iraklion CRETE KASOS

TURKEY

Zonguldak Bartin Cide Inebolu Ince Burun Sinop Salayd

Eregli Azdavay Devrekâni Boyabat Bafra Sinop Körfezi

Karabük Kastamonu Duragan Samsun Terme

Bolu Gerede Çerkes Kargi Vezirköprü Çarsamba

Mudurnu Kizilcahamam Cankiri Alagöz Merzifon Amasya Erbaa

Beypazari ANKARA Çubuk Çorum Alaca Turhal Niks

Kirikkale Yozgat Sorgun Zile Tokat

Kaymaz Polatli Bâla Keskin Yerköy Sival

Sivrihisar Kaman Kirsehir Sofular Bogazliyan Gemerek

Emirdag Yenice Mucur Bünyan Elbi

Cihanbeyli Tersakan Gölü Tuz Gölü Avanos Kayseri Gür

Bolvadin Nevsehir Ürgüp Erciyes Dagi 3 916 m Pinarbasi

Sarayönü Aksaray Yesilhisar Develi

Konya Hasan Dagi 3 253 m Nigde Cappadocia Saimbeyli

Beysehir Gölü Bor Ala Dagi 3 734 m Yahyali

Cumra Karapinar Ulukisla Kahraman Maras

Eregli Karaman Aladag Kozan Kadirli

Tarsus Ceyhan Osmaniye

Ermenek Icel (Mersin) Adana Dörtyol

Silifke Karatas Iskenderun Iskenderun Körfezi Kirikhan

Kizilcali Hatay (Antioch) Alepp (Halat)

Cape Apostolos Andreas Idlib

Rizokarpason Al Ladhiqiyah (Latakia) Ma'arrat an Nu'r

Cape Kormakitis Leonarisson Jablah

Morfou LEFKOSIA (NICOSIA) Baniyas Har

CYPRUS Ammochostos (Famagusta) Tartus

Lefkara Larnaka Tartous

Páfos Lemesos (Limassol) Cape Greko Him

Cape Gata Trâblous (Tripoli) Bcharre 3 088 m Hermel Qaryate

Batroûn Baalbek Nabk

Jbail (Byblos) Lebanon Mts Anti-Lebanon

BEIRUT LEBANON DAMASCUS

Saïda (Sidon) Al Qunaytirah

MEDITERRANEAN SEA Sour Lake Tiberias Golan Heights As Suwe

'Akko Teverya (Tiberias) Dar'a Salkhad

Haifa Nazareth Irbid Jarash

Netanya Al Ghawr Zarqa

Al Bardi Nablus AMMAN Al A

Sidi Barrani Ramallah Jericho Mt Nebo

Bîr el Thalâtha Rashid Dumyat TEL-AVIV-YAFO Rehovot Jerusalem Jordan

Marsa Matruh Alexandria Ashqelon Bethlehem PALESTINE

El-Daba Port Said Gaza Hebron Masada Dead Sea

Bir Fuâd Damanhur El-Mansura Rafah Beersheba Sedom (Sodom) Karak Qatranah

El-Alamein Tanta Romani El-Arish ISRAEL Tafilah

Nasr Shibin El-Kom El-Ballâh Qeziot JORDAN

EGYPT Minûf Suez Canal Negev Shawbak

Nile CAIRO Great Bitter Lake Petra Jafr

El-Giza Suez Ma'an

Sinai El Kuntilla Al Quwayrah

0 50 100 miles

0 100 200 km

142

H I J K L M N

BLACK SEA

GEORGIA

DAGESTAN

ARMENIA

AZERBAIJAN

NAKHICHEVAN

IRAN

IRAQ

SYRIA

PONTUS MTS

ZAGROS MTS

TALIS DAGLARI

Mesopotamia

Kurdistan

Anaklla
Poti
Kutaisi
Samtredia
Khashuri
Gori
Tianeti
Telavi
Kumukh
Derbent
Kobuleti
Borjomi
Mtskheta
TBILISI
Rustavi
Tsnori
Zagatala
Bazar-Dyuzi 4 480 m
Quba
Muqtadir
Batumi
Khulo
Qax
Davaçi
Siyazan
Trabzon (Trebizond)
Rize
Pazar
Artvin
Ardahan
Posof
Stepanavan
Agstafa
Zagatala
Mingäçevir Su Anbari
Babadag 3 632 m
Ordu
Tirebolu
Çildir Gölü
Gyumri
Kars
Tsnori
Gänca
Yevlax
Bärdä
Göyçay
Agsu
Kürdämir
BAKI
Gölkoy
Kackar Dagi 3 937 m
ARMENIA
Sabirabad
Saatli
Älät
Susehri
Köse Dagi 3 577 m
Kelkit
Ispir
Oltu
Narman
Aragats 4 090 m
Sevan
Kamo
YEREVAN
Lake Sevan
Imisli
Askale
Erzurum
Kagizman
Igdir
Artashat
Ararat
Xankandi
Goris
Biläsuvar
Calilabad
Nefiçala
Erzincan
Kemah
Pülümür
Agri
Tutak
Buyuk Agri (Mt Ararat) 5 165 m
Dogubayazit
Maku
Naxçivan
Culfa
Qazangöldag 3 829 m
Qandaran-bashi 2 886 m
Garmi
Masalli
Yardimli
Arapkir
Bingol Daglari 3 649 m
Hinis
Patnos
Tendürük Dagi 3 542 m
NAKHICHEVAN
Markan
Qal'eh Dagh 2 241 m
Iri Dagh 2 841 m
Kuyeh
Lerik
Anbaran
Keban Baraji
Hekimhan
Elazig
Palu
Bingol
Bulanik
Malazgirt
Mus
Memrut Dagi
Lake Van
Ahta Dagi 2 750 m
Ozalp
Khvoy
Marand
Tasuj
Kuhha ye Sabalan 4 810 m
Ardabil
Maden
Hani
Lice
Mus
Tatvan
Van
Qotur
Hirabit-D. 3 550 m
Salmas
Sharafkhaneh
Tabriz
Sarab
Malatya
Ergani
Bitlis
Hosap
Gevas
Sikefti
Sheikh Bazit Dagh 2 781 m
Kuh-e Sahand 3 710 m
Kara D. 3 630 m
Torkaman
Khalkhal
Bandar-e Anzali
Diyarbakir
Batman
Silvan
Sirvan
Catak
Baskale
Sivelan
Yüksekova
Orumiyeh
Lake Urmia
Maragheh
Azaran
Mianeh
Adiyaman
Besni
Siverek
Karacali Dag 1 919 m
Kurtalan
Pervari
Samdi Dag 3 811 m
Oshnoviyeh
Kaju
Kuh-e Qareh Urgan 2 232 m
Rasht
Sanliurfa (Edessa)
Viranşehir
Kiziltepe
Mardin
Midyat
Beytüssebap
Çukurca
Amadiyah
Zab-e Küchek
Mahabad
Bowkan
Kuh-e Qareh Dash 2 925 m
Zanjan
Sürüç
Harran
Ceylanpinar
Nusaybin
Ain Divar
Zakho
Dahuk
Aqrah
Ranya
Sar Dasht
Saqqez
Zarrineh
Chardagh
Soltaniyeh
Sirdan
Mulla Ali
Qazvin
Manbij
Maskanah
Ar Raqqah
Al Hasakah
Tall'Uwaynat
Sinjar
Nineveh
Tall'Afar
Al Mawsil
Arbil
Koi Sanjaq
Sar Dasht
Bijar
Qutiabad
Hesar
Assad
Ash-Shadadah
Nahr al-Khabur
Euphrates
Az Zab al-Kabir
Altin Köprü
Taqtaq
As Sulaymaniyah
Sanandaj
Khosrowabad
Razan
Nowbaran
Dayr az Zawr
Busayrah
Wadi ath-Tharthar
Ashur
Kirkuk
Halabja
Sirván
Paveh
Ravansar
Hamadan
Zareh
Mayadin
Ash Shadadah
As Fachan
Qadir Karam
Maydan
Qeshlaq
Kangavar
As Sukhnah
Tuz Khurmatu
Kifri
Qasr-e-Shirin
Kermanshah (Bakhtaran)
Harsin
Nahavand
Arak
Tadmur (Palmyra)
Salihiyah
Fuhaymi
Al Haditha
Samarra
Al Muqdadiyah
Gilan-e Gharb
Eslamabad-e Gharb
Oshtorinan
Abü Kamal
Balad
Ba'qubah
Ilam
Sarneh
Ransa
Khorramabad
Khaal Baghdadi
Mehran
Amirabad
Shandrukh
Sarab-e Meymeh
Abdanan
Kuh-e-Takht Apan 3 353 m
Ar Rutbah
Ar Ramadi
Al Habbaniyah
BAGHDAD
Tigris
Jassan
Nasrian-e-Pa'in
Zard Küh 4 547 m
Al Iskandariyah
Karbala
Al Kut
Shaykh Sa'd
Al Kumayt
Dezful
Shithathah
Babylon
Al Hillah
Al Hayy
Al-Gharraf
Masjed Soleyman
Al Kufah
An Najaf
Al-Diwaniyah
Ar Rifa'i
Qal'at Salih
Al Amarah
Susangerd
Turayf
Judaidat al Hamir
Ash Shinafiyah
Qaryat al Gharab
Ash Shatrah
An Nasiriyah
Al'Uzay
Hoveyzeh
Ahvaz
Ramhormoz
Judayyidat Ar'ar
As Samit
As Samawah
Euphrates
Ur
Suq ash Shuyukh
Al Qurnah
Karun
Badanah
'Ar'ar
Al'Ashuriyah
Ash Shabakah
Hammam
Al Qusayr
Al Basrah
Shatt al-Arab
Bandar-e Khomeyni
Sakäkah
Al'Uwayqilah
As Salman
Birkat 'Athamin
Al Busayyah
Hawr al Hammar
Abadan
Khosrowabad
Qalib Baqur

Firat
Dicle
Tigris
Euphrates

H I J K L M

143

Afghanistan • Iran

TURKMENISTAN

Karakum Desert

BAKI

Neficala

Alät

CASPIAN SEA

Krasnovodskiy Zaliv

Kuuli-Mayak
Darta
Turkmenbashi
Cheleken
Koturdepe
Nebitdag
Gumdag
Gazandzhyk
Gyzylarbat
Khodzhakala
G.Khasardag 1 616 m
Aydere
Megin
Byuzmeyin
ASHGABAT

Kirpili
Sernyy Zavod
Murzechirla
Bakhardok
Cheshme 2-y
Mary

KOPET DAG

Kharaki
Atrak
Bojnurd
Shirvan
Quchan
Kuh-e-Hazar Masjed 3 146 m
Chanaran
Sarakhs

Chekishlyar
Gorgan
Minudasht
Skah Pasand
Dasht
Sad-Kharv
Sabzevar
Neyshabur
Mashhad
Sang Bast
Tedzhen

Bandar-e Anzali
Rasht
Bandar-e Torkeman
Gorgan
Noyek
Ryabad
Shafi'abad
Mayamey
Emamrud
Khan Bagh
Turan
Eslam Qal'eh
Safid Sagak

Sakht-Sar
Tonkabon
Amol
Babol
Ghaem Shahr
Damghan
Torbat-e-Heydariyeh
Torbat-e Jam

Sirdan
Mulla Ali
Qazvin
Zanjanrü
Hesar
Takht-i-Suleiman 4 819 m
ELBURZ MTS
Damavand 5 604 m
Surkhabid
Sang-e Sar
Riza
Kashmar
Sangan
Nasrabad

Razan
Karaj
Afjeh
Damavand
Semnan
Torud
Khorasan

Zareh
Nowbaran
Zarand
Kilan
Eyyanaki
Abdollahabad
Mo'alleman
Dasht-e Kavir
Tusharik

Qom
Kavir
Karim Khanch
Kumel
Chashmeh ye Palasi
Deh Kavir
Ab Khur
Bejestan
Kuh-e Kalat 2 605 m
Borun

Jannatabad
Eyn or Rashid
Siryan

Arak
Kijh e Aliabad 3 356 m
Kashan
Si Chah
Tabas
Sarab

Mahallat
Gask
Avaz

Khomeyn
Qasami
Robat-e Abgarm
Homand

Aligudarz
Kuh-e-Takht Apan 3 353 m
Khunsar
Daran
Na'in
IRAN
Kuh-e Nay Band 2 992 m
Nay Band
Sib Chah
Sahlabad
Kuh-e-Baran 2 561 m

Zard Küh 4 547 m
Chadegan
Esfahan
Najafabad
Basiran

Masjed Soleyman
Shahr-e Kord
Qomisheh
Kharanaq
Zarigan
Dasht-e Lut
Shah Kuh 2 729 m
Qa'emabad

Shalamzar
Kuh-e Kukalai 4 298 m
Tarqan
Esfandaran
Kuh-e Khowrnag 3 197 m
Darband
Kuh-e Darband 8 000 m
Bala Howz

Dehdez
Manj
Kuh-e Alijuq 3 724 m
Khar Kuh 3 512 m
Yazd
Taft
Bafq
Ravar
Tabasin
Heydarabad
KUH-E PALANG

Ramhormoz
Dishmuk
Shir Kuh 4 074 m
Kulvand
Shürab

Behbehan
Abarqu
Anar
Zarand
Kuhpayeh 3 142 m
Malgazul
'Aliabad

Bandar-e Khomeyni
Kuh-e Dinar 4 432 m
Abadeh
Deh Bid
Bavanat
Rafsanjan
Kerman
Deh-i Gul
Nosratabad
Garagheh
Kuh-e Malek

Deh-Dasht
Kakun
Moryhab
Kuh-e Masahun 3 600 m
Mashiz
Nabid
Keshit
Gorg
Zahed

Basht
Kuh-e Barm Firuz 3 673 m
Kor
Kuh-e Laleh Zar 4 374 m
KUH-E JEBAL BAREZ
Lengbarut
Shuru

Cham-e Zeydun
Arsanjan
Tashk
Sa'adatabad
Rabor
Bam
'Azizabad
Nazil

Baba Kalan
Marv Dasht
Daryacheh-ye Tashk
Baft
Khabr
Rigan

Hesar
Guyom
Zarqan
Persepolis
Sirjan
Baluchistan

Shiraz
Kazerun
Kavar
Neyriz
Tall-e Halal
Gaz Saleh
KUH-E SHAH SAVARAN
Giran Rig 2 548 m
Kuh-e Bazmc 3 489 m

Shapür
Helleh
Daryacheh-ye Bakhtegan
Boluk
Gazbor
Bazman

Borazjan
Abadeh
Fasa
Darab
Bushehr
Firuzabad
Khafr
Kuh-e Furgun 3 279 m
Kuh-e Gireh 5 190 m
Rig Mati

Rishahr
Jahrom
Kul
Kuh-e Gireh
Kahn'Ali

KHARG
Mand
Juyom
KUH-E KHONJ
Shamil

Kangan
Kur Deh
Anveh
Kuh-e Hormoz 2 804 m
Bandar-e Abbas
Jaghin

Manifah
Khidru
Bastak
Minab

Kerman ... *(region labels)*

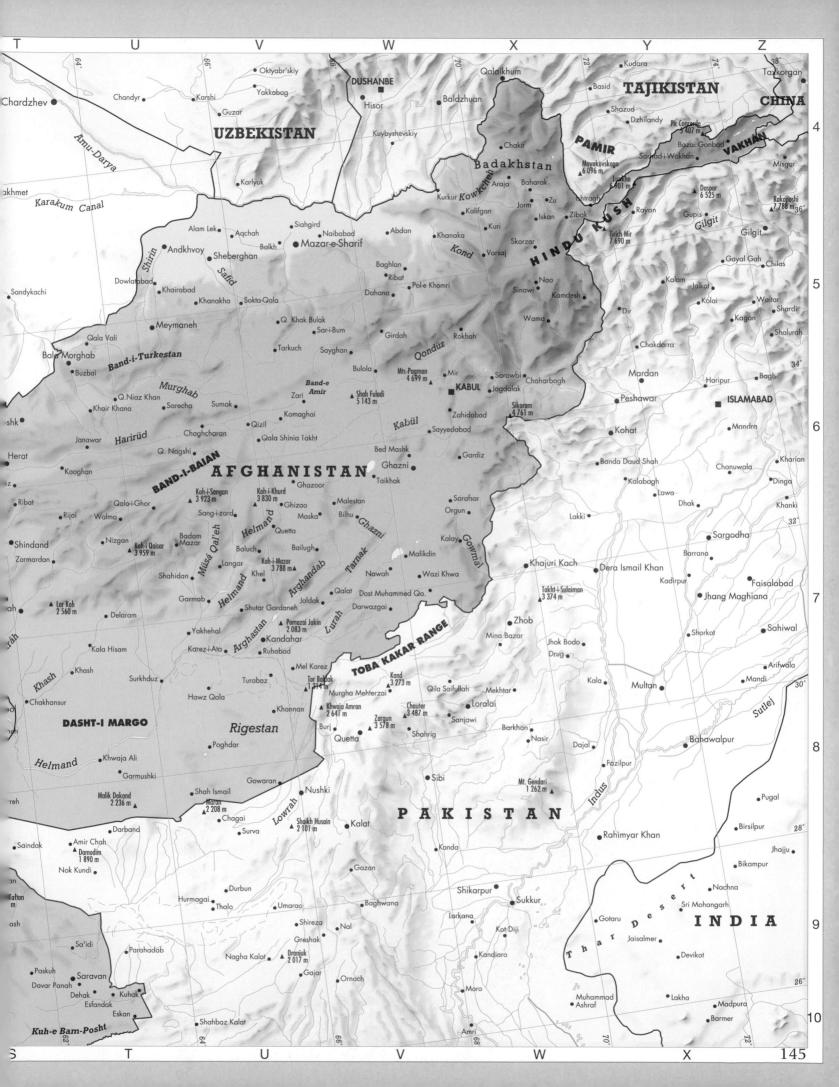

Tropic of Cancer

Dezful
Sarab-e Meymah
Abdanan
Nosrian-Pa'in
Amirabad
Mehran
Shandikh
Jassan

Susangerd
Ahvaz
Hoveyzeh
Karun
Al Amarah
Al Qurnah
Al Basrah
Abadan
Khosrowabad
Shatt al-Arab
Kuwait Bay

KUWAIT CITY
Al Jahrah
Al Fuhayhil
Al Fuhayhil

KUWAIT

As Sahaf
Mulayjah
Hanidh
Qaryat as Sufla
Ash Shumlul

Ad Dahna

RIYADH
(Ar Riyad)

Al Jufayr

Al Amarah
Al Kumayt
Al'Uzay
Shaykh Sa'd
Al Hayy
Qal'at Salih
Ash Shatrah
An Nasiriyah
Hawr al Hammar

As Summan

Al Artawiyah

Al Kut
Al-Gharraf
Ar Rifa'i
Ur
Suq ash Shuyukh
Al Qusayr
Al Busayyah

Al' Abtiyah
Al Ma'daniyat

Al Wari'ah

Shaqra

Jassan
Al'Uzay
At-Diwaniyah
Qaryat al Gharab
Euphrates
An Nasiriyah
Al Qusayr

Hafar al Batin

Al Kahfah
Ar Rass
Buraydah

Nejd

BAGHDAD
Tigris
Karbala
Babylon
Al Hillah
An Najaf
Al Kufah
Ash Shinafiyah
As Samawah
Hammam
Birkat 'Athamin
Nisab

Qalib Baqur
Raghwah
Linah
Aba ad Dud

Unayzah

Shubramiyah
Ash 'ariyah

Ar Ramadi
Al Habbaniyah
Al Iskandariyah
Shithathah
Qaryat al Gharab
As Samawah
Al Samit

Rafha
Al-Hajarah

Turabah

Al Jubb
As Safra
Samirah

Nuqrah

Ad Dafinah

Ar Rutbah
Judaidat al Hamir
Al'Ashuriyah
Al'Uwayqilah

Ha'il
Mawqaq
Jabal Shammar

Saudi Arabia

Ar Rutbah
Badanah
'Ar'ar
Judayyidat Ar'ar
Sakakah

Jubbah
Al Khalf

An Nafud

Al Khaif

Arabian

Turayf
Ithra
Al'Assafiyah
Tayma'

Medina

Peninsula

DAMASCUS
Al Qunaytirah
As Suwayda
Salkhad
Al Azraq
Al Hawja
Al Mughayra'
Al Qalibah
Al Bada'i
As Sawrah
Bi'r al Amir
Bi'r Haymir
Al Hamra'
Bi'r Mubayrik

Golan Heights
Dar'a
Jarash
Zarqa
AMMAN
Mt Nebo

JORDAN

Al Hazm
Al Uthayli
Al Akhdar
Bi'r Aba al Ajjaj

Hanak
Umm Lajj
Bi'r Nabt

Hijaz

Sour
Akko
Haifa
Nazareth
Teverya
Nablus
Ramallah
Jerusalem
Bethlehem
Hebron
Jericho
Irbid
Jordan
Al Ghawr
Dead Sea
Sedom
Karak
Qatranah
Tafilah
Shawbak
Petra
Ma'an
Jafr

Al Quwayrah
Al Mudawwarah
Ar Ramlah
Hajj
Tabuk
J. Dubbogh 2349 m
Al Muwaylih
Madci'n Salih
As Sawrah
Duba
Qal'at al Azlam

Yanbu'al Bahr

EGYPT

Netanya
Rehovot
TEL-AVIV-YAFO
Ashqelon
Gaza
Beersheba
Rafah
ISRAEL
Geziot
Negev
Masada
El Kuntilla
Eilat
Bi'r Taba
Aqaba
Al Humaydah
Jabel al Lawz 2579 m
J. Dafaf 2098 m
Sharmah
Al Muwaylih
Sharmah

Ras'Banas

Gebel Hamata 1977 m

Quseir

Nuweiba
el Muzeina
Dahab
Ra's ash
As Sawrah
Maqna
Madia Tiran
Ofira
Gulf of Aqaba

Mesopotamia

SUDAN

ERITREA

ETHIOPIA

DJIBOUTI

YEMEN

RED SEA

Gulf of Aden

Lake Tana

Asir

Ramlat Sab'atayn

JABAL TUWAYQ

FARASAN ISLES

DAHLAK ARCHIPELAGO

Wadi Hajr

Wadi Bana

Wadi al Jawf

Wadi Najran

Wadi Zabid

Wadi ad Dawasir

Wadi Tathlith

Wadi Bishah

Atbara

Bab al-Mandab

SAN'A'

ASMARA

TA'IZZ

Amd • Al Qarn • Al Hawra • Irqah
Zamakh • Al 'Abn Baqun • Fakhdh 1619 m • Al Mahfid • Hisn Bal'id
Sharawrah • Wudayah • Arqyn 985 m • J. Mirmal 1939 m • Lawdar • Shuqrah
Mushayriqah • Boyhan al Qisab • Harib • Ma'rib
Soyh • J. Thamar 1512 m • Al Bayda
Najran • Hayjan • Rada' • Al Darbah • Musoymir • Madinat ash Sha'b • Aden
Zahran • Khamir • Khamir • Al 'Uri • Taqar 3090 m
Harad • Midi • Hayran • Manaldjah • Hays • Dhubab • Am Nabiyah
Abu 'Arish • Al Fiaqu • Az Zuhrah • Hamra • Al Joh al Astal • Al Turbah • Khozor • Anghar • Obock
Ad Darb • Al Luhayyah • Al 'Uri • Al Hudaydah • Al Khawkhah • Moulhoule
Sabya • Sajid • Kamaran • Ed • Bethil • Assab
Bahr • Hassis • Farasan • Bahar-Assolf • Dahyori • Musa Ali 2063 m
Khamis Mushayt • Abha
Marran • Ash Shuqayq • Al Qa' • Tio • Ghiriffo
Al Qahmah • Quz • Hali • Ed
Dawqah
Tathlith
Bi'r Ibn Sarrar
Hamdah
Qasr Himam • Sulayyimah
Al Khurmah • Bi'r Buraym
Al Lith • Homdanah • Mersa Teklay • Massawa • Adi Ugri • Adigrat
Sa'diya • Shadad • Archico • Af Abed • Adwa • Aksum
Mecca • Mastabah • Uodgan • Rendakoma • Ros Dashen 4620 m
Usfan • Ar Rayyan • Argadom • Baden • Mokada 2295 m • Gonder
Dahaban • Jeddah • Bi'r Mujayrimah • Adi Gemtela
Qadimah • Dukambiya • Odas • Sittona
Port Sudan • Suakin • Sebderat • Tudlok
Dungunab • J. Askeinib 1104 m • Kassala • Gedaref
Halaib • Jebel Asoteribo 2216 m • Salalah • Sinkat • Hadaliya • Metema
Oyo • Jebel Erba 2216 m • Imasa • Hadaliya
Togni • Ogrein • Adarot • Gadamai • Umadam • Dukambiya

DASHT-I MARGO

Malik Dokand 2 236 m

Lar Koh 2 550 m
Delaram
Kala Hisam
Khash
Surkhduz
Khwaja Ali
Garmushki
Darband
Parahadab

Helmand
Khash
Farah
Ka'ata
Farah
Zabo
Sekuha
Bandani

Amir Chah
Damodan 1 890 m
Nok Kundi
Saindak
Zirreh

Chakhansur

Kuhak
Saravan
Esfandak
Eskan
Sa'idi
Dehak
Davar Panah
Paskuh
Kuh-e Bam-Posht
Bepatan
Rask
Kohrad
Gowatar
Ra's Al Hadd

KUH-E PALANGAN

Kuh-e Buran 2 561 m
Qa'emabad
'Aliabad
Kuh-e Malek Siah 1 643 m
Garagheh
Zahedan
Shuru
Nazil
Adiz
Rezvan
Kuh-e Taftan 4 042 m
Khash
Kuh-e Bazman 3 489 m
Bazman
Karevandar
Mand
Kahrad

IRAN

Dasht-e Lut

Shah Kuh 2 729 m
Basiran
Sahlabad
Homand
Qasami
Sib Chah
Robate Abgarm
Kuh-e Nay Band 2 992 m
Nay Band

Baluchistan

Heydarabad
Malgazul
Nosratabad
Gorg
Lengbarut
'Azizabad
Rigan
Dehi Gul
Keshit
Nabid
Bam
Gazbor
Rig Mati
Kahn'Ali

KUH-E SHAH SAVARAN

Giran Rig 2 548 m
Guh Kuh 2 185 m
Pugunzi
Suruk
Pey Beshk
Kalak

Gulf of Oman

MUSCAT
Matrah
Al Mintirib
Daghmar
Sur
J. Khadar 2 151 m

AL HAJAR ASH SHARQ

Kuh-e Darband 8 000 m
Darband
Ravar
Kerman
Kuhpayeh 3 142 m
Rabor
Baft
Khabr
Kuh-e Gireh 5 190 m
Jaghin
Shamil
Gaz
Berizak
Kangan
Jask

KUH-E JEBAL BAREZ

Kuh-e Laleh Zar 4 374 m
Mashiz
Zarand
Rafsanjan
Sa'dalabad
Sirjan
Gaz Saleh
Boluk
Kuh-e Furgun 3 279 m
Qeshm
Lavan
Minab

Al Husayfin
Al Khaburah
Barka
JABAL AKHDAR
Jabal Kawr 2 719 m
Maskin
Mufi
Nazwa

Kuh-e Mashun 3 600 m
Anar
Talle Halal
Khabr
Darab
Kul
Bandar-e Abbas
Laft
Kumzar
J. al Harim 2 081 m
Dibba al Hisn
J. Adhan 2 128 m
Al Masna'a

Shürab
Kharanaq
Zorigan
Bafq
Kuh-e Khawrtog 3 197 m
Kulvand
Neyriz
Darryacheh-ye Tashk
Bastak
Maragh
Bandar-e Lengeh
Kangan
Mina Jebel Ali
As Sadr
Al 'Ayn
Al Fujayrah
Al Quraiyah

Na'in
Taft
Sib Kuh 4 074 m
Yazd
Khar Kuh 3 512 m
Abarqu
Darryacheh-ye Bakhtegan
Neyriz
Tashk
Arsanjan
Juyom
Anveh
KUH-E KHONJ
Bandar-e Chiru
Lazeh

Sharjah
Ajman
Dubai
Jaziral al Hamra'
Hamriyyah
Ruweis
Al Mirfa

Esfanderan
Deh Bid
Bavanat
Moryhab
Persepolis
Abadeh
Zarqan
Kor
Kavar
Khafr
Kur Deh
Khidru
Kangan

ABU DHABI
Al Mirfa

UNITED ARAB EMIRATES

Ad Dafrah

Kuh-e Barm Firuz 3 673 m
Marv Dasht
Shiraz
Abadeh
Guyom
Firuzabad
Jahrom
Mand

Shalamzar
Dehdez
Manj
Kuh-e Alijuq 3 724 m
Basht
Kuh-e Dinar 4 432 m
Kakun
Kazerun
Borazjan
Fasa
Helleh

Esfahan
Najafabad
Qomisheh
Tarqan
Shahr-e Kord
Abarqu
Deh-Dasht
Baba Kalan
Behbehan
Hesar
Rishahr
Bushehr
Shapur
Indapur

Ad Dammam
Al Khobar
Dhahran
Al Jubayl

BAHRAIN
AL MANAMAH
Al Hadd
Ras Tannurah
Al Uqayr

QATAR
DOHA (AD DAWHAH)
Umm Sa'id
Dukhan
Umm Bab

Hasa
Al Mubarraz
Al Hufuf
Buqayq
Haradh
Kharit

Aligudarz
Khunsar
Daran
Chadegan
Masjed Soleyman
Ramhormoz
Bandar Khomeyni
Manifah

Zard Kuh 4 547 m

The Gulf

Tropic of Cancer

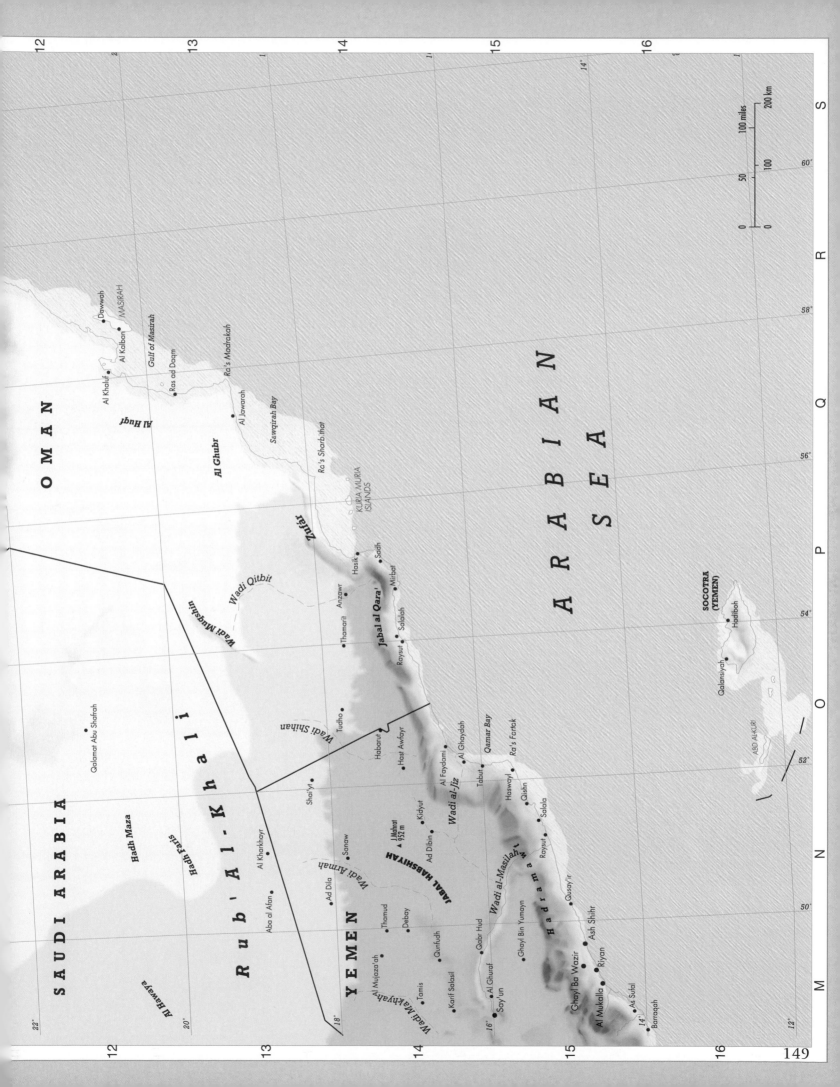

SAUDI ARABIA

OMAN

YEMEN

Rub' Al-Khali

ARABIAN SEA

Al Hawaya
Qalamat Abu Shafrah
Hadh Maza
Hadh Fajis
Aba al Afan
Al Kharkhayr
Ad Dila
Sanaw
Sonaw
Shai'yn
Habarut
Tudho
Wadi Shihan
Wadi Qitbit
Wadi Mughshin
Thamarit
Anzawr
Hasik
Sadh
Mirbat
Zufar
Jabal al Qara'
Raysut
Salalah

Al Mujazza'ah
Tamis
Thamud
Debay
Qunfudh
Karif Salasil
Qabr Hud
Al Ghuraf
Say'un
Ghayl Bin Yumayn
Ghayl Ba Wazir
Al Mukalla
As Sufal
Barraqah
Riyan
Ash Shihr
Qusay'ir
Wadi al-Masilah'
Hadramawt
Raysut
Salala
Qishn
Haswayl
Tabut
Qamar Bay
Ra's Fartak
Al Ghaydah
Al Faydami
Wadi al-Jiz
Hast Awfayr
JABAL HABSHIYAH
J.Mahrat
▲ 952 m
Kidyut
Ad Dibin
Wadi Armah
Wadi Makhyah'

Dawwah
MASIRAH
Al Kalban
Gulf of Masirah
Al Khaluf
Ras ad Daqm
Ra's Madrakah
Al Jawarah
Sawqirah Bay
Ra's Sharb Ithat
Al Hugf
Al Ghubr

KURIA MURIA
ISLANDS

SOCOTRA
(YEMEN)
Hadiboh
Qalansiyah
ABD AL KURI

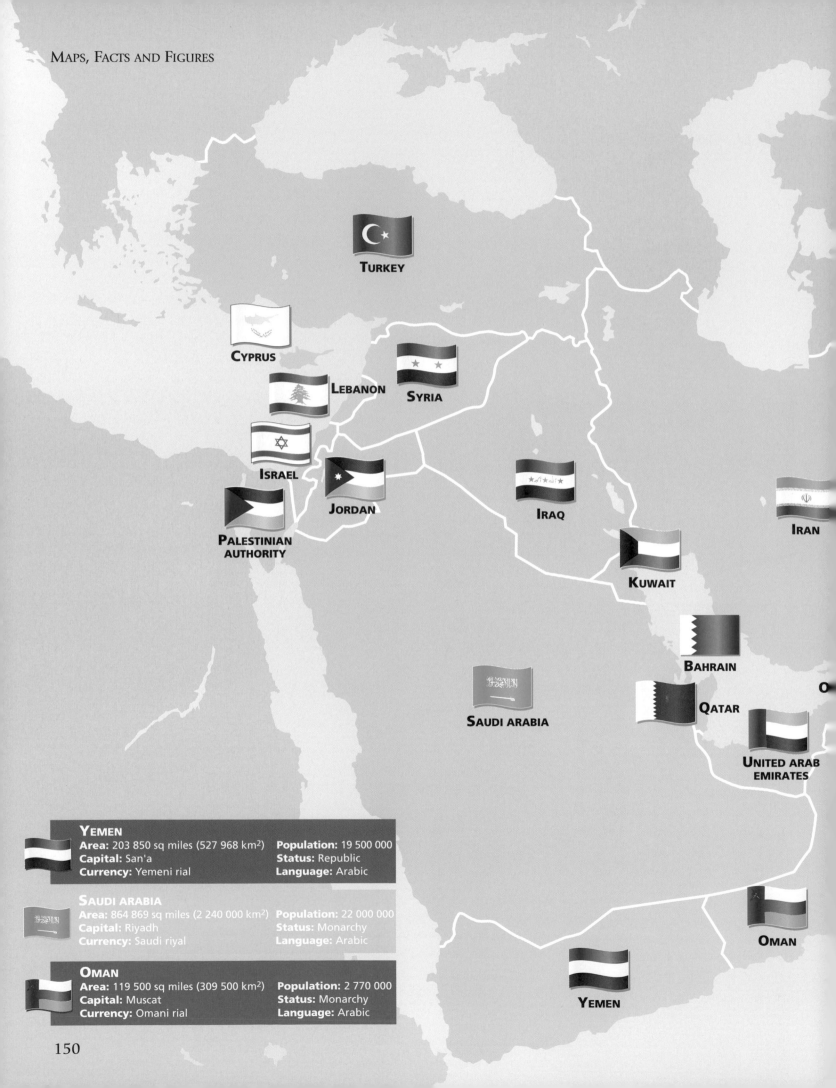

TURKEY

CYPRUS

LEBANON

SYRIA

ISRAEL

JORDAN

IRAQ

IRAN

PALESTINIAN AUTHORITY

KUWAIT

BAHRAIN

SAUDI ARABIA

QATAR

UNITED ARAB EMIRATES

O

YEMEN
Area: 203 850 sq miles (527 968 km²) **Population:** 19 500 000
Capital: San'a **Status:** Republic
Currency: Yemeni rial **Language:** Arabic

SAUDI ARABIA
Area: 864 869 sq miles (2 240 000 km²) **Population:** 22 000 000
Capital: Riyadh **Status:** Monarchy
Currency: Saudi riyal **Language:** Arabic

OMAN
Area: 119 500 sq miles (309 500 km²) **Population:** 2 770 000
Capital: Muscat **Status:** Monarchy
Currency: Omani rial **Language:** Arabic

OMAN

YEMEN

The Middle East

'The Middle East' is a singularly unevocative term for one of the most varied and exciting regions of the world. This fascinating area extends from the ancient Fertile Crescent to the arid deserts of the Arabian peninsula, from the Mediterranean to the foothills of the Himalayas.

AFGHANISTAN
Area: 251 773 sq miles (652 225 km²)
Capital: Kabul
Currency: Afghani
Languages: Dari, Pashtu
Population: 22 930 000
Status: Provisional government

IRAN
Area: 636 296 sq miles (1 648 000 km²)
Capital: Tehran
Currency: Iranian rial
Population: 65 540 000
Status: Islamic republic
Language: Persian

TURKEY
Area: 300 948 sq miles (779 452 km²)
Capital: Ankara
Currency: Turkish lira
Population: 69 630 000
Status: Republic
Language: Turkish

SYRIA
Area: 71 498 sq miles (185 180 km²)
Capital: Damascus
Currency: Syrian pound
Population: 17 131 000
Status: Republic
Language: Arabic

CYPRUS
Area: 3572 sq miles (9251 km²)
Capital: Nicosia
Currency: Cypriot pound
Population: 710 000
Status: Republic
Languages: Greek, Turkish

The Turkish Republic of Northern Cyprus has been recognised only by Turkey since 1983.

LEBANON
Area: 4036 sq miles (10 452 km²)
Capital: Beirut
Currency: Lebanese pound
Population: 3 600 000
Status: Republic
Language: Arabic

ISRAEL
Area: 8473 sq miles (21 946 km²)
Capital: Jerusalem (disputed)
Currency: New Israeli shekel
Population: 6 580 000
Status: Republic
Languages: Hebrew and Arabic

PALESTINIAN AUTHORITY
Area: 2402 sq miles (6220 km²) (of which 2263 sq miles/5860 km² West Bank)
Seat of Authority: Gaza
Currency: New Israeli shekel
Population: 2 895 683 (of which 1 192 207 in Gaza Strip)
Status: Palestinian authority
Languages: Arabic, English and Hebrew

JORDAN
Area: 37 738 sq miles (97 740 km²)
Capital: Amman
Currency: Jordanian dinar
Population: 5 330 000
Status: Monarchy
Language: Arabic

IRAQ
Area: 169 235 sq miles (438 317 km²)
Capital: Baghdad
Currency: Iraqi dinar
Population: 24 570 000
Status: Republic
Language: Arabic

KUWAIT
Area: 6880 sq miles (17 818 km²)
Capital: Kuwait
Currency: Kuwaiti dinar
Population: 2 260 000
Status: Monarchy
Language: Arabic

BAHRAIN
Area: 268 sq miles (695 km²)
Capital: Manama
Currency: Bahraini dinar
Population: 700 000
Status: Monarchy
Language: Arabic

QATAR
Area: 441 659 sq miles (11 437 km²)
Capital: Doha
Currency: Qatari riyal
Population: 600 000
Status: Monarchy
Language: Arabic

UNITED ARAB EMIRATES
Area: 30 000 sq miles (77 700 km²)
Capital: Abu Dhabi
Currency: UAE dirham
Population: 2 940 000
Status: Federal state, Monarchies
Language: Arabic

AFGHANISTAN

A region of aridity and austerity

The rich valleys of Mesopotamia, the mild Mediterranean seaboard and the Yemeni monsoons: these are the exception, rather than the rule, in what is largely an area of searing aridity and inhospitable terrain.

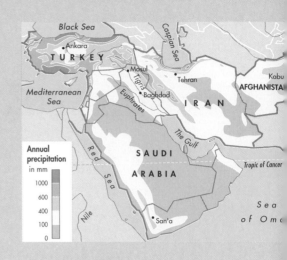

Situated between 20° and 60° longitude and 30° and 40° North, this vast region includes all the countries of Arab western Asia. It also embraces non-Arab nations such as Turkey, Israel, Iran and Afghanistan. The Middle East forms part of a continuous landmass with Africa, but their natural histories are very different.

Desert lands

Much of Turkey has a Mediterranean climate, as do Cyprus and the coastal regions of Lebanon, Syria and Israel, while the south-west corner of the Arabian Peninsula is brushed twice a year by monsoon rains. But aridity is the region's defining climatic characteristic, especially in the more southerly and eastern areas; some of the driest deserts in the world are found here. The most inhospitable conditions are in the deep Arabian interior, in the Rub al-Khali or 'Empty Quarter', and in the Iranian plateau.

Climatic conditions can vary considerably within individual countries: Baghdad, for example, receives only 5.3 in (135 mm) of rainfall a year, compared with 14 in (356 mm) falling on Mosul, higher up the Tigris valley in northern Iraq. In some areas, the rainfall deficit is partly made up by the incidence of snow – even if it falls only in the highest, most remote and inaccessible mountain areas. And in the regions where the headwaters gather, the annual spring snowmelt does much to boost the volume of water flowing in the great rivers.

A tortured terrain

Three geotectonic plates collide at the heart of the Middle East, the African and Arabian plates driving northward into the Anatolian plate. The rugged mountain ranges of Turkey, and the Elburz and Zagros mountains of Iran, were all forced upwards by an impact whose effect is still felt in the region's frequent devastating earthquakes. Farther to the east, the impact of India against the Asian landmass has thrown up the Himalayas, the effect rippling westward to form the peaks of the Hindu Kush. In between these heights lie the most extraordinary declivities: the lower Jordan Valley lies almost 1300 ft (400 m) below sea level, while farther along the same fault line the Red Sea reaches oceanic depths.

TEMPERATURES			
	Highest	Lowest	Range
Qatar	46°C (115°F)	15°C (59°F)	31°C (56°F)
Bahrain	39°C (102°F)	18°C (64°F)	21°C (38°F)
Iran (plateau)	40°C (104°F)	–20°C (–4°F)	60°C (108°F)

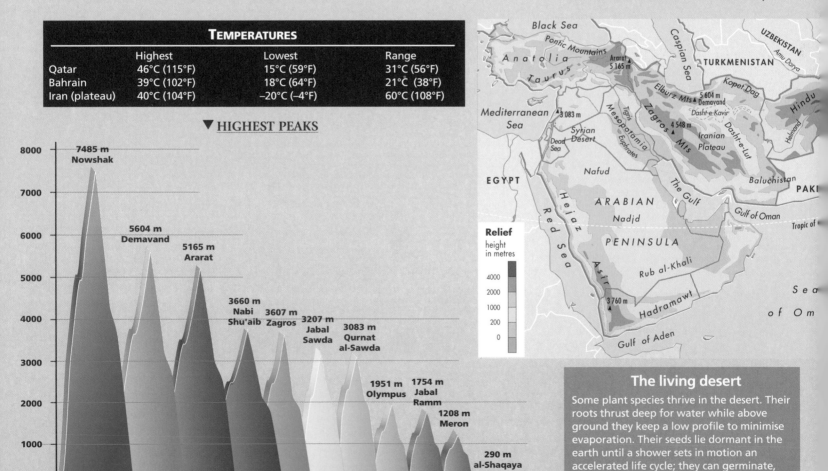

▼ __HIGHEST PEAKS__

7485 m Nowshak
5604 m Demavand
5165 m Ararat
3660 m Nabi Shu'aib
3607 m Zagros
3207 m Jabal Sawda
3083 m Qurnat al-Sawda
1951 m Olympus
1754 m Jabal Ramm
1208 m Meron
290 m al-Shaqaya

■ Afghanistan ■ Turkey ■ Iraq ■ Lebanon ■ Jordan ■ Kuwait
■ Iran ■ Yemen ■ Saudi Arabia ■ Cyprus ■ Israel

The living desert

Some plant species thrive in the desert. Their roots thrust deep for water while above ground they keep a low profile to minimise evaporation. Their seeds lie dormant in the earth until a shower sets in motion an accelerated life cycle; they can germinate, grow, flower and reproduce in hours. Among the plants live insects, rodents and snakes.

A range of cultures and life chances

A meeting-point of different religious, linguistic and cultural traditions, the Middle East has experienced conflict for much of its history. But in the 21st century a youthful population stands poised to turn that very diversity into a rich resource for future prosperity – if the region's problems can be overcome.

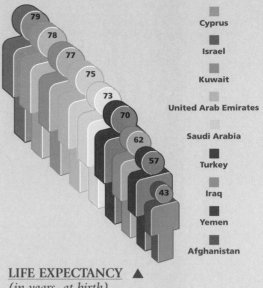

LIFE EXPECTANCY ▲
(in years, at birth)

Legend: Cyprus, Israel, Kuwait, United Arab Emirates, Saudi Arabia, Turkey, Iraq, Yemen, Afghanistan

SCHOOLING AND ILLITERACY

Not all states direct the same resources towards the task of educating their young populations. Some are still a long way from offering schooling on any extensive scale.

12-17-year olds at school		Illiteracy:	male	female
Qatar	78%	Cyprus	1.1%	3.7%
United Arab Emirates	67%	Israel	2.6%	6.2%
Saudi Arabia	51%	Turkey	5.7%	21.4%
Kuwait	50%	Kuwait	15.0%	18.3%
Yemen	37%	Saudi Arabia	15.4%	29.2%
Iraq	33%	Qatar	19.9%	17.4%
Afghanistan	n/a	United Arab Emirates	24.0%	18.5%
		Yemen	29.5%	69.9%
		Iraq	44.1%	75.6%
		Afghanistan	n/a	

Life expectancy

Iraq, once a land of petro-plenty, now has African levels of infant mortality, while Afghanistan, poor to begin with, has declined even further into misery. In some more fortunate states, however, buoyed up by oil revenues or international trade, the standard of living as indicated by the index of infant mortality compares favourably with that of the advanced industrial democracies.

Falling mortality levels in the Middle East in recent years have not been matched by any corresponding drop in birthrates, resulting in a sharp increase in population. Wider demographic trends are hard to establish with any certainty: local crises in countries such as Yemen, and more recently Iraq and Afghanistan, have created too much statistical turbulence for generalised remarks to be made with real confidence. Bitterly fought on the battlefield, the Arab-Israeli struggle has also had its demographic front. Despite continuing Jewish settlement in the Occupied Territories, the higher Palestinian birthrate seems set to ensure that the colonists remain in the minority. Cyprus and Turkey, like the rulers of the United Arab Emirates, have introduced programmes of birth control.

THE AGE PYRAMID ▼

FERTILITY AND INFANT MORTALITY RATES

	Fertility index	Infant mortality (per 1000)
Cyprus	1.9	8
Turkey	2.3	38
Kuwait	2.6	11
United Arab Emirates	3.1	11
Iraq	4.2	63
Saudi Arabia	5.4	20
Yemen	6.1	62
Afghanistan	6.8	161

LIFE EXPECTANCY BY REGION
(in years, at birth)

Eastern Mediterranean:	73.4
Arabian Peninsula:	70.6
Fertile Crescent:	69.8
Asian countries:	57.3

Young countries

In most Middle Eastern countries, young children far outnumber the old. If these states are to realise their hopes for future prosperity, this young generation must be educated, which means major investment in modern schooling. In some poor but densely populated countries, the arrival on the job market of a new generation of school leavers has imposed an insupportable burden on underfunded welfare systems.

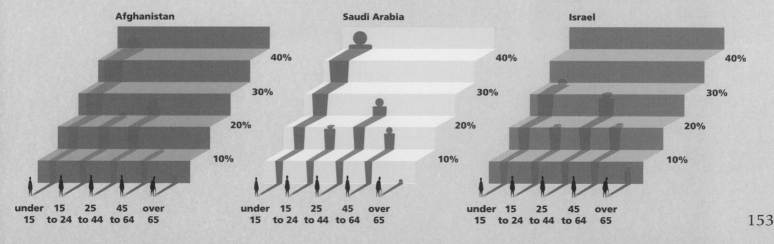

Afghanistan — Saudi Arabia — Israel

under 15 · 15 to 24 · 25 to 44 · 45 to 64 · over 65

Population distribution

The density of populations in the Middle East is for the most part dictated by geographical factors. Coastal plains are crowded, while desert regions are virtually uninhabited. Water has always been scarce, so populations have historically congregated along fertile river valleys. Some mountain regions have become busy centres for minority populations who saw them as safe strongholds – for example, the many Maronite Christian villages in the hills of northern Lebanon, the Druse and Alawi Shiite settlements of Lebanon and Syria, and the Kurdish heartlands of eastern Turkey.

The Middle East has been a region of great cities since antiquity: Islam's early converts soon transcended their nomadic origins to adapt to this urban tradition. Today several metropolises have in excess of a million inhabitants, though in some respects the rise of smaller, secondary cities has been more significant. These have helped to slow the widening gap between outlying regions and national centres, bringing development (especially in oil and related industries) to undeveloped areas. But remote rural areas are still being left behind, the rigidity of their social structures a brake on enterprise. The drift of disaffected youth to the cities threatens to leave them stranded in their stasis.

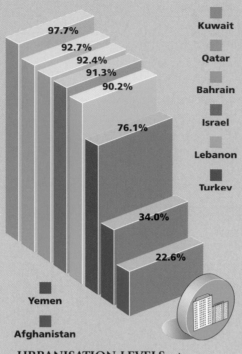

URBANISATION LEVELS ▲
(by percentage)

- Kuwait 97.7%
- Qatar 92.7%
- Bahrain 92.4%
- Israel 91.3%
- Lebanon 90.2%
- Turkey 76.1%
- Yemen 34.0%
- Afghanistan 22.6%

A babel of languages

The languages of the Middle East belong to three groups: Indo-European, Altaic or Turkic, and Semitic. The best-known Indo-European tongues are Kurdish, Persian and Pushtu (spoken through much of southern Afghanistan), though the picture is complicated by a large number of regional sub-languages and dialects.

The Indo-European languages date back 6000 years or more, but they do not have quite the same continuously traceable pedigree enjoyed by the Semitic tongues. The ancestry of Arabic and Hebrew can be followed all the way back to the Akkadian known from inscriptions produced in Mesopotamia around 2500 BC.

Named after the Altai Mountains of Central Siberia, the Altaic languages were spoken by nomadic invaders, most famously the Mongols and the Turks. Modernised in the 1920s by order of Atatürk, Turkish is now written in the Latin alphabet, rather than the Arabic alphabet used since the Turks first converted to Islam.

Some Middle Eastern countries are linguistically mixed: in Iran, not only Persian but Kurdish, Turkish, Azeri, Baluchi, Arabic, Armenian – and many other tongues – are spoken. Elsewhere there may be uniformity: one can travel the length and breadth of Yemen, for example, without hearing any language other than Arabic.

Christian communities of the Middle East

Independent Churches
Syrian Orthodox Church (with West Syriac rite)
In Syria: 150 000 adherents
Assyrian Church (with West Syriac rite)
In Iraq and Syria: some 50 000 adherents

Orthodox Church
Melchite Orthodox Church (with Byzantine rite and Arabic liturgy)
In Lebanon, Syria, Jordan, Israel and Egypt: 800 000 adherents

Catholic Churches
Maronite, Melchite Catholic and Chaldean Churches
In Lebanon, Syria, Israel, Jordan and Iraq: 400 000 adherents
Syrian Catholic Church (with West Syriac rite): 100 000 adherents
Coptic Catholic Church: 100 000 adherents

Middle Eastern languages

Indo-European: Iran and adjacent areas of Iraq and Turkey; the Afghan languages Pashtu and Dari are both varieties of Persian.

Altaic (Turkic): Turkey and Northern Cyprus; Azeri is spoken on the Caspian coast of Iran.

Semitic: Arabic in the Arabian Peninsula and the Fertile Crescent; Hebrew in Israel.

The Kurds

Current estimates suggest that there are about 25 million Kurds. They have no state of their own. Some 50 per cent live in Turkey, 25 per cent in Iran, 20 per cent in Iraq and 3.5 per cent in Syria. In Turkey, Syria and north-west Iran, the Kurdish dialect *Kurmanji* is written in the Latin alphabet; *Sorani* in Iraq uses Arabic script.

ISLAMIC DIVISIONS			
	Sunni	Shiite	Ibadi
Iran	15%	85%	
Lebanon	20%	30%	
Oman	40%		60%
Iraq	43%	52%	
Bahrain	60%	40%	
Kuwait	75%	25%	
Afghanistan	80%	20%	
Saudi Arabia	97%	2%	

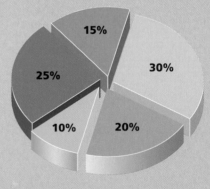

- 15%
- 30%
- 25%
- 20%
- 10%

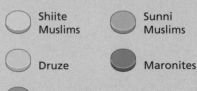

- Shiite Muslims
- Sunni Muslims
- Druze
- Maronites
- Other Christians

RELIGIOUS DIVISIONS ▲ IN LEBANON

Islam and others

Almost 90 per cent of the population in the Middle East professes adherence to Islam; the remaining 10 per cent belongs to Judaism (in Israel) or to the various Christian Churches. Despite this overwhelming majority, Islam is not as monolithic as it might seem, because it is itself divided both along national and sectarian lines. While 90 per cent of Muslims follow the Sunni tradition, this still leaves a vociferous minority of Shiites (who in Iran comprise the majority of the population), as well as a small Ibadi community found largely in Oman. There are other divisions, too – those between Arabs, Persians and Turks, for example. Indeed, the more closely one studies the region's peoples, the harder it becomes to generalise. The State of Israel is by no means populated only by Jews – and within its Palestinian minority is a sub-minority of Christians.

Entering the global economy

As the world price for oil has declined, oil-producing countries have made efforts to strengthen their economies by diversifying – and some states never had significant oil reserves in the first place. All countries, meanwhile, must do what they can to find a still more precious liquid: water.

The Arab League was founded in 1945 by Egypt, Syria, Iraq, Jordan, Lebanon, Yemen and Saudi Arabia; today it has 20 member nations. But the Middle East has changed much in half a century, and a long list of councils and committees now oversees the economic life of the region. Established in 1960, OPEC (Organisation of Petroleum Exporting Countries) is now a mere shadow of its former self. In the 1970s it sent shock waves through the industrialised nations when it raised oil prices in protest against Western support for Israel. OPEC remains a significant organisation despite the increasing importance of the more regionally centred and politically conservative GCC (Gulf Cooperation Council), set up by Saudi Arabia in 1981.

Turkey has looked westward in recent decades, firm in its NATO membership, despite mutterings from Islamic radical elements, and a cofounder of OECD (Organisation for Economic Cooperation and Development) in 1961. For years now, Turkey has pursued membership of the European Union (EU), although its human rights record and its role in Cyprus remain sticking points.

Trouble spots
The Middle East has seldom been out of the news in recent times. Apart from the intractable Arab-Israeli struggle, there have been territorial disputes over oil reserves, and increasingly impatient competition for water resources. The economic benefits of oil, fabulous as these may have been, have too often been cancelled out by the demands of a frenetic regional arms race.

INTERNET CONNECTIONS ▼
(per 1000 inhabitants)

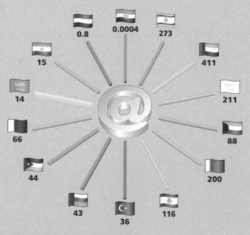

0.8   0.0004   273
15   411
14   211
66   88
44   200
43   36   116

The Middle East online
Conservative elements in many states have shown a profound suspicion of modern mass media communications and information technology. But almost all states in the region have allowed their scientists and students some degree of international collaboration and Internet access.

Flashpoints
Israel: Caught in a cycle of conflict with the Palestinians of the Occupied Territories.
Iraq: Claims Kuwait as its own '19th province'; branded a 'terrorist state' by USA.
Syria: Longstanding enemy of Israel, which annexed Syrian Golan Heights in 1981.
United Arab Emirates: Still in conflict with Islamic Iran over ownership of 'Three Islands' in Strait of Hormuz, first occupied by forces of the Shah in 1971; locked in legal battle with Saudi Arabia over precise positioning of the frontier line between the two countries.
Kuwait: Iraq is not the only neighbour with designs on Kuwait: Saudi Arabia lays claim to parts of its coastal waters.
Yemen: At odds with Oman in a frontier dispute and with Saudi Arabia over maritime boundaries in the Red Sea.
Cyprus: Northern half of island (including part of Nicosia) under Turkish occupation since 1974.
Turkey: Sole sponsor of TNCR (Turkish Republic of Northern Cyprus); in dispute with Syria over water rights and boundary issues; virtually at war with its own minorities, notably Kurds.
Saudi Arabia: In dispute with UAE and Qatar over land frontiers and with Yemen over maritime boundaries.

Proportion of GDP spent on defence *(as percentage)*

4.6
5.0
9.5
14.1

Imports of conventional arms *(as a percentage of world total)*

Turkey
United Arab Emirates
Israel
Saudi Arabia

4.2
5.5
11.5
12.4

A REGION UNDER ARMS ▲

STUDENTS EDUCATED OVERSEAS			
United Arab Emirates:	23.8%	Yemen:	15.9%
Oman:	21.1%	Kuwait:	14.0%
Bahrain:	20.3%	Qatar:	12.0%
		Iraq:	1.5%

ISRAELI IMPORTS AND EXPORTS *(in billions of US dollars)* ▼

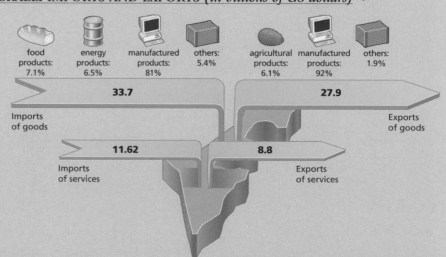

food products: 7.1%
energy products: 6.5%
manufactured products: 81%
others: 5.4%

agricultural products: 6.1%
manufactured products: 92%
others: 1.9%

33.7   27.9
Imports of goods   Exports of goods

11.62   8.8
Imports of services   Exports of services

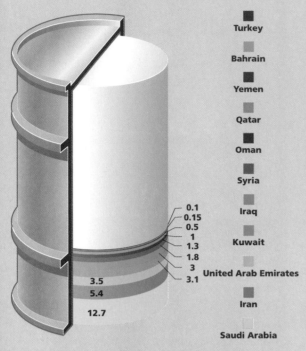

Turkey
Bahrain
Yemen
Qatar
Oman
Syria

0.1
0.15
0.5
1
1.3
1.8
3
3.1

Iraq

Kuwait

United Arab Emirates

3.5
5.4
12.7

Iran

Saudi Arabia

PETROLEUM PRODUCTION ▲
Total production for the Middle East:
1 099 689 000 metric tonnes.

A global market
The Middle East's main commercial links are still with the European Union (EU) countries and the United States, but Asia has become an increasingly important – and in some cases the predominant – trading partner.

Middle Eastern oil: still a winner
Since the 1950s, oil has been one of the great export assets of the region, a major source of revenue – and sometimes of contention. With 65 per cent of the world's known oil reserves and 30 per cent of global production between them, Saudi Arabia, Iran and the United Arab Emirates rank among the top ten producers in the world. Iraq would have been another member of this exclusive club, but its oil industry has had to contend with the crippling effects of international sanctions imposed in the wake of the 1991 Gulf War. Although oil reserves are no longer the huge source of revenue they once seemed to be, and the producing economies have all been working hard to diversify, there is no doubt that oil remains a very valuable resource.

FOREIGN TRADE	
Producers	Clients
Afghanistan	
Asia: 67%	Asia: 43%
CIS: 13.3%	EU: 30.9%
EU 12.8%	Others: 26.1%
Others: 6.9%	
Cyprus	
EU: 47%	EU: 27%
USA: 19%	Middle East: 23%
Asia: 18%	Others: 50%
Others: 16%	
Israel	
EU: 51%	USA: 32%
USA: 18.8%	EU: 30.2%
Asia: 11%	Asia: 18%
Others: 19.2%	Others: 19.8%
Lebanon	
EU: 47.5%	Middle East:45.6%
Asia: 22%	EU: 22%
USA: 9.2%	Others: 32.4%
Others: 21.3%	

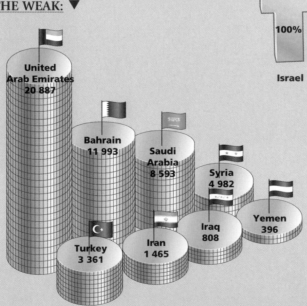

GROSS DOMESTIC PRODUCT, FROM THE STRONG TO THE WEAK: ▼ SOME EXAMPLES
(per inhabitant in US$)

United Arab Emirates 20 887
Bahrain 11 993
Saudi Arabia 8 593
Syria 4 982
Yemen 396
Iraq 808
Iran 1 465
Turkey 3 361

100% Israel
96% Jordan
93% United Arab Emirates
86% Iraq
69% Yemen

ACCESS TO DRINKING WATER ▲

Water shortage
Always a problem for communities in the region, water is becoming a cause of contention between states whose growing populations require ever-increasing amounts. Once seen as an issue of military strategy, Israel's occupation of the Golan Heights has gained extra significance as their watershed has grown steadily in importance. Turkey has been involved in acrimonious disputes with Syria and Iraq over its interference with the flow of the Tigris and Euphrates. Desalination plants are out of the question for all but the rich oil monarchies, while conservation does not come easily to populations just getting used to Western-style consumerism.

Other resources
Agriculture remains an important area of economic activity in the countries of the ancient Fertile Crescent. In Syria, some 30 per cent of the working population is employed in a sector that has been much modernised in recent years. Irrigation has made agriculture possible in many desert areas.

Tourism has been a big growth area, both Turkey and Cyprus vying for their share of the Mediterranean package trade. Red Sea and Gulf resorts have succeeded in enticing a new breed of jet-setting tourists, offering stupendous golf courses and marinas as well as some of the world's most luxurious hotels. Cultural tourism continues to grow modestly; the region can offer unrivalled sights, but political instability has militated against more sustained development.

MIGRATION TO THE RICH OIL-PRODUCING STATES	
	Non-native workers
Gulf States	42.8%
United Arab Emirates	67.7%
Qatar	76.2%
Kuwait	82.0%

Immigration
An irony of the modern Middle East is that those states richest in oil tend to be the most thinly populated. In the Gulf States in particular, an extraordinary standard of living for the few has had to be supported by a large population of migrant workers, many from Asia. For the most part young, male and unattached, these migrants represent a potentially disruptive element in societies which, however much they may need foreign workers, remain reluctant to accord them rights of citizenship.

Index

Page numbers in *italics* denote illustrations. The letter and number references in brackets are the co-ordinates for places in the map section, pp. 142-9.

Acknowledgments

Abbreviations: t = top, m = middle, b = bottom, l = left, r = right.

FRONT COVER: view of Hagia Sophia, Istanbul – DIAF/
J. Sierpinski.
BACK COVER: Yemeni fisherman inspect their catch – GAMMA/
N. Jalot.

Pages 4/5: ALTITUDE/Y. Arthus-Bertrand; 6: COSMOS/SPL/
Planetary Visions/Geosphere Project-T. Van Sant; 8: DIAF/
N. Wheeler; 9t: ALTITUDE/Y. Arthus-Bertrand; 9b: EXPLORER/
D. Henquet; 10t: HOA QUI/N. Thibaut; 10b: DIAF/C. Senechal;
11b: GAMMA/Agence Mission; 12t: ALTITUDE/Y. Arthus-
Bertrand; 12b: HOA QUI/P. & C. Weisbecker; 13: ALTITUDE/
H. Hiscocks; 14t: HOA QUI/M. Jozon; 14b: HOA QUI/
X. Richer; 15tl: BIOS/R. Puillandee; 15b: BIOS/M. Gunther;
16t: BRIDGEMAN ART LIBRARY PARIS/British Museum,
London; 16m: BRIDGEMAN ART LIBRARY PARIS/Ashmolean
Museum, Oxford; 16b: DIAF/N. Wheeler; 17tr: BRIDGEMAN
ART LIBRARY PARIS/Musée du Louvre, Paris;
17m: BRIDGEMAN ART LIBRARY PARIS/The Detroit Institute
of Arts; 17bl: BRIDGEMAN ART LIBRARY PARIS/Musée du
Louvre, Paris; 17br: BRIDGEMAN ART LIBRARY PARIS;
18tl, m: BRIDGEMAN ART LIBRARY PARIS/British Library,
London; 18tr, br: BRIDGEMAN ART LIBRARY PARIS/Musée du
Louvre, Paris; 19tr: CORBIS-SYGMA/D. Bartruff;
19m: ALTITUDE/Y. Arthus-Bertrand; 19b: BRIDGEMAN ART
LIBRARY PARIS/Lithograph after James Fergusson; 20t: HOA
QUI/NF/Carteret; 20ml: GAMMA/C. Boisvieux;
20mr: BRIDGEMAN ART LIBRARY PARIS/National
Archaeological Museum, Naples; 20bl: BRIDGEMAN ART
LIBRARY PARIS; 20br: BRIDGEMAN ART LIBRARY
PARIS/Bibliothèque nationale de France, Paris; 21m: CORBIS-
SYGMA/R. Perry; 21bl, br: BRIDGEMAN ART LIBRARY PARIS;
22tl: RAPHO/K. Nomachi; 22hr: BRIDGEMAN ART LIBRARY
PARIS/British Library, London; 22b: ASK IMAGES/TRIP;
23t: ASK IMAGES/TRIP/C. Rennie; 23m, b: BRIDGEMAN ART
LIBRARY PARIS/Bibliothèque nationale de France, Paris;
24tl: BRIDGEMAN ART LIBRARY PARIS/Royal Asiatic Society,
London; 24tr: ALTITUDE/Y. Arthus-Bertrand;
24ml: BRIDGEMAN ART LIBRARY PARIS/Bibliothèque
nationale de France, Paris; 24mr: DIAF/G. Guittot; 24b: HOA
QUI/S. Grandadam; 25tr: BRIDGEMAN ART LIBRARY PARIS/
Janissaire, by William Page, 1823/Victoria & Albert Museum,
London; 25m: BRIDGEMAN ART LIBRARY PARIS/British
Library, London; 25b: BRIDGEMAN ART LIBRARY PARIS/Le
Camp de Daud-Pascia, engraving after Luigi Mayer, 1806/
Stapelton Collection; 26tl: CORBIS-SYGMA/P. Bois;
26tr: GAMMA/R. Rickelsberg; 26m, b: L'ILLUSTRATION;
27tr: GAMMA/N. Quidu; 27m: GAMMA/E. Rad; 27b: GAMMA/
G. Merillon; 28/29: GAMMA/IRIS/E. Rad; 30: EXPLORER/P. Le
Floch; 32t: DIAF/B. Morandi; 32b: HOA QUI/G. Boutin;
33m: HOA QUI/C. Sappa; 33b: EXPLORER/P. Wysocki;
34t: GAMMA/K. Daher; 34m: HOA QUI/G. Guittard;
34b: GAMMA/P. Maître; 35l: DIAF/TPC/C. Bowman;
35r: EXPLORER/T. Mauger; 36tl: HOA QUI/A. Gerard;
36tr: GAMMA/S. Sibert; 36b: ALTITUDE/Y. Arthus-Bertrand;
37t: EXPLORER/L.-Y. Loirat; 37m: GAMMA/LIAISON/D. Gair;
37b: HOA QUI/C. Boisvieux; 38t: HOA QUI/NF/Serena;
38b: ALTITUDE/Y. Arthus-Bertrand; 39t: GAMMA/C. Boisvieux;
39b: EXPLORER/T. Mauger; 40t: DIAF/R. Mazin; 40m: GAMMA/
C. Vioujard; 40b: HOA QUI/Le Monde; 41t: ALTITUDE/
Y. Arthus-Bertrand; 41b: DIAF/D. Thierry; 42t: RAPHO/
G. Sioen; 42m: ALTITUDE/Y. Arthus-Bertrand; 42b: RAPHO
SAFIR/Kazemi; 43tr: RAPHO/G. Sioen; 43b: DIAF/B. Morandi;
44tl: ASK IMAGES/E. Doumic; 44b: HOA QUI/C. Valentin;
45t: HOA QUI/G. Boutin; 45bl: BIOS/M. Gunther; 45br:
DIAF/B. Morandi; 46: HOA QUI/C. Boisvieux; 48t: ALTITUDE/
Y. Arthus-Bertrand; 48bl: GAMMA/CGA/F. Demulder;
48br: ALTITUDE/Y. Arthus-Bertrand; 49tl: GAMMA/C. Vioujard;
49tr: EXPLORER/R. Nowitz; 49b: GAMMA/E. Rad; 50m: DIAF/

Y. Travert; 50bl: EXPLORER/R. Mattes; 50br: HOA QUI/
F. Latreille; 51t: ALTITUDE/Y. Arthus-Bertrand; 51m: HOA QUI/
C. Boisvieux; 51b: GAMMA/SPOONER/K. Arkell; 52tl: GAMMA/
C. Vioujard; 52tr: GAMMA/N. Jalot; 52b, 53m: HOA QUI/
Y. Gellie; 53b: HOA QUI/C. Valentin; 54t: COSMOS/WOODFIN
CAMP/R. Azzi; 54m: GAMMA/E. Bouvet; 54b: GAMMA/
J. Burlot; 55tr: GAMMA/C. Hires; 55b: GAMMA/L. Van der
Stock; 56t: HOA QUI/Y. Gellie; 56bl: HOA QUI/C. Valentin;
56br: HOA QUI/Y. Gellie; 57t: GAMMA/P. Renault;
57m: GAMMA/J.-C. Francolon; 57b: GAMMA/C. Boisvieux;
58t: Anders Blomqvist/Lonely Planet Images; 58b: GAMMA/
CONTRASTO/W.-S. Lamm; 59t: HOA QUI/STOCKSHOOTER;
59m: HOA QUI/C. Valentin; 59bl: ASK IMAGES/D. Guilloux;
59br: HOA QUI/P. Roy; 60: RAPHO/K. Nomachi; 62t: HOA
QUI/M. Troncy; 62m: GAMMA/SAOLA/I. Simon; 62b:
GAMMA/C. Boisvieux; 63t: ALTITUDE/Y. Arthus-Bertrand; 63bl:
HOA QUI/Le Monde; 63br: HOA QUI/J.-D. Joubert; 64t: HOA
QUI/B. Gerard; 64m, b: COSMOS/WOODFIN CAMP/B.
Iverson; 65t: RAPHO/G. Sioen; 65b: ALTITUDE/Y. Arthus-
Bertrand; 66m: EXPLORER/S. Frances; 66b: DIAF/E. Planchard;
67tl: DIAF/G. Simeone; 67tr: DIAF/Y. Travert; 67m: HOA
QUI/C. Valentin; 67b, 68tl, tr: DIAF/Y. Travert; 68bl: DIAF/
G. Simeone; 68br: DIAF/J. Sierpinski; 69t: COSMOS/A. Keller;
69m: COSMOS/WOODFIN CAMP/B. Boutrit; 69b: HOA QUI/
NF/Serena; 70t: HOA QUI/S. Grandadam; 70m: HOA QUI/
N. Thibaut; 70b: DIAF/B. Morandi; 71t: GAMMA/A.-C. Lefevre;
71b: COSMOS/P. Maitre; 72t: GAMMA/C. Hires; 72m: GAMMA/
P. Maitre; 73tl, tr: DIAF/G. Durand; 73b: HOA QUI/B. Perousse;
74/79: HOA QUI/W. Buss; 74m: GAMMA/E. Baitel; 74mtl: DIAF/
R. Bouquet/Janusz Korczak and the children of the ghetto,
sculpture by Boris Sektzier, 1978; 74mtr: HOA QUI/
E. Simanor/Architect Joseph Klarwein; 74mb, b: GAMMA/
E. Baitel; 75t: ASK IMAGES/S. Attal; 75ml: DIAF/B. Morandi;
75mr: CORBIS-SYGMA/E. Bouvet; 75bl, bm: GAMMA/E. Baitel;
76tl: DIAF/G. Guittot; 76tr: HOA QUI/E. Simanor; 76ml: HOA
QUI/NF/Serena; 76mm: GAMMA/SAOLA/B. Brecelj;
76b: CORBIS-SYGMA/A. Gyori; 77m: DIAF/Y. Travert;
77bl: COSMOS/FOCUS/T. Krausz; 77br: HOA QUI/W. Buss;
78tl: GAMMA/E. Baitel; 78tm: DIAF/G. Guittot; 78tr: CORBIS-
SYGMA/E. BOUVET; 78ml: ASK IMAGES/C. Esther;
78mm: GAMMA/E. Baitel; 78mrt: DIAF/B. Morandi;
78mrb: CORBIS-SYGMA/E. Bouvet; 78bl: COSMOS/M. Sergere;
78bm: HOA QUI/P. Roy; 78br: HOA QUI/G. Guittard;
79tl: GAMMA/E. Baitel; 79tm: ASK IMAGES/S. Attal;
79tr: sculpture by Claes OLDENBURG "Apple core, 1992"
aluminium and paint on enamel (2 x 2 x 3 m) – HOA QUI/
S. Grandadam/Museum of Israel, given by The Morton and
Barbara Mandel Fund, the Mandel Associated Foundations,
Cleveland, and the artist to the American Friends of the
Museum of Israel; 79m: DIAF/J. Sierpinski; 80t: GAMMA/
N. Quidu; 80m, b, 81t: GAMMA/LIAISON/Peterson; 81b: HOA
QUI/Le Monde; 82t: ALTITUDE/Y. Arthus-Bertrand; 82b: HOA
QUI/Le Monde; 83t: HOA QUI/B. Perousse; 83m: GAMMA/
C. Vioujard; 83b: GAMMA/P. Renault; 84: GAMMA/C. Boisvieux;
86t: HOA QUI/F. Latreille; 86m: COSMOS/FOCUS/G. Menn;
86b: COSMOS/KATZ PICTURES/T. Stoddart; 87t: GAMMA/
P. Aventurier; 87m: GAMMA/LIAISON/Yurman; 87b: CORBIS-
SYGMA/P. Robert; 88t: GAMMA/FIGARO MAGAZINE/G. NOËL;
88b: DIAF/D. Thierry; 89tl: HOA QUI/C. Valentin; 89tr: HOA
QUI/B. Perousse; 89b: GAMMA/SAOLA/Bonnier; 90t, m, b, 91tr,
b: GAMMA/M. Lounes; 92t: GAMMA; 92bl: GAMMA/ABC
AJANSI; 92br: GAMMA/LIAISON/Peterson; 93tl: GAMMA/
C. Boisvieux; 93mr: GAMMA/S. Nackstrand; 93b: GAMMA/
N. Quidu; 94t: GAMMA/E. Baitel; 94m: GAMMA; 94b: RAPHO/
M. Serraillier; 95t: GAMMA/C. Boisvieux; 95m: DIAF/Pratt-
Pries; 95b: COSMOS/P. Maitre; 96t: GAMMA/E. Rad;
96m: GAMMA/E. Baitel; 96b: HOA QUI/W. Buss; 97m: RAPHO/
K. Nomachi; 97b: RAPHO/J.-M. Armani ; 98t: COSMOS/

ANZENBERGER/C. Akkam; 98m: RAPHO/F. Elkoury;
98b: GAMMA/FIGARO MAGAZINE/G. NOËL; 99t: COSMOS/
STRATUS/M. Buhrer; 99b: HOA QUI/Y. Gellie; 100t: GAMMA/
C. Boisvieux; 100m: DIAF/B. Morandi; 100b: GAMMA/FIGARO
MAGAZINE/G. Buthaud; 101t: EXPLORER/GEOPRESS;
101bl: ALTITUDE/Y. Arthus-Bertrand; 101br: DIAF/N. Wheeler;
102t: EXPLORER/D. Clément; 102m: HOA QUI/NF/Serena;
102bl: DIAF/A. Even; 102br: DIAF/J.-P. Garcin; 103t: DIAF/
J.-D. Sudres; 103b: GAMMA/LIAISON/D. Gair; 104tl: GAMMA/
Reza; 104tr: DIAF/B. Morandi; 104bm: EXPLORER/T. Mauger;
105t: GAMMA/L. Maous; 105m: DIAF/J. Sierpinski;
105b: GAMMA/P. Renault; 106t: GAMMA/C. Vioujard;
106m: DIAF/G. Guittot; 106b: HOA QUI/M. Troncy;
107tr: GAMMA/N. Quidu; 107b: HOA QUI/Y. Gellie;
108: GAMMA/M. Deville; 110t: HOA QUI/X. Richer;
110m: COSMOS/WOODFIN CAMP/R. Azzi; 110bl: COSMOS/
Kehoane; 110br: GAMMA/Reza; 111t: COSMOS/S. Sibert;
111m: EXPLORER/M. Carbonare; 112t: HOA QUI/Y. Gellie;
112m: COSMOS/DOT/H. Horenstein; 112b: GAMMA/
A. Benainous; 113t: COSMOS/WOODFIN CAMP/R. Azzi;
113b: COSMOS/R. Smolan; 114tl: HOA QUI/E. Bernager;
114tr: GAMMA/P. Renault; 114b: HOA QUI/Y. Gellie; 115t: HOA
QUI/NF/Carteret; 115b: HOA QUI/Y. Gellie; 116t: DIAF/
J.-P. Garcin; 116bl, br: GAMMA/C. Boisvieux; 117t, m: GAMMA/
E. Rad; 117b: VANDYSTADT/G. Vandystadt; 118t: ASK IMAGES/
C. Esther; 118b: JACANA/K. Amsler; 119t: HOA QUI/M. Jozon;
119b: HOA QUI/C. Valentin; 120: DIAF/B. Merle; 122t: DIAF/
B. Morandi; 122b: HOA QUI/ NF/Carteret; 123t: HOA QUI/
Y. Gellie; 123bl, br: GAMMA/A. Duclos-R. Gaillarde;
124tl: DIAF/Y. Travert; 124tr: DIAF/ B. Morandi; 124b: DIAF/
F. Soreau; 125t: GAMMA/Reza; 125m: HOA QUI/W. Buss;
125b: EXPLORER/Fiore; 126t: ASK IMAGES/P. Meunier;
126m: HOA QUI/C. & J. Lenars; 126b: CORBIS-SYGMA/R.-T.
Nowitz; 127tm: ASK IMAGES/D. Guilloux; 127tr: CORBIS-
SYGMA/R.-T. Nowitz; 127b: CORBIS-SYGMA/C. Heller;
128t: RAPHO/G. Gerster; 128m: GAMMA/E. Baitel;
128b: DIAF/B. Morandi; 129tl: COSMOS/ S. Sibert; 129tr: HOA
QUI/W. Buss; 129b: EXPLORER/G. Thouvenin;
130t, b: COSMOS/ S. Sibert; 131t: HOA QUI/Y. Gellie;
131m: EXPLORER/G. Thouvenin; 131b: GAMMA/V. Prado;
132t: COSMOS/WOODFIN CAMP/R. Azzi; 132m: GAMMA/
J.-C. Gisbert; 132b: GAMMA/U. Andersen; 133t: BRIDGEMAN
ART LIBRARY PARIS/National Museum of India, New Delhi;
133b: GAMMA/E. Baitel; 134t: BRIDGEMAN ART LIBRARY
PARIS/LAUROS-GIRAUDON/ Bibliothèque nationale, Tunis;
134m: ASK IMAGES/TRIP/H. Rogers; 134b: HOA QUI/W. Buss;
135t: GAMMA/V. Prado; 135m: INSTITUT DU MONDE
ARABE/P. Maillard/The Sea, by Chafik Abboud; 135b: INSTITUT
DU MONDE ARABE/P. Maillard/Composition, by Dhia Al
Azzaoui, 1986; 136t: CORBIS-KIPA/Film Sacred, by Amos Gitaï,
1999; 136bl: CORBIS-KIPA/Film Wedding in Galilee, by Michel
Khleifi, 1987; 136br: CORBIS-KIPA/Film Yol (The Way), by
Yilmaz Güney, 1982; 137t: EXPLORER/M. Carbonare;
137m: ASK IMAGES/P. Meunier; 137b: GAMMA/SAOLA/
Bonnier; 138t: DIAF/J.-D. Sudres; 138ml: COSMOS/R. Freerck;
138mr: COSMOS/ANZENBERGER/M. Horvath; 138b: GAMMA/
N. Quidu; 139l: COSMOS/R. Freerck; 139r: GAMMA/S. Sibert;
140/141: COSMOS/FOCUS/T. Hegenbart.

Printed and bound in Europe by Arvato Iberia
Colour separations: Station Graphique, Ivry-sur-Seine